T0301340

The Growth of Service Industries

The Growth of Service Industries

The Paradox of Exploding Costs and Persistent Demand

Edited by
Thijs ten Raa

Associate Professor of Economics, Tilburg University, The Netherlands

Ronald Schettkat

Professor of Economics, Utrecht University, The Netherlands

Edward Elgar
Cheltenham, UK • Northampton, MA, USA

Published by
Edward Elgar Publishing Limited
Glensanda House
Montpellier Parade
Cheltenham
Glos GL50 1UA
UK

Edward Elgar Publishing, Inc.
136 West Street
Suite 202
Northampton
Massachusetts 01060
USA

A catalogue record for this book
is available from the British Library

Library of Congress Cataloguing in Publication Data

The growth of service industries : the paradox of exploding costs and persistent demand /edited by Thijs Ten Raa and Ronald Schettkat.
    p. cm.
   Includes index.
   1. Service industries—Management. 2. Service industries—Cost control. 3. Corporations—Growth. I. Raa, Thijs ten. II. Schettkat, Ronald.

  HD9980.A2G76   2000
  658–dc21

                                00–047676

ISBN 1 84064 422 2

Typeset by Manton Typesetters, Louth, Lincolnshire, UK.
Printed and bound in Great Britain by MPG Books Ltd, Bodmin, Cornwall.

Contents

Figures

Tables

Contributors

Eileen Appelbaum is the Research Director of the Economic Policy Institute in Washington, USA.

William Baumol is Professor and Director at the C.V. Starr Center for Applied Economics, New York University and Senior Research Economist and Professor Emeritus at Princeton University, USA.

Esra Erdem is a junior economist at Corpus Christi College, Oxford University, UK.

Andrew Glyn is a senior lecturer and fellow of Corpus Christi College, Oxford University, UK

Stephen Machin is Professor of Economics at University College London, and Research Director at the Centre for Economic Performance, London School of Economics, UK.

Joe Mattey is a senior economist at the Federal Reserve Bank of San Francisco, USA.

Pierre Mohnen is Professor of Economics at the University of Quebec in Montreal, Canada.

Joachim Möller is Professor of Economics at the University of Regensburg, Germany.

Thijs ten Raa is Associate Professor of Economics at Tilburg University, the Netherlands.

Giovanni Russo is Assistant Professor of Economics at Utrecht University, the Netherlands.

Ronald Schettkat is Professor of Economics at Utrecht University, the Netherlands.

Foreword

Thijs ten Raa and Ronald Schettkat

The surprising vigour of the service sector puzzles policy makers and economists alike. Policy makers struggle with the question of whether they should put a lid on public service budgets as the costs of their provision rise. Economists are puzzled by the interplay of slow service and fast goods productivity growth and wonder why the demand for services is so persistent. This book is intended to address both readerships and serves as a useful introduction to service productivity analysis.

Services such as education, cultural activities, and health services are under budgetary pressure. If budgets for services are held constant, but the prices go up, there is a problem. The very existence of some services is under threat. Many economists take this as a fact of life. In their view, if commodities become more expensive, there will be less demand. What is puzzling, however, is that services do not become more costly because their provision becomes less efficient. In a seminal article Baumol (1967) diagnosed the 'disease' of the services as a lagging of productivity growth, compared to manufacturing. The success of technical progress in industry makes manufactured goods ever less expensive and thus increases the *relative* price of services, however unintentionally. Services do not require increasing quantities of resources, but the same amount of resources able to generate ever increasing quantities of manufactured goods is needed to produce services. The absolute resource cost of services does not go up, but the opportunity cost of services does, that is the number of manufactured products foregone.

While Baumol (1967) showed that there is no need to reduce the amount of services we consume, one certainly expects that the pressure on the services mounts as their relative price goes up. Yet this is not what has happened. The services sectors of advanced economies show surprising vigour. The employment of ever larger shares of the labour force comes as no surprise; this phenomenon is a direct consequence of the low productivity performance we just noted. But the fact that the real service share of GDP is also growing or is at least stable is puzzling. The paradox of the services is that, in spite of their exploding costs, demand persists.

A small number of experts from Europe and North America has been invited to address the paradox. What are the facts? Do services really suffer from the cost disease? Is the contribution to the economy in terms of employment, income, or output nonetheless stable? If so, how can we explain the persistence of the services? A very lucid introduction to the cost disease and the persistence of the services is provided by William J. Baumol in Chapter 1 of this volume. In the light of recent data and new economic mechanisms explored in this book he displays ground-breaking optimism as regards the role of the services in modern economies.

In order to organize the analysis of the services, all contributors to this volume received a list of potential resolutions of the service paradox. The possible explanations range from accounting issues to supply and demand effects and are presented by the editors in a simple, two-sector model of the economy in Chapter 2. Three possible explanations are conceptual, involving the appropriate measurement of the service productivity and the service share. The remaining four explanations are economic–behavioural. The first effect is a supply effect: the capacity of the service sector to absorb labour that is surplus to the manufacturing sector because of increased automation. The second is related, but takes into account international trade. Technological progress abroad may shift the domestic comparative advantage to the services. Last, but not least, there are two demand effects. The income effect, a preference for services by richer consumers, may tilt advancing economies towards the services despite the fact that they are becoming costlier. The substitution effect, the replacement of services by manufactures, would seem to predict a reduction of the service share, but this trend may not last as consumers reach saturation point.

The supply-side of the services sector is addressed in the next part of the book, Part 2, 'Supply-side reasons for employment shifts'. In Chapter 3, Erdem and Glyn provide some very useful statistics and analysis of employment in the services. The first supply effect, that the services sector acts as a sponge that absorbs labour supply, is documented and found to be very real. It is particularly relevant to female labour supply. The other supply effect, acting through international trade, is also investigated in an OECD framework by Machin in Chapter 4, but does not resolve the paradox of the services. Machin analyses the fascinating implications of the service sector for skill requirements.

Part 3 investigates the cost disease of the services for the USA (Chapter 5 by Mattey) and Canada (Chapter 6 by Mohnen and ten Raa). The potential conceptual resolutions of the service paradox, dealing with the appropriate measurement of productivity and the real service share, are inspected, but found to carry little weight. The role of demand is more important.

Part 4 focuses on demand effects. In Chapter 7 Appelbaum explores the relationship between demand analysis and the service paradox. An interesting further twist is given in an input–output framework by Russo and Schettket in Chapter 8, matching service activity to final product categories. The ultimate test for demand effects to explain the persistence of the services requires the estimation of income and price elasticities and this is masterfully done in Chapter 9, by Möller.

What is fascinating about the above analyses of the services is that the results all point to the same resolution of the service paradox. The use of appropriate productivity and share measures may soften the coexistence of the cost disease, but not by much. International trade has the potential to explain the persistence of the service share, but this line of reasoning is not conclusive either. However, demand, and particularly income effects, are important and resolve the paradox. The concluding chapter extracts a useful list of stylized facts about the modern service sectors. The new perspective provides a clear understanding of the coexistence of the cost disease and the persistence of service demand.

This project has been supported by the Netherlands Science Foundation, the Department of Economics and Policy Studies of Utrecht University, and the Department of Econometrics of Tilburg University.

REFERENCE

Baumol, William J. (1967), 'Macroeconomics of unbalanced growth: the anatomy of urban crisis', *American Economic Review*, **57** (3), 415–26.

PART I

The amazing vigour of the services

1. Paradox of the services: exploding costs, persistent demand

William J. Baumol[1]

Between 1981 and 1991 the University's health insurance costs ... increased by 635%. This rapid and continuing inflation parallels the experience of most employers in the nation ... among [the] reasons ... Doctors' and hospitals' charges for each procedure and operation increase each year at a rate that exceeds the rise in the cost of living. (Karen Bradley, Director of Personnel, New York University, Memorandum to the Staff, October 7, 1991.)

There were twelve postal deliveries on weekdays in Kentish Town [then in suburban London] at that time [the 1860s] and one on Sundays. (Kapp (1972), p. 48n.)

Three basic facts characterize the economic history of much of the service sectors of the world's industrialized economies. First, the costs (and prices) of the services have been rising faster than those of other commodities, and have been doing so persistently and cumulatively as far back as the available statistical data go. Second, the amount spent on the services and their share of national income has also been rising persistently. And, third, so far as can be measured, the overall product of the service sector as a share of national income has remained more or less constant. That is, consumers have spent a larger and larger share of their incomes on those services, but the amount of service they received in return has just about kept up with the overall amount of other products they obtained.[2] This roughly constant share of services output, together with their rapidly rising share of GDP (and of the labour force of each industrial nation), is something of a paradox.

These facts raise the obvious question: Why? Why do service prices seem virtually always to be ahead of other products in terms of the speed with which their prices rise? Why does this not affect their share of the outputs of the economies? And why are consumers willing to spend an ever-greater share of their incomes on these services despite their exploding prices? This book seeks to provide answers to these questions. It contains a number of papers presented at a conference held in Amsterdam in the autumn of 1998. Many of these papers provide new empirical and analytical evidence testing the cost disease hypothesis and exploring it further. It is, therefore, appropriate to begin the volume with a review of the concept, its logic and the character of the sorts of pertinent evidence that were available previously. That is the purpose of this introductory chapter.

It is thirty five years since William Bowen and I (1966) first reported our analysis of what we called the 'cost disease of the performing arts' – the disease of persistently and cumulatively rising costs – with its profoundly disturbing implications for the future.[3] Soon after, we realized in general terms that it applied to a variety of other services (we now call them 'stagnant services') including health care, education, restaurant services, library and legal services, police protection, auto repair and a number of others. The cost implications for the future that flowed from the analysis have been amply confirmed by subsequent developments. The same is true of the implications for demand, which from the earliest writings on the subject were recognized to depend on the way in which purchasers are affected by the rising incomes that have accompanied the increasing costs. It was surmised then, largely from unsystematic observations, that these demand effects are likely to vary from one service to another, a surmise that the data subsequently obtained also appear to confirm.

More recently, the analysis has attracted attention in discussions of health care, where scarcely any industrial country is immune from its financial pressures. Here, the discussion begins with a review of the empirical evidence. Then, after a very brief summary of the cost-disease analysis and its applicability to health-care costs, the discussion turns to the record of the demand response and to some policy implications.

1   THE COST CRISIS OF HEALTH CARE, EDUCATION, AND SOME OTHER VALUABLE SERVICES

The exploding costs of health care are obviously causes of widespread concern. The history of their costs is therefore a matter of importance in itself, but we focus on it here because it is typical of the costs of the other handicraft services – that is, of services in which direct human effort is not easily replaced by machines.

It is often noted that the cost per capita (or cost as a share of average income) of health care in the USA is considerably higher than that in most other countries. We can be fairly certain from the statistical evidence that this is true, despite the well-known pitfalls besetting comparison of prices in different countries with their different currencies. The shortcoming of this conclusion, in my view, is not that it may be inaccurate, but that it focuses upon the wrong issue. The pain society experiences from the costs of health care and education is not caused primarily by their *levels* at some particular date but, rather, from their *growth rates*. What makes the problem so difficult to deal with is the fact that high as these costs may have been yesterday, they are considerably higher today, and will be substantially higher still tomorrow. Note that this does not refer to price inflation, but to what economists call 'real price increases', that is, rates of price increase *above and beyond* the rate of general inflation of prices in the economy.

The magnitude and persistence of the rates of growth of these real prices are striking. In the postwar period from 1948 to 1995 in the USA, the annual rate of increase in the price of a physician's services (the price charged by the doctor to the patient) was more than 5.5 per cent per annum, compared to an average annual increase of a little under 4 per cent per year in the government's measure of overall inflation, the Consumer Price Index, or CPI (see Figure 1.1 for the graphs of these two series). This difference may not seem very large, but over the 47 years in question it means that the price of a doctor's services has increased by approximately 1200 per cent in absolute terms, or more than 100 per cent in terms of dollars of constant purchasing power. In Figure 1.1 we see how the price of physicians' services (upper curve) has cumulatively outstripped the economy's rate of inflation (lower curve).

Over the same period, in the USA, the price of a hospital room increased even more rapidly, by a considerable margin, than the cost of a visit to a

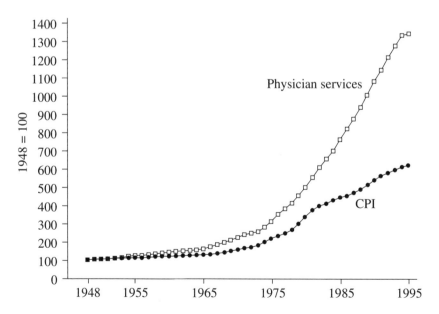

Figure 1.1   Price indices: physician services vs. CPI, 1948–95

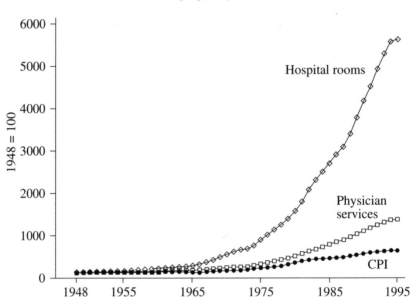

Figure 1.2   Price indices: hospital rooms, physician services and CPI,
1948–95

physician. The cost of a hospital room is reported by the US Bureau of Labor
Statistics to have risen at an average annual rate of 8.6 per cent compounded,
which over the 47-year interval cumulated to a 5500 per cent increase. This
amounts to about an 800 per cent rise in terms of dollars of constant purchasing power – that is, after full correction for the economy's overall inflation
during this time interval. Figure 1.2 reports the hospital-room cost data and
shows how it makes the rise in real price of a physician visit seem modest by
comparison.

Increases of this magnitude clearly constitute a serious threat to the quality
of medical care that middle and lower-income persons, whether older or
younger, can afford. In an affluent society such as ours, that is dedicated to
promoting the general welfare – including the provision of medical care
meeting some minimum standard of acceptability – the rising price of medical care clearly represents a problem of the utmost importance.[4]

The cost of education has shown patterns very similar to those of medical
care. Education expenditure per student has also risen steadily and cumulatively at a rate markedly outstripping that of inflation. It increased 348 per
cent in terms of dollars of constant purchasing power in the postwar period,
which works out to an average increase of 7.4 per cent per year for the
postwar years, between that of a physician visit (5.5 per cent) and that of a

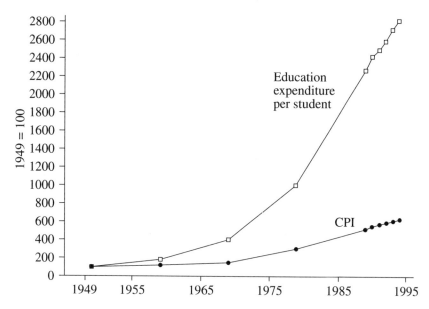

Figure 1.3   Price indices: education expenditure per student vs.
CPI, 1949–95

hospital room (8.6 per cent). Figure 1.3 (constructed from data from the US Department of Education) reports the information. Costs of higher education exhibit similar patterns.

There remains the question of whether the problem of steadily growing real cost of health care and education is an issue only in the USA. It has been suggested that other countries exercise firmer control over their medical costs, and continue to offer better and more affordable public services. There is, undoubtedly, much truth to this, and it reflects, among other influences, a variety of public policies – a greater commitment to social services financed by tax rates far higher than those in the USA, stricter controls on the fees charged by physicians, and so on. Still, it must be remembered that there are few industrialized countries in which similar complaints about *rates of cost increase* are not heard.

Let us, then, examine what the international data show for a number of the services that are subject to the cost disease. There exists a profusion of follow-up studies of the issue for the case of the performing arts. Hence, there is an abundance of clear and unambiguous evidence that bears on the subject. Over the years a number of researchers have collected systematic evidence on costs and cost trends for non-commercial theatres in the USA, UK, Australia, Sweden, Russia and other countries, in other live performing arts and in other economic activities with analogous attributes. (See, for example, Baumol and Bowen (1966), Blaug (1976), Throsby and Withers (1979), Ford Foundation (1974), Frey and Pommerehne (1989), Felton (1994), and Throsby (1994). Much of this material can be found in Towse (1997)). All of the evidence, some of it going back more than a century, confirms that costs of the live performing arts, whether measured in terms of cost per performance or cost per attendee, have risen persistently and cumulatively at a rate almost always exceeding the economy's rate of inflation.

For other economic activities, international statistics for the required comparisons are surprisingly difficult to obtain. In part, this is attributable to measurement problems. There are a number of services, such as those of government, whose outputs are very hard to measure or even to define and observe. Others, such as health care, are so heterogeneous that the statistics are likely to be exceedingly difficult to compare from one country to another. Still, we have been able to obtain some such data for education and health care.

Figures 1.4a, 1.4b and 1.4c show the cost of education per student for six countries: Japan (1965–89); UK and Germany (1965–90); and Canada, France

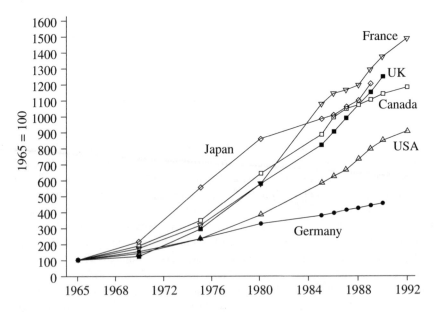

Notes:
Japan: 1965–89.
UK & Germany: 1965–90.

Figure 1.4a   Price indices: six countries, nominal education expenditure per student, 1965–92

and the USA (1965–92).[5] The figures simply show indexes (1965 = 100) of total expenditures by educational institutions divided by total enrolment. Figure 1.4a provides indexes uncorrected for inflation (that is, nominal expenditure per student). It shows that, for the most part, education costs rose at a substantial rate throughout most of the period. Since 1965 is selected as the base year, all of the countries are given the same initial point. In these terms, with no correction for the different rates of inflation in the different countries, we see that foreign education expenditures grew at a more rapid rate than in the USA in all but one country – Germany. But this may be attributable to the fact that over the period inflation in the USA was slower than that in most other countries.

We correct for the effects of inflation in the usual way, by dividing each country's nominal figure by the corresponding value of its overall price index (the GDP deflator) for each year for which statistics are reported. The resulting indexes of *real* education cost per student are shown in Figure 1.4b. Here we see that, despite the deflation of the numbers, the curves generally remain upward sloping, meaning that cost of education per student rose faster than

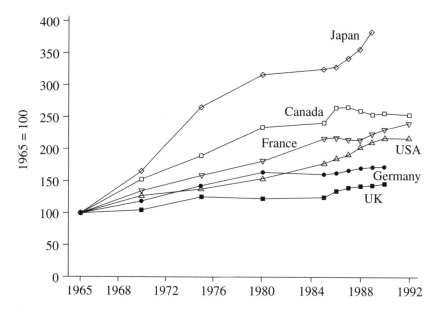

Notes:
Japan: 1965–89.
UK & Germany: 1965–90.

Figure 1.4b   Price indices: six countries, real education expenditure per student, 1965–92

the general price level. Moreover, we see that in three of the six countries this cost rose more rapidly than it did in the USA.

Figure 1.4c sums up the results. The height of the bar for each country shows the average rate of increase of *real* education costs per annum in that country. We see once more that each of these countries suffers from the problem of rising real costs, and that, in terms of the rate of increase, the USA is below the middle, with Japan, Canada and France having the dubious distinction of being ahead, and Germany and the UK lagging behind.

We also have some comparative health-care cost figures, for whatever they may be worth. In 1990 (updated 1993) the OECD provided, as they put it, 'At a more aggregate level, a new "total" medical-consumption price index...' (1990, p. 122). This price index is calculated for the years 1960 to 1993 for a number of countries, including all of the major free-market industrial countries. In all of them the nominal health-care price index rose rapidly, as is hardly surprising. As Figure 1.5a (analogous to Figure 1.4c for education) indicates, per-capita health care prices rose more rapidly than prices in general. That is, the real cost per person of medical care rose (and rose quite

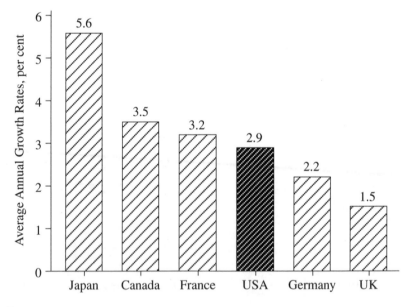

Notes:
Japan: 1965–89.
UK & Germany: 1965–90.

Figure 1.4c   Average annual growth rates of real education expenditure per pupil, 1965–92, six countries

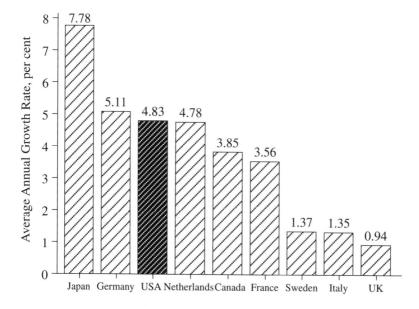

Figure 1.5a   Average annual growth rates of real health expenditure per capita, 1960–93, nine countries

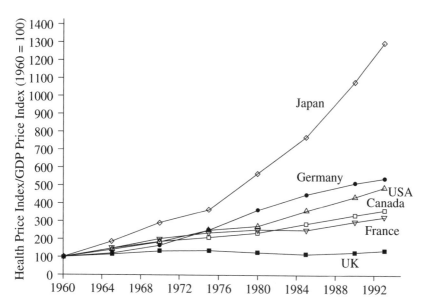

Figure 1.5b   Price indices: real per capita health expenditures, 1960–93, six countries

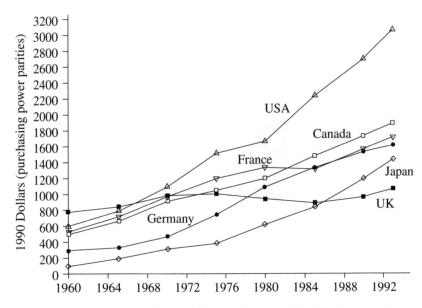

Figure 1.5c　　Real per capita health expenditures: 1960–93, six countries

steadily), with the US rate of increase exceeded by both Japan and Germany. Figure 1.5b also illustrates these growth trends for each country.

At least two conclusions are suggested by our quick review of the data. First, it should be clear that the health care or educational systems of other countries provide no sure models for a quick cure of the problem of rising real cost of those services in a market-controlled industry, such as health care in the USA. Second, the universality and persistence of the problem – the fact that it has endured for four decades at the very least, and has beset many countries – indicate that it lies deeper than the particular administrative or other institutional arrangements adopted in any one country. Let us, then, inquire into at least one possible source of the rising-cost phenomenon.

2　THE PERSISTENCE OF PRODUCTIVITY-GROWTH DIFFERENTIALS AND THE COST DISEASE

The issue is surely complex, and no single explanatory hypothesis can pretend to account for a set of problems whose roots are undoubtedly sociological and psychological as well as economic. Still, there is one influence that goes far in accounting for the difficulties that have just been described, and that at the same time at least suggests appropriate general directions for government policy to deal with the problem. It should be kept in mind that the following discussion focuses throughout, not upon the *level* of costs, but upon their real *rates of increase*. There are many influences, actual or alleged, notably lawsuits against doctors and others involved in health care, lack of competitiveness in the profession and high earnings of physicians, that clearly may help to explain those cost levels in the USA, but I am aware of none beside the one about to be described that seems to account for the many countries in which *growth* in health and education costs persistently outpaces the rate of inflation.

It is hardly surprising that, while overall productivity in the industrial world has been growing rapidly, the pace of growth in different industries has varied substantially. What is more unexpected is the persistence of the pattern of differences in productivity growth between economic sectors. A given sector of the economy does not usually fluctuate haphazardly between periods of relatively slow and relatively rapid advance in productivity. Rather, the industries in which productivity was expanding slowly a century ago are, by and large, the very ones in which productivity growth is still slow today. And the endurance of productivity stagnancy in those industries has given them a distinctive price history that is the fundamental symptom of the cost disease of the personal services. This cost disease phenomenon occurs when the services, in a class that will presently be described, are plagued by cumulative and persistent rises in their costs, increases that normally exceed to a significant degree the corresponding rate of increase for commodities generally, that is, almost always outstrip the economy's rate of inflation.

The common element that characterizes all the stagnant services is the handicraft attribute of their supply processes. None of them has, at least so far, been fully automated and liberated from the requirement of a substantial residue of personal attention by their producers. That is, they have resisted reduction in the amount of labour used per unit of their output. Not that the growth rate of their labour productivity has always been zero. On the contrary, in almost every case there has been some rise in the productivity of these personal services with the passage of time; but over longer periods it has been far slower than the rate of productivity increase characteristic of the economy as a whole. That is why we call them the stagnant services.[6]

There are at least two reasons why rapid and persistent productivity growth has eluded the stagnant services. First, some of them are inherently resistant to standardization. Before one can undertake to cure a patient or to repair a broken piece of machinery it is necessary to determine, case by case, just what is wrong and the treatment must then be tailored to the individual case. The manufacture of thousands of identical automobiles can be carried out on an assembly line and much of the work done by industrial robots, but the repair of a car just hauled to a garage from the site of an accident cannot be entrusted completely to automated processes. A second reason why it has been difficult to reduce the labour content of these services is the fact that in many of them quality is, or is at least believed to be, inescapably correlated with the amount of labour expended on their production. Teachers who cut down the time they spend on their classes or who increase class size, doctors who speed up the examination of their patients, or a police force that spends less time walking through their assigned neighbourhoods are all judged to be shortchanging those whom they serve. This, then, is why the stagnant services have consistently not experienced steady and substantial productivity growth, that is, reduced labour content. To see the implications for costs and prices, let me return to a (slightly edited) quotation from our earliest description of the relationship (Baumol and Bowen 1966, pp. 167–71).

Let us imagine an economy divided into two sectors: one, the progressive sector, in which productivity is rising, and another, the stagnant sector, in which productivity is constant. Suppose the first economic sector produces automobiles, and the second, performances of Mozart quartets. Let us assume that in automobile production, where technological improvements are possible, output per work-hour is increasing at an annual rate of 4 per cent, while the productivity of quartet players remains unchanged year after year. If wages in the automobile industry match the rise in productivity, then the one effect on cost is exactly offset by the other – total cost and output both rise by the same percentage. As a consequence, labour cost *per unit* (the ratio between total labour cost and total output) remains absolutely unchanged. This process can continue indefinitely, with auto workers earning more and more each year, but cost per car remaining stationary. Matters are very different in quartet performance. Suppose that the quartet players' wages, though below that of the auto workers, maintain their relative position. What does this situation imply for the costs of quartet performance? If the earnings of string players increase by, say, 4 per cent per year while their productivity remains unchanged, it follows that the direct labour cost per unit of their output must also rise at 4 per cent. Moreover, there is nothing in the nature of this situation to prevent the cost of performance from rising indefinitely and at a compounded rate.

Ordinary price inflation plays no role in the logic of our analysis. So long as the wages of musicians in this two-sector economy continue to increase at all, the cost of a live performance will rise, cumulatively and persistently, relative to the cost of an automobile, whether or not the general price level in the economy is changing. The extent of the increase in the relative cost of the performance will depend directly on the relative rate of growth of productivity in the automobile industry. Moreover, though it is always tempting to seek some villain to explain such a cumulative run of real price increases, there is no guilty party here. Neither wasteful expenditure nor greed plays any role. It is the relatively stagnant technology of live musical performance – its inherent resistance to productivity improvements – that accounts for the compounding rise in the cost of performance of quartets.

It will be evident that this analysis is applicable to many other personal services. In particular, the services that have been labelled 'stagnant' all appear to have difficulties persistently impeding growth in their productivity very similar to those facing the musicians in our parable. Clearly, health care has taken giant steps in quality improvement over the decades, but while the amount of physician time spent per patient-visit or per illness may have declined somewhat, it has done so only marginally. In education there has been no great change in class size, and therefore no large variation in number of students served per teacher-hour, and it is widely judged that there has been little if any improvement in quality. The output of an hour of police protection, or an hour of postal delivery time, or an hour of street-cleaning time has probably been enhanced by the use of motor vehicles in terms of territory covered, but the increase has probably been modest (criminal productivity has also been 'enhanced' by the use of motor vehicles), and certainly has not been continuous and cumulative. The productivity of trial lawyers and actors or musicians engaged in live performances has risen to a minuscule degree at most, and while automotive repair services have done somewhat better, the increase in their productivity has still been well below that of manufacturing, as the data demonstrates. Conditions in the insurance industry are very similar. This follows directly from what has just been said, for the purchaser of an insurance policy simply is acquiring a bundle of several stagnant services – health care, auto repair, legal services, and so on, and as we have just noted, productivity growth in the supply of each of these services has surely lagged. A final class of stagnant activities to be noted here is particularly significant in terms of the state of society. The care of poor people, government welfare, and related programmes seem to benefit from no significant source of productivity growth – they appear to remain fundamentally unchanged, handicraft activities.

The conclusion is that all of these services suffer from a rise in their costs that is terrifyingly rapid and frighteningly persistent.[7] They threaten the strained budgets of the individual families, the municipalities and the central governments of the entire industrialized world. And, as the resulting financial problems grow more serious, it is understandable that spending on these services is cut back or, at most, increased by amounts barely sufficient to keep up with the overall price inflation in the economy. But since the costs of the stagnant services are condemned to rise, persistently and cumulatively, with greater rapidity than the rate of inflation of the economy, the consequence is that the supply of these services tends to fall in quantity and quality.

3   THE SHARE OF THE SERVICES IN NATIONAL INCOME

Next, let us consider what has happened to demand for the services and the amounts of those services actually received by consumers, relative to the volume of the other outputs they obtain. We will find that, taken in total, this amount has not increased significantly, as is implied by those who argue that the industrial countries are turning into service economies. Nor, at the other extreme, and perhaps more surprisingly, is the overall quantity of the services demanded and actually obtained by consumers declining substantially – it is not driven downward by the very substantial rise in their relative prices. That is, consumers have not been driven by rapidly and persistently rising prices to cut down on the quantities of the services they purchase. It is, indeed, true that the share of American GNP constituted by the total market value of the outputs of the service sector has been rising sharply. But that is merely an illusion created by the relative rates of inflation in the service and manufacturing sectors, and bears no resemblance to the behaviour of their *real* outputs. We have already seen clear evidence that, on the average, the prices of the services have been rising far more rapidly than those of manufactured goods. If one deflates the output figures for these two sectors, adjusting each with its own price index to construct estimates of their real outputs, one finds that, at least in the USA, *the share of the real outputs of the services relative to that of manufacturing simply has not been rising.* In the past three or four decades in the United States the combined output of services such as product repair and household help as well as education, health care, and telecommunications has, of course, gone up, as the nation became wealthier. But the outputs of industrial products, if anything, rose even a bit faster. The main point here is that this record of real output composition hardly comports with the allegation that the preferences of American consumers are turning sharply toward the services and dragging the economy's output proportions along. Rather, the real proportion of output of the two sectors has remained approximately constant.

There is a second body of evidence, which uses comparisons of the outputs of wealthier and poorer countries, that pertains directly to the conjecture that rising wealth drives consumer preferences away from manufactured goods and toward the services. International price data indicate that other industrialized countries are also paying high relative prices for their services, so that those services also constitute a fairly large proportion of their gross domestic product (GDP), calculated at nominal, that is, inflation unadjusted, market prices, even though the actual volume of such service outputs consumed in those countries is not unusually large. The opposite price pattern has been characteristic of poorer countries. In general, then, we should anticipate a systematic pattern that gives the impression that the richer and more productive an economy is, the higher is the share of the services in its GDP, that is, the closer that country will have approached becoming a service economy. We should also find that the apparent relationship becomes considerably weaker or disappears altogether once one corrects for the price illusion introduced by the differences in price behaviour of manufactures and services in the poorer and richer countries. That is, after correcting for the false perception of high service output in richer countries (which stems from the higher relative price of services in such economies), we should not be surprised that the services' *real* share of output does not have any clear relationship to the level of prosperity of a country. The true relationship may even be the reverse of what it appears to be, with low-wage/cheap-services countries devoting larger real shares of their incomes to the services than do the rich countries where high wages make service outputs relatively costly to buy.

The empirical evidence is provided by excellent cross-sectional international data for 1975 contributed by Robert Summers (1985). Real (inflation-adjusted) gross domestic product per capita, the services' proportion of total real GDP expenditures, and their proportion of total nominal

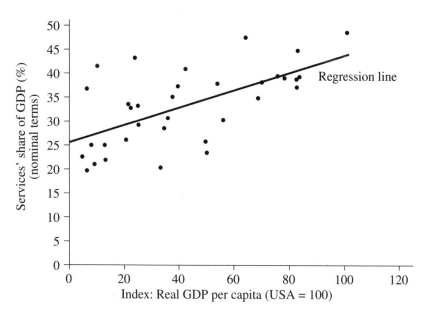

Source: Summers (1985).

Figure 1.6a   Nominal (unadjusted for inflation) share of services vs. per-capita income, 1975, 39 countries

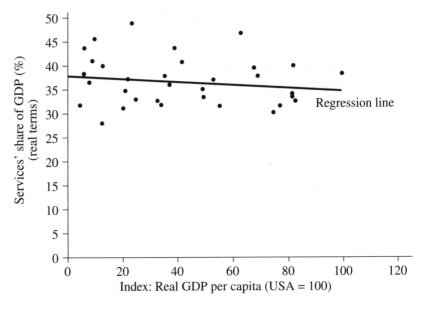

Source: Summers (1985).

Figure 1.6b   Real (inflation-adjusted) share of services vs. per-capita
income, 1975, 39 countries

(*un*adjusted for inflation) GDP expenditures were collected for a sample of
34 countries, ranging from very poor countries, such as Malawi and India,
to highly industrialized states, like Germany and the USA. Our price observations imply, as we have seen, that if the real share of GDP devoted to
services remains roughly constant among countries, the nominal share devoted to services will rise with real GDP per capita because the relative
prices of services are higher in wealthier than in poorer countries. Figures
1.6a and 1.6b show patterns completely consistent with these predictions:
in real terms, the share of GDP devoted to services remained roughly
constant as real income per capita increased, whereas, in nominal terms, the
share of total expenditures in the services grew markedly with income. This
result (which is also confirmed in a later paper by Summers and Heston,
1988 obviously is completely consistent with the conclusion that it is largely
an illusion that the USA and other prosperous countries are becoming
'service economies'.

4 SOME RECENT DEVELOPMENTS IN RELEVANT TECHNOLOGY, EVIDENCE AND THEORY

As has always happened in recent centuries, technological change has continued to affect the productivity of the services. Nothing in the analysis reported here claims that productivity improvement is impossible for any or all of the services. On the contrary, there are services, such as telecommunications, that have long been leaders in their rate of growth of productivity. Even in the services most affected by the cost disease such improvements have occurred. The productivity of actors, musicians and dancers has surely been raised by air transportation that reduces the time they must spend travelling between performance locations. Computers, television and film have at least made it possible to obtain productivity increases in education. In health care, there are a number of examples of technologically provided reductions in the labour employed in a given procedure.

There is good reason to expect that computer technology will materially raise productivity in a number of services, particularly those, such as the financial industries, in which record-keeping and related activities constitute a significant portion of their costs. However, it is to be noted that evidence of the productivity contribution of computers has only just begun to emerge. Until recently, to paraphrase Robert Solow's quip, the contribution of computers was evident everywhere except in the statistics. The latest data have begun to attribute some productivity benefits to computerization, but so far they are relatively modest. This need not presage a dim future for such productivity benefits. Both the steam engine and electrification made revolutionary contributions to manufacturing productivity, but in both cases decades were required before either had a major effect on the economy.

In any event, the issue for the cost disease is not whether productivity in the affected services can increase at all. Evidently it does increase in many such fields, perhaps almost everywhere. Rather, the issue is whether productivity growth in these laggard sectors can overtake that experienced in other fields. So long as there is no full catch-up, the costs of these laggard sectors can be expected to continue to *rise relative to the costs of the sectors in which it is growing more rapidly.* Moreover, the costs of the persistent relative laggards must then continue to rise more rapidly than the economy's overall price level. This must be so, since that price level corresponds to a weighted average of the costs of the two sectors – that in which it grows faster than the average and that in which it grows more slowly. I have seen no evidence leading me to expect such a revolutionary improvement in productivity growth in the laggard activities. Computers will undoubtedly help their growth, but I see no reason to believe that it will enable their speed to catch up with that of the growth vanguard. And until that happens, we can expect the cost disease to continue roughly as it has been.

I turn next to a few remarks on recent literature related to the cost-disease phenomenon. Since my writings on the cost disease first appeared, there have been a number of valuable studies of the pertinent empirical evidence. This is not the place for an extensive survey. Several of the chapters in this volume clearly constitute such studies. (For another recent example, see Fase and Winder 1999.) Generally, the evidence has not been inconsistent with the analysis, and at least some of it has been highly supportive. Empirical work that has been critical of the analysis has, so far as I am aware, never claimed to have shown that the theory is incorrect, but has argued, rather, that it downplays some other important influences that have contributed materially to the rising costs of some of the services.

There have also been some pertinent theoretical developments. Perhaps the most noteworthy is an important theorem by Nick Oulton of the Bank of England (forthcoming). In the cost-disease model, if the stagnant sector supplies only final products, a shift of the economy's inputs from the 'progressive sector' (the sector with rapid productivity growth) to the slow-growth 'stagnant sector' can be expected to reduce the average productivity growth of the economy. This result seems quite obvious intuitively, and it is generally, indeed trivially, correct.

However, a significant share, perhaps even the bulk of the shift of the labour force into the stagnant services, is not into the production of final products but into the supply of intermediate goods. The evidence indicates that most of the substantial rise in jobs in the USA since the Second World War has been provided by information-related services, whose outputs are used substantially, if not predominantly by other industries, as inputs to their own activities. In sum, a substantial share of this shift of the labour force has been into intermediate goods, rather than final products. Specifically, as Oulton points out, much of the growth in input use by the stagnant sector does, indeed, occur in business services and other intermediate output sectors of the economy.

It is here that Oulton's surprising and significant result applies. His theorem asserts that a shift of primary inputs, such as labour or raw material, from the progressive sector to the portion of the stagnant sector that produces intermediate outputs rather than final products tends to *increase* the economy's growth rate of productivity. This will be true so long as the stagnant sector has any positive growth in its productivity, however small.

The result is counterintuitive, because it suggests that productivity growth can be raised by increasing the share of the economy's primary inputs used *in the slow-growth sectors*. The explanation of the result is, however, straightforward. Suppose there is some growth of the productivity of a primary input turning out a stagnant sector's intermediate product that is used, in turn, in the progressive sector. This increases the growth rate in the net productivity *of the primary input* used both directly and indirectly by the progressive sector. It does so by reducing indirectly the primary input (labour) per unit of stagnant input used by the progressive sector, which serves as a supplement to the independent labour-productivity growth rate within the progressive sector. I illustrate the argument using a two-sector model, with relatively stagnant sector 1 providing intermediate input to progressive final-product sector 2. I assume perfect competition, for simplicity.

Let

y_i = the output of sector i
L_i = the primary input quantity used by sector i, where $L_1 + L_2 = L$ (constant)
p_i = the price of the sector's output
G_i = the growth rate of the productivity of the primary input used directly by sector i (with $0 < G_1 < G_2$, so that sector 1 is the relatively stagnant sector)
w = primary input price, and
* denote the (natural logarithmic) growth rate of the pertinent variable.
Then we have for the production functions of the two sectors
$y_1 = F_1(L_1, t)\ y_2 = F_2(y_1, L_2, t)$.
The growth rate of productivity in the economy is
$$(y_2/L)^* = y_2^* - L^* = y_2^* = (1/y_2)(\partial y_2/\partial t) + (y_1/y_2)(\partial y_2/\partial y_1)(1/y_1)(\partial y_1/\partial t)$$
$$= G_2 + (p_1 y_1/p_2 y_2)G_1 = G_2 + (wL_1/wL)G_1 = G_2 + (L_1/L)G_1.$$

This is Oulton's result. It shows that the economy's growth rate of primary input productivity is a rising function of L_1/L, the share of primary input in the stagnant sector, provided that $G_1 > 0$. The last line of algebra follows from the perfect competition assumption, which tells us that relative output price equals the marginal rate of transformation of the two outputs, $p_1/p_2 = (\partial y_2/\partial y_1)$ and the zero profit condition, $p_1 y_1 = wL_1$ and $p_2 y_2 = wL_2 + p_1 y_1 = wL$.

5   HAS RISING COST NOT AFFECTED DEMAND?

It would seem from the statistics just summarized that rising prices have not induced consumers to *decrease* (or to increase) their demand for services. As prices have risen, the public have simply accepted the higher cost of the services to them, and added approximately enough to the amount they spent on the services to make up for the rise in prices. That is, while overall demand for services has not increased, contrary to what is often believed, apparently consumers have stubbornly continued to buy about as much service as before, relative to other things, no matter how much prices rose.

That is, indeed, true of services overall, but by lumping all the services together we conceal more than we reveal, for the demands for the different services have behaved very differently from one another. Once we examine the pattern the explanation will virtually suggest itself. The fact is that some services have actually experienced some rise in demand despite sharply rising prices, while others have virtually disappeared.

The clearest example of a disappearing service is the fate of full-time personal service, the maids and butlers that used to work every day in every upper-class and many middle-class homes. In the USA their disappearance began early:

> ... the number of persons throughout the country employed in household service dropped from 1,851,000 in 1910 to 1,411,000 in 1920, while the number of households enumerated in the census rose from 20.3 million to 24.4 million ... in the country as a whole the number of paid domestic servants per 1,000 population dropped from 98.9 in 1900 to 58 in 1920 (Cowan 1997, p. 350).

In Europe such developments were far behind those in the USA, perhaps not really taking off until the 1950s. But today in France, Germany, the Netherlands and the UK, among others, full-time household help is as rare as it is in the USA. The explanation is undoubtedly complex and involves many elements, including changing attitudes of both employers and employees, social pressures and many other causes. However, one influence is particularly noteworthy in terms of the discussion here. In the household, and particularly in the kitchen and the laundry, labour-saving innovation has proved possible. First, there was hot running water, the electric iron and the sewing machine. After those, electric washing machines, clothes dryers and dishwashers, vacuum cleaners and a host of other new mechanisms have greatly reduced the effort required for each task, though, according to Cowan, the net effect has not been a reduction in the amount of time housewives have been spending on household tasks.

Thus, it is simply untrue that demands have failed to respond to rising service prices. They have been affected, but the effects have differed from one type of service to another. At the opposite extreme from the declining employment of household servants has been the expanding consumption of health care and educational services. Almost everywhere in the world there has been an increase in the share of the population receiving primary, secondary and university education (see, for example, Baumol, Blackman and Wolff 1989, pp. 196–8). In the industrial countries, the resources devoted to health care, including the number of doctors and nurses, have grown considerably faster than the population.[8]

Part of the explanation, of course, is that in many countries health care and education are provided by government as largely free services, so that users of these services did not directly experience the effects of the price increases. But they did have to pay the taxes to cover the rising costs, a connection that did not go unnoticed by taxpayers and politicians. Moreover, there has also been a steady rise in the use of these services in the USA, where they are generally privately supplied, and consumers pay the rising prices directly.

The obvious explanation for the rising consumption of these services, despite their rising cost, is a double one. First, these are services that people consider critical for their welfare, and particularly for the welfare of their children. Here, the rising difference between the earnings of more educated members of the labour force and those that are less educated is surely relevant. Second, it has not proved possible in these fields to invent new technology that permits 'do-it-yourself' education and health care. There has been no industrial revolution *of this sort* in these fields such as occurred in the household.

6   TOWARD VIABLE POLICY: CAN WE AFFORD ABUNDANT HEALTH CARE AND EDUCATION?

The pervasive fiscal difficulties that threaten quality of life in the industrialized countries have many roots. However, the evidence that has been presented here indicates that a considerable share of the problem is attributable to the cost disease. If inflation proceeds at a rate of, say, four per cent per year, but cost of education per pupil and other municipal services rise at a rate of six per cent, then a tax base that expands only a little faster than the rate of inflation is sure to lead to growing financial problems for the agency that finances schooling. Also, in the USA medical costs and insurance premiums that rise considerably faster than the rate of inflation year after year would appear to put such vital services beyond the reach of all but the wealthiest families. If the main cause of this predicament is, indeed, the nature of the technology of the supply of these services, and the course of development of such technology does not lend itself to easy modification, then the implication would seem grim indeed.

Yet, I shall argue now, far from there being no exit, the very structure of the problem is such as to offer society all the resources requisite for its solution. Contrary to appearances, we can afford ever more ample medical care, ever more abundant education, ever more adequate support of the indigent, and all this along with a growing abundance of private comforts and luxuries. It is an *illusion* that we cannot do so, and the main step needed to deal effectively with the fiscal problem underlying the growing public squalor is to overcome that illusion. This conclusion may strike the reader as implausible in light of all that has been said. Yet, the conclusion is inescapable, if only our future productivity record bears any resemblance to that of decades past which brought the USA and the rest of the industrial world ever-better health care and ever-more education, despite rising costs. There are two fundamental reasons why this must be so.

6.1 First Reason for Optimism: The Small, but Positive, Growth Rate of Productivity in the Stagnant Services

It is important to recognize that, regardless of their value as expressed in terms of money, wages are really increasing only when it takes fewer hours of labour to earn the wages needed to purchase a given set of goods. As I will show now, that is precisely true of the stagnant services. Their money prices are indeed rising ever higher, and their exchange rate against manufactured goods is constantly increasing, just as has been shown here. But in the number of hours of labour it takes to acquire them, over the longer run, their cost is decreasing steadily, even if relatively slowly. If this is so, the view that we cannot afford them is simply the result of what economists call 'money illusion' – confusion of the appearance given by trends in money prices with the reality of ability to afford the services.

But how can that be? The answer is that even the most stagnant of services is undergoing *some* productivity growth – lowly, and not very steadily, but some growth nevertheless. The cost disease analysis does not claim otherwise; it merely observes that productivity in the stagnant services grows substantially *more slowly* than that of the economy overall. To illustrate the point, let me return to my favourite example. If, in the earlier parable, the hypothetical Mozart string quartet had been scored for a half-hour performance, then its performance in 1990 required two person-hours of labour, just as it did in 1790, when it might have been written. Thus, there is apparently no scope for the slightest increase in labour productivity.[9] Yet that is only an illusion. To see why, consider a recent performance by a Viennese group of musicians played in Frankfurt am Main. A trip from their Austrian home base to the German auditorium surely would normally have taken no more than several hours in 1990. But when Mozart made the trip in 1790 it required six days of extreme discomfort (and, at that, Mozart wrote that he was surprised at the speed of the journey).[10] Certainly, technical progress has reduced the number of hours of labour required to provide a unit of the output in question, thus raising the labour productivity of every itinerant performer, even in live performance (and we know that performers are virtually all itinerant).

This example clearly suggests that there is no service whose productivity is untouched by technical progress to some degree. The consequent rise in labour productivity means, by definition, that it requires ever less labour time to produce a unit of such a service. And every resulting reduction in labour time spent in producing the service means that those purchasing the service must expend that much less labour-time to acquire the wherewithal needed to purchase it. That is the sense in which even education and medical care have really grown slowly but steadily cheaper, even as they appear to become steadily more unaffordable. Productivity growth in the stagnant services means that their real costs are steadily, if slowly, declining despite the dramatic inflation in their money prices. However, this, at best, can only make a minor contribution toward solution of the politico-budgetary problems that stem from the cost disease. More powerful aid must come from a second source.

6.2   Second Reason for Optimism: Productivity Growth in the Entire Economy means we can Afford more of Everything

There is a good deal more to the optimistic side of the cost-disease story. Even if it were true that productivity in the stagnant services was not increasing at all, their rising prices still could not put them beyond the reach of the community. On the contrary, it would remain true that society could afford ever more of them, just as it has in fact been getting ever more of the health care and education that seem steadily to become, to an ever greater degree, too expensive to afford.

As was pointed out some time ago by David Bradford (1969), in an economy in which productivity is growing in almost every sector and declining in none, it is a tautology that consumers can have more of every good and service. To achieve this goal, some *limited* quantity of the inputs used to produce goods whose productivity is growing relatively quickly (the 'progressive' outputs) need merely to be transferred into the production of the stagnant services. Then productivity growth will still permit expansion of the progressive output quantities, despite the limited decline in their inputs, while the outputs of the stagnant service will grow because more input is devoted to their production. To achieve such a goal – ever-greater abundance of everything – society must change the proportions of its income that it devotes to the different products. If this is true, only money illusion can cause us to believe that consumers as a group cannot afford to pay the rising costs of education, health care, and other such services.

An analogy can perhaps make the optimistic character of the basic conclusion clearer. Suppose we think of the public's consumption of goods and services as the purchase of a bundle containing many components, just as the purchase of a car includes the acquisition of seats, tyres, steering wheel, and so forth. Imagine that the price of steering wheels is increasing rapidly, but that because of the decline in the costs of the other components, cars (equipped with steering wheels) grow less expensive every year. Would one really conclude that steering wheels are growing unaffordable?

NOTES

1. Sue Anne Batey Blackman's invaluable assistance in the preparation of this piece adds to my heavy debt to her. I am, of course, extremely grateful to the organizations that supported the research: the Alfred P. Sloan Foundation and the C.V. Starr Center for Applied Economics.
2. If the economy provided only two easily measurable outputs – a manufactured good such as a TV set, and a service such as a concert performance by an orchestra – then what the statement would mean is that the ratio of number of TV sets produced to the number of concerts performed would remain roughly constant. Of course, service outputs are usually difficult to measure, so that what is meant here is approximate constancy of the total nominal value of services supplied, divided by an index of *service* prices relative to the corresponding index of outputs of all other commodities.
3. As we have emphasized from the beginning, we were not the originators of the cost disease idea. We have repeatedly cited the work of Jean Fourastié ([1949] 1963) as an early and noteworthy contribution in the field. Our primary contribution, if any, is to call attention to the profound implications of the cost disease for society, ranging from the financial troubles of the arts to the availability of health care to the general public. The author's participation in the political battles over health care legislation in the US is illustrative. On this, see Senator Daniel Patrick Moynihan's *Baumol's Disease* (1993). For an extensive set of my writings on the subject (with several co-authors), see Ruth Towse, (ed.) (1997).
4. There have, of course, been some offsetting, beneficial developments. Growing scientific knowledge and improved medical techniques indisputably mean that patients are getting better care for their money than they were forty years ago. More than that. To the extent that innovation has reduced the length of treatment some illnesses require, expenditure *per illness* must have risen correspondingly less quickly than cost per patient-day.
5. The data for the USA include expenditures of all educational institutions, public and private, at all levels. The expenditure figures for the other countries are confined to public institutions, which constitute the bulk of their educational institutions.
   The US figures are from US Department of Education, while the source for the statistics for the other countries is the United Nations Educational, Scientific and Cultural Organization (UNESCO). The general price indexes – the gross domestic product (GDP) deflators – come from the Organization for Economic Cooperation and Development (OECD).
6. This explanation is supported by the available data on crude labour productivity growth in higher education, or labour productivity figures unadjusted for changes in the quality of the product. According to the 1995 Digest of Education Statistics, in 1869–70 there were 563 institutions of higher learning in the USA, with 52 286 degree students enrolled and 5553 faculty members – in other words, 9.4 students per faculty member. In 1992–93 there were 3638 institutions of higher learning with 14 486 315 students and 835 000 faculty members – in other words, 17.3 students per faculty member. This means that crudely measured labour productivity (the number of students taught per teacher) grew over the course of those 123 years at an annual rate of one-half of one per cent. This is only one-quarter of the average rate of growth of labour productivity in the US economy as a whole, which is some two per cent a year.
7. The cost disease analysis also has an implication that may help to account for the high relative *level* of health care cost in the USA. It must be remembered that, despite wide-

spread impressions to the contrary, productivity levels in most other countries still remain well below those in the USA. If that is so, we should expect the graphs for their medical costs as well as those for other stagnant services to have intertemporal shapes very much like those shown for the USA in Figures 1.1–1.3, but that their heights should not yet have reached the levels of the American figures. The point is that we are all going rapidly uphill, but the USA began climbing earlier.

8. The Organization for Economic Cooperation and Development reports '...a strong rise in the physician-to-population ratio' in its member-countries (for instance, in France the number of active physicians per 1000 population doubled between 1970 and 1990, with similar rises in other OECD countries (see OECD, 1993, p. 166). The *Statistical Abstract of the United States* reports that between 1960 and 1996 the number of physicians per 100 000 of population in the USA rose from 151 to 239, and the number of nurses climbed from 293 per 100 000 population in 1960 to 815 in 1996 (see *US Department of Commerce*, 1998).

9. Or even for any increase in total factor productivity, for that matter; the latter appears frozen by the fact that the same number of instruments, the capital equipment, was required at the two dates.

10. Letter of September 28, 1790.

REFERENCES

Baumol, William J. and Alan S. Blinder [1982] (1999), *Economics: Principles and Policy,* San Diego: Harcourt Brace Jovanovich.

Baumol, William J. and William G. Bowen (1966), *Performing Arts: The Economic Dilemma,* New York: Twentieth Century Fund.

Baumol, William J., Sue Anne Batey Blackman and Edward N. Wolff (1989), *Productivity and American Leadership: The Long View,* Cambridge, Mass.: MIT Press.

Blaug, Mark (1976), 'Rationalizing social expenditures – the arts', in Mark Blaug (ed.), *The Economics of the Arts,* London: Martin Robertson, pp. 132–47.

Bradford, David (1969), 'Balance on unbalanced growth', *Zeitschrift für National Ökonomie,* Vol. 29, pp. 291–304.

Cowan, Ruth Schwartz (1997), 'The "industrial revolution" in the home: household technology and industrial change in the 20th Century', in S.H. Cutcliffe and T.S. Reynolds (eds), *Technology and American History,* Chicago: University of Chicago Press.

Fase, M.M.G. and C.C.A. Winder (1999), 'Baumol's Law and Verdoorn'a Regularity', *De Economist,* **147** (3), 277–91.

Felton, M.V. (1994), 'Preliminary Evidence on the Existence of the Cost Disease in the Performing Arts', Paper presented at the Midwest Economic Association Meetings, unpublished, Indiana University Southeast, New Albany, Indiana.

Ford Foundation (1974), *The Finances of the Performing Arts,* Vol. I, New York: The Ford Foundation.

Fourastié, Jean [1949] (1963), *Le Grand Espoir du XXe Siècle* [The Great White Hope of the 20th Century], Paris: PUF, 1949, Gallimard, 1963.

Frey, B.S. and W.W. Pommerehne (1989), *Muses and Markets. Explorations in the Economics of the Arts,* Oxford, UK: Blackwell.

Hay, Ian (1992), *Money, Medicine, and Malpractice in American Society,* New York: Praeger.

Heston, Alan and Robert Summers (1988), 'A New Set of International Comparisons of Real Product and Price Levels. Estimates for 130 Countries: 1950–1985', *The Review of Income and Wealth,* **34** (1), 1–25.

Kapp, Yvonne (1972), *Eleanor Marx*, New York: Pantheon Books.

Moynihan, Daniel Patrick (1993), *Baumol's Disease*, New York State and the Federal Fisc: XVII, Fiscal Year 1992, Published in Association with the Taubman Center for State and Local Government, John F. Kennedy School of Government, Harvard University, July 29.

National Center for Education Statistics (1992), *Digest of Education Statistics 1992*, Washington, DC: US Dept. of Education, October.

Noether, Monica (1986), 'The growing supply of physicians: has the market become more competitive?', *Journal of Labor Economics*, **4** (4), 503–37.

Organization for Economic Cooperation and Development (OECD) (1990), *Health Care Systems in Transition: The Search for Efficiency*, Paris OECD.

Organization for Economic Cooperation and Development (OECD) (1993), *OECD Health Systems, Facts and Trends, 1960–1991*, Paris: OECD.

Organization for Economic Cooperation and Development (OECD) (1995), *Health Data 1995*, Paris: OECD.

Oulton, Nick, 'Must the Growth Rate Decline?', London, 1999, (forthcoming).

Poggi, Emil J. (1964), *The American Theater: An Economic Study, 1870–1931*, unpublished dissertation: Columbia University.

Ryan, Paul (1992), 'Unbalanced growth and fiscal restriction: public spending on higher education in advanced economies since 1970', *Structural Change and Economic Dynamics*, **3** (2), 261–88.

Scheiber, G.J. and J.-P. Poullier (1987), 'Trends in international health care spending', *Health Affairs*, Vol. 6, Fall, pp. 105–12.

Scheiber, G.J., J.-P. Poullier and L.M. Greenwald (1991), 'Health care systems in twenty-four countries', *Health Affairs*, Vol. 10, Fall, pp. 22–38.

Scitovsky, Tibor and Ann Scitovsky (1959), 'What price economic progress?', *Yale Review*, Autumn.

Summers, Robert (1985), 'Services in the international economy', in Robert P. Inman (ed.), *Managing the Service Economy*, Cambridge: Cambridge University Press, pp. 27–48.

Throsby, D.C. (1994), 'The production and consumption of the arts: a view of cultural economics', *Journal of Economic Literature*, **32** (1), March, pp. 1–29.

Throsby, D.C. and G.A. Withers (1979), *The Economics of the Performing Arts*, London and Melbourne: Edward Arnold.

Toffler, Alvin (1964), *The Culture Consumers*, New York: St. Martin's Press.

Towse, Ruth (ed.) (1997), *Baumol's Cost Disease: The Arts and Other Victims*, Cheltenham, UK and Northampton, Mass.: Edward Elgar.

United Nations Educational, Scientific and Cultural Organization (UNESCO), *Statistical Yearbook*, Paris: various issues.

US Department of Commerce, Bureau of the Census (1995), *Statistical Abstract of the United States 1995* (115th edition), Washington, DC: US Government Printing Office.

US Department of Commerce, Bureau of the Census (1998), *Statistical Abstract of the United States 1998* (118th edition), October.

US Department of Education, *Digest of Education Statistics*, Washington, DC: National Center for Education Statistics.

US Department of Labor, Bureau of Labor Statistics (1995), *CPI Detailed Report*, January, Washington, DC: US Government Printing Office.

2. Potential explanations of the real share maintenance of the services

Thijs ten Raa and Ronald Schettkat

1 INTRODUCTION

The problem of the services is that productivity growth is low compared to that in industry. We may thus expect that services become expensive relative to manufactured goods and, therefore, price themselves out of the market. Surprisingly, at least to narrow-minded economists such as us, this does not happen. The share of the services in advanced economies is stable, or even growing. And this is not just a price effect. In other words, modern economies do not depict a shrinking real share of the services which is constant in dollars because of the ever increasing price of services. No, the real share itself is also stable. And because of the price increase, services consume ever increasing shares of our budgets.

The purpose of this chapter is to understand the issue in terms of a model. The model will be simple yet rich enough to clarify conceptual issues and to identify potential explanations. The conceptual issues are the appropriate measures of productivity growth and real shares. We will argue that instead of measuring the growth of productivity in terms of output per worker, it is better to use the concept of total factor productivity (TFP) growth. We will also argue that instead of measuring the service share as a percentage of national income, it is better to take it as a percentage of the national product. And yes, it makes a difference, even though national income and national product are equal! Services constitute part of national income as a sector of activity and part of the national product as commodities. At the sectoral level, however, the identity of product and income does not hold.

Once we have straightened out the concepts, some potential resolutions of the service paradox – exploding costs, persistent demand – suggest themselves. Suppose, for example, that services become more costly in terms of labour input, but not in terms of total factor input. In other words, labour may replace another input, such as capital. Then the paradox would be 'resolved' by the sheer fact that upon close inspection services have not become more costly. In short, the first potential explanation of the service paradox would be: 'Get your productivity measure right, use TFP'. We shall see that the distinction between intermediate (business) and final (personal) commodities (services) foreshadows itself in the appropriate weighting of service and industry TFP-rates. The second potential explanation of the paradox would be, therefore: 'Get your sectoral weights right, use Domar aggregation'. Also, suppose that services constitute a stable share of national income, but not of the national product. This, as we will see below, signifies a services shift from final to intermediate demand. Once more, the paradox would be 're-solved' by an appropriate redefinition of a constituent part, namely 'real share'. The third potential explanation of the service paradox would be, therefore: 'Get your share measure right, use products'.

Although it will prove extremely useful to make these distinctions between various productivity and share measures, they do not exhaust the potential explanations of the service paradox. There are four more potential explanations of the amazing vigour of the services. All are price effects and are of a supply or demand nature. To get a good grasp of these potentially important mecha-nisms, we must first analyse the price effects of differential productivity growth. We will do so in the context of a Mickey Mouse model of the economy, featuring only two sectors, industry and a service sector. The interrelationship between the sectors is simple: industry employs services, but the service sector uses no industry products. The simplifications are made for expository reasons only. For a general analysis we refer to ten Raa (1995). Once the model is presented we will review all the potential explanations of the service paradox.

2   A MICKEY MOUSE MODEL OF DIFFERENTIAL PRODUCTIVITY GROWTH

The subtleties surrounding both total factor productivity growth and the service share in the economy are microeconomic and escape our attention in a Solow (1957) growth model. The least we need to consider in the economy are two sectors, say industry (I) and services (S). The economy transforms factor inputs, labour and capital, into final commodities, goods and services. Final commodities are used for final consumption: household consumption, government consumption, investment, and net exports. There is also interme-diate consumption, but goods used by industry or services do not count towards the national product. It is only the net output of commodities one is interested in, because if we would include, say, the wheat used by bakers in the national product, then we would double count it, once as wheat and once as bread. Moreover, our national product would be sensitive with respect to disaggregation. If the baker supplies bread to restaurants, we would further

Table 2.1   Input–output accounts

	Industry	Services	Final demand	Total output
Industry	0	0	G	G
Services	B	0	P	$B + P$
Labour	L_I	L_S		
Capital	K_I	K_S		

double count by adding restaurant bread to baker's bread. Now the exclusion of intermediate inputs from our measure of the gross national product has far-reaching consequences for the services. Basically, personal services belong to the national product, but business services do not. Table 2.1 illustrates this.

The first column in Table 2.1 depicts the inputs used by sector I: For simplicity we assume that the intermediate goods are zero. Services, however, are used as an input, denoted by B (for business services). The other inputs are labour and capital, in both sectors. (For simplicity we assume that the intermediate service input is zero in the services sector.) The first row in Table 2.1 depicts the distribution of output of goods. By assumption, all output is for final demand, denoted G (for goods). For the service sector, however, output is divided between intermediate demand, B, and final demand, P (for personal services).

Later on we shall introduce prices, but for the time being let us assume that all values in Table 2.1 are nominal, in current dollars. Then the financial balance of industry reads, equating revenue (the first row sum) and costs (the first column sum, incorporating profit in the cost of capital)

$$G = B + L_I + K_I \tag{2.1}$$

Similarly, the financial balance of the service sector reads

$$B + P = L_s + K_s \tag{2.2}$$

Adding equations (1) and (2) we obtain

$$G + P = L_I + K_I + L_S + K_S \tag{2.3}$$

Equation (2.3) is the macroeconomic identity of the national product and national income. The national product is defined by the final consumption of goods and services: G plus P. The national income is what accrues to the factor inputs: $L_I + K_L$ in industry and $L_S + K_S$ in the service sector. Notice that business services, B, do not count towards the national product. They cancelled out in the summation of (2.2) and (2.3). Yet the activity of providing business services generates national income. This can be seen by considering the extreme case where all service activity is for business ($P = 0$). Then the national product (G) is divided between industry ($L_I + K_I$) and services ($L_S + K_S$). (It is even conceivable that all income accrues to the services: $L_I = K_I = 0$.) The point is that the identity of national product and income holds only in the aggregate, but not at the sectoral level.

Intermediate inputs (business services in Table 2.1) also play a tricky role in productivity analysis, the subject to which we turn now. Roughly speaking, productivity is output per input. Taking differences it follows that productivity growth is output growth minus inputs growth. However, all this is now meant to be in real terms. If output grows faster than input only because of consumption price inflation, but not in volume, we do not speak of productivity growth. To illustrate the distinction, let Table 2.1 now be in real terms, or volumes, and denote the prices of goods, services, labour, and capital by p_I, p_S, w, and r. We may allow for different wage rates in industry and the service sector, so that we have w_I and w_S, and similarly for the rental rate of capital. The financial balances now read

$$p_I G = p_S B + w_I L_I + r_I K_I \qquad (2.4)$$

and

$$p_S (B + P) = w_S L_S + r_S K_S \qquad (2.5)$$

Dividing by total outputs, G and $B + P$, respectively, and introducing input–output coefficients, we obtain the unit cost relations,

$$p_I = p_S a_{SI} + w_I l_I + r_I k_I \qquad (2.6)$$

and

$$p_S = w_S l_S + r_S k_S \qquad (2.7)$$

where the input–output coefficients are obviously defined by

$$a_{SI} = B / G, \quad l_I = L_I / G, \quad k_I = K_I / G \qquad (2.8)$$

for the goods, and by

$$l_S = L_S / (B + P), \quad k_S = K_S / (B + P) \qquad (2.9)$$

for the services. Since productivity is 'output per input', productivity growth must manifest itself as a reduction of input–output coefficients. We shall uncover this correspondence as follows. First we define sectoral productivity growth as a weighted sum of input–output coefficient reductions. Then we define total factor productivity growth by the so-called Solow residual. Finally we prove that TFP-growth is a Domar weighted average of sectoral productivity growth.

Industry productivity growth is defined by

$$\pi_I = -(p_S da_{SI} + w_I dl_I + r_I dk_I)/p_I \tag{2.10}$$

It is a weighted average of input–output coefficient reduction rates, $-da_{SI}/a_{SI}$, $-dl_I/l_I$, and $-dk_I/k_I$, where the weights are the cost shares, $p_S a_{SI}/p_I$, $w_I l_I/p_I$, and $r_I k_I/p_I$, which sum to unity because of (2.6). Similarly, service productivity growth is defined by

$$\pi_S = -(w_S dl_S + r_S dk_S)/p_S \tag{2.11}$$

The problem of low service productivity growth, relative to industry, can now be denoted as

$$\pi_S < \pi_I \tag{2.12}$$

Some of the questions we address in this book are the following. Is (2.12) a serious problem? And what are the consequences for prices and demand shares? As a first step, let us aggregate the sectoral productivity growth rates into a TFP-growth figure. The latter is defined by Solow (1957) as the residual between output growth and input growth. Output refers to the net output of the economy, the commodities used for final consumption, G and P. The value is the gross domestic product,

$$GDP = p_I G + p_S P \tag{2.13}$$

Business services are not included, because they are intermediate inputs. The national income identity, derived for nominal values (with all prices unity) in (2.3), now becomes

$$p_I G + p_S P = w_I L_I + r_I K_I + w_S L_S + r_S K_S \tag{2.14}$$

On the right-hand side of (2.14) we find the inputs, labour and capital, valued by their prices. The residual between output growth and input growth is defined by

$$TFP = (p_I dG + p_S dP - w_I dL_I - r_I dK_I - w_S dL_S - r_S dK_S)/GDP \quad (2.15)$$

The two leading terms on the right-hand side of (2.15) are goods and services growth. Because of the division by GDP we have a weighted average of the output growth rates with the weights given by the value shares of goods and services in (2.13):

$$\frac{p_I G}{GDP}\frac{dG}{G} + \frac{p_S S}{GDP}\frac{dS}{S} \quad (2.16)$$

The remaining four terms are a weighted average of the input growth rates with the weights given by the value shares of labour and capital in (2.14), using (2.13).

The role of business services is delicate. If industry economizes on business services, it shows in industry productivity growth, namely the leading term of (2.10), but it does not show directly in TFP, (2.15). We will now aggregate industry and service productivity growth into TFP growth and check what exactly is going on. We claim that

$$TFP = \frac{p_I G}{GDP}\pi_I + \frac{p_S(B+P)}{GDP}\pi_S \quad (2.17)$$

Before proving the claim, notice that TFP-growth is a weighted average of the sectoral productivity growth rates, but that the weights sum to more than unity. If we delete B from (2.17), then the weights sum to unity because of (2.13).

The proof of (2.17) is as follows. Multiplying through by GDP, substituting (2.15), (2.10), and (2.11), we must show that

$$p_I dG + p_S dP - w_I dL_I - r_I dK_I - w_S dL_S - r_S dK_S =$$

$$-(p_S da_{SI} + w_I dl_I + r_I dk_I)G - (w_S dl_S + r_S dk_S)(B+P) \quad (2.18)$$

Substituting (2.8) and (2.9), the left-hand side of (2.18) becomes

$$p_I dG + p_S d(B+P-a_{SI}G) - w_I d(l_I G)$$

$$-r_I d(k_I G) - w_S d[l_S(B+P)] - r_S d[k_S(B+P)] \quad (2.19)$$

Applying the product rule of differentiation, the coefficient of dG becomes $p_I - p_S a_{SI} - w_I l_I - r_I k_I = 0$ by (2.6), the coefficient of $d(B + P)$ becomes $p_S - w_S l_S - r_S k_S = 0$ by (2.7), and the remaining terms are precisely the right hand-side of (2.18). This completes the proof of claim (2.17).

The weights attached to sectoral productivity growth in (2.17) sum to 1 + p_SB/GDP. This is the so-called Domar ratio of our Mickey Mouse economy. The aggregation rule holds under general circumstances, see Hulten (1978). Equation (2.17) shows that service productivity growth must be attached to a disproportionate weight. For example, if in (2.13) GDP is split equally between goods and services, $p_IG = p_SP$, not an unrealistic assumption for OECD economies, then (2.17) becomes

$$TFP = 0.5\pi_I + (0.5 + p_SB/GDP)\pi_S \qquad (2.20)$$

Now let us return to the problem of the services, low productivity growth (2.12). Equation (2.20) reveals that the problem may be diminished to some extent by the boost we ought to give to the contribution of service productivity growth to TFP-growth. The boost is given by the business services, B.

What is going on here is an often overlooked distinction between the ditributions of the national product and value added. The national product is p_IG goods plus p_SP services. Value-added, however, is $p_IG - p_SB$ in industry plus $p_S(B + P)$ in the service sector. Sectoral productivity growth is defined as the cost reduction relative to sectoral output. In the service sector the latter amounts $B + P$. A cost reduction of say 1 per cent of $p_S(B + P)$ may look modest, but it may well amount to a solid 2 per cent in terms of p_SP, the service share of the national product. One might say that the Domar aggregation rule takes care of the elimination of the intermediate inputs, such as business services. The inclusion of business services in the denominator of the service productivity growth measure understates the contribution of the sector to TFP-growth.

3   PRICE AND QUANTITY EFFECTS OF LOW SERVICE PRODUCTIVITY GROWTH

Whatever the appropriate weight we ought to give to service productivity growth, a negative differential compared to industry productivity growth means that the relative price of services goes up, at least for competitive economies. This is a consequence of the definitions of sectoral productivity growth, (2.10) and (2.11). Sectoral productivity growth rates measure cost reductions. The full costs of goods and services are given by (2.6) and (2.7), where profits are incorporated in the cost of capital. In the light of these cost relations, low service productivity growth, (2.12), implies an increase in the relative price of services. This phenomenon is called the cost disease, see Baumol (1967). The instinct of economists is that a higher relative price of services means a lower share of demand, at least in real terms. Services would price themselves out of the market. What are the quantity effects of differential productivity growth? We distinguish four, namely two supply and two demand effects. Let us discuss each of them.

3.1 The Domestic Supply Effect

The mirror image of low service productivity growth is high industry productivity growth. Technical progress in industry releases factor inputs that can be employed in industry itself, the service sector, or a combination of the two. However, the mix of the released factors must match the factor intensity of the receiving sector or combination of sectors. For example, if industry undergoes a process of labour-saving technical change, then additional activity of the labour-intensive sector is required to absorb replaced workers. This will be the service sector. It is not difficult to capture this effect in the model.

Abstracting from market failures such as externalities or increasing returns to scale, the competitive allocation of goods and services will be efficient. If we invoke a representative consumer, efficiency means that utility is maximized subject to resource and technology constraints. Assuming substitutability of the goods and services, labour and capital will be fully utilized. Denote the stocks by L and K, respectively. Then

$$(l_I + l_S a_{SI})G + l_S P = L, (k_I + k_S a_{SI})G + k_S P = K \qquad (2.21)$$

Here each constraint shows the factor input requirements of industry, business services, and personal services, respectively. The constraints are represented by straight lines in the space of goods and personal services; see Figure 2.1.

The steep curve in Figure 2.1 represents the capital constraint, reflecting the relative capital intensity of goods production. A flat curve represents a labour constraint. The outer labour constraint is obtained by labour-saving technical progress in industry, a reduction in l_I or a_{SI}, where the latter reflects a saving of business services. Although this outward shift of the frontier implies an increase of the capacity of labour in terms of goods production (the horizontal intercept moves right in Figure 2.1), the optimum allocation (at the intersection point with the capital constraint) moves left. The labour-saving process prompts a reallocation from goods to services. The reduction in labour requirements is equivalent to a greater labour endowment and its utilization requires a greater level of activity of the labour-intensive sector, the services. In short, the service sector may act as a sponge that absorbs excess labour.

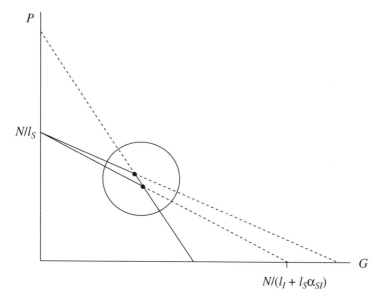

Figure 2.1   The production possibility frontiers and the optimum allocations

3.2   The International Supply Effect

The domestic supply effect holds irrespective of the shape of the utility function, but subsumes a closed economy. Open economies, however, may allocate resources across sectors independently of the proportions desired by consumers. Figure 2.2 zooms in on the old and new allocations depicted in Figure 2.1 and shows for each the budget line with points of the same value, given the world prices.

The slope of either budget line reflects the terms of trade. In Figure 2.2 the terms of trade are in between the opportunity costs of services (in terms of goods) at the sections of the production possibility frontier to the left and to the right. The two commodities, goods and services, are in the so-called cone of diversification, a term of international trade theory. If, however, the terms of trade become more extreme, with the budget lines more horizontal or vertical, it becomes profitable to supply a corner point comprising just goods or just services. This is the case of specialization. The non-produced commodity would be imported. Sustained productivity differentials between goods and services in a national economy which are not matched by the rest of the world may knock off services. Conversely, if dramatic technological progress in manufacturing occurs abroad, the comparative advantage at home may shift towards the services.

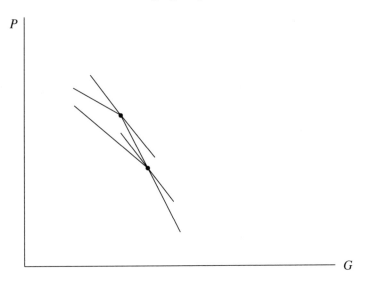

Figure 2.2   Enlargement and terms of trade

3.3   The Income Effect

The two straight, parallel lines in Figure 2.2 are essentially budget lines. Maximization of utility subject to these budget lines yields demand in either situation, before and after the technical change. If consumers demand goods and services in fixed proportions (have Leontief utility functions), the reduction of goods production in the new situation, on the outer production possibility frontier, will be supplemented by an increase in goods imports. It is more likely, however, that they will demand disproportionally many services. The reason is not that consumers must adapt to the new mix of output, but that many services are 'luxury' commodities, which are in greater demand as the standard of living rises. The preferences of consumers are such that age lengthening health services and other personal services become much more important as the budget goes up.

The fact that the budget lines in Figure 2.2 are parallel reflects our implicit assumption that the world terms of trade are not affected by the technology shock in the country under consideration.

3.4   Limit to the Substitution Effect

If the economy is not small and open, but closed or large enough to trigger general equilibrium effects, then the increase in the service opportunity cost given by the flatter production possibility slope in Figure 2.1 will result in a higher price of the service.

The extreme case of a closed economy shows the mechanism quite explicitly, particularly when the labour-saving change in industry is due to a reduction in the business service requirement, a_{SI}. The unit cost relation for industry, (2.6), illustrates that the relative price of the goods, p_I/p_S, will go down. (The wage and rental rates may vary as well, but this amounts to second order effects which do not affect the conclusion, at least for smooth utility functions.) For the general case of open economies with, however, general equilibrium effects through world markets, the lower relative price of goods will induce consumers to demand more of them. This is the substitution effect of differential productivity growth. While the supply and income effects increase the volume of services, the substitution effect increases the volume of goods. In principle, this process may continue unchecked, unless consumers reach saturation.

4 POTENTIAL RESOLUTIONS OF THE SERVICES PARADOX

The service sector suffers from low productivity growth; economists predict that services will price themselves out of the market. Yet the real share of services is stable. The paradox of the services – exploding costs yet persistent demand – is a puzzle. This chapter has provided a theoretical framework for an understanding of the problem. The analysis has proceeded from the measurement of productivity growth and real shares of GDP to the price and quantity mechanism. It is important to distinguish final and intermediate output. The latter, particularly business services, do not contribute to GDP in the product sense, but their productivity gains must be multiplied by a Domar factor to assess the true contribution. The analysis suggests a number of potential resolutions of the service paradox. The first three are conceptual, the last four are economic-behavioural.

4.1 The Inclusion of Capital

Most statements of the services productivity paradox are in terms of labour productivity. This goes back to Baumol (1967) who argued that it is difficult to imagine the performance of, say, a violin quartet with fewer person hours. Labour, however, is not the only input. It is conceivable that one could economize on the auditorium. The inclusion of capital in the measurement of productivity has the potential to correct the performance of the service sector favourably. In this chapter we have included the capital input theoretically and this will be persued in the empirical part of this volume. If the service sector has a better performance in terms of TFP than in labour productivity, then the paradox would be a measurement problem.

4.2   The Weighting of Sectoral Productivity Rates

Sectoral productivity growth is measured by relative cost reductions, irrespective of the destination of output of a sector. However, if a sector produces a large amount of intermediate inputs, such as business services, then cost reductions which are modest in terms of all output may be important in terms of the net output of the economy, GDP. Formally this is taken care of by attaching a Domar weight to the sectoral productivity growth rate. It reflects the indirect importance of a sector. This correction of the service productivity growth measure is the second potential resolvant of the paradox.

4.3   What Real Share?

Closely related is the appropriate measure of the service share in the economy. When we say the real share is stable, we often refer to the share of the service sector in national income. This, however, may well be stable even if services price themselves out of the market, for example by outsourcing of in-house manufacturing activities. What we should measure is the service share of the national product. Although the distinction is immaterial from a macroeconomic point of view, it matters at the sectoral level. Thus, the third potential resolution of the service paradox involves the appropriate measurement of the service in the product accounts.

4.4   The Absorption of Labour

This is the first economic, behavioural effect, referred to as the supply effect in section 3. If there is limited substitutability between factor inputs such as labour and capital, but markets work smoothly, then labour-saving technical progress in industry releases manpower which can only be absorbed by an expansion of other sectors, the services. This is a general equilibrium mechanism. The productivity growth is equivalent to a wider abundance of labour and that dampens its price and hence that of the services.

4.5   International Specialization

Relative cost fluctuations between goods and services may shift the comparative advantages of economics and thus prompt reallocations of activity. Even if services become more costly, they may attract more comparative advantage because of stronger developments in a partner economy. In short, changes in the trade position of an economy may explain the services paradox.

4.6   Income Effects

TFP-growth is paramount to an increase in the standard of living and richer consumers may just find services more important. This effect may thus counter the substitution effect of costlier services pricing themselves out of the market.

4.7   The End of Substitution

An increase in the relative price of services will prompt consumers to substitute goods. This is perhaps the most important price effect that economists have in mind when they address the cost disease. However, there may be a limit to substituting goods. At some point consumers become saturated with goods, while in terms of services the sky is the limit.

5   CONCLUSION

The logic that an increase in cost should reduce the share of services is simplistic. True, there is the so-called substitution effect, but there are other reasons, all consistent with the presence of substitution effects, that may counter and thus resolve the paradox. Income effects, general equilibrium effects, including international trade, and conceptual measurement issues may dominate the substitution effect. Moreover, the latter may be insignificant once consumers become saturated with goods.

REFERENCES

Baumol, William J. (1967), 'Microeconomics of unbalanced growth: the anatomy of urban crisis', *American Economic Review*, **57** (3), 415–26.
Hulten, Charles R. (1978), 'Growth accounting with intermediate inputs', *Review of Economic Studies*, **34** (3), 308–50.
Solow, Robert M. (1957), 'Technical change and the aggregate production function', *Review of Economics and Statistics*, **39** (3), 312–20.
ten Raa, Thijs (1995), *Linear Analysis of Competitive Economies*, LSE Handbooks in Economics, Hemel Hempstead: Harvester Wheatsheaf.

PART II

Supply-side reasons for employment shifts

3. Employment growth, structural change and capital accumulation

Esra Erdem and Andrew Glyn[1]

Declining agriculture and, more recently, deindustrialization and the expansion of services have shaped the labour market performance of individual OECD countries. It is now widely accepted that there is a strong structural component to unemployment and non-employment in OECD countries. This chapter examines the post-1950 patterns of structural change in a slightly longer perspective. One objective is to highlight the differing labour market experience of men and women. A second focus is on the relation between capital stock growth and the pattern of employment. Section 1 presents and analyses the longer-run trends. Section 2 examines the relationship between structural change and employment performance as a whole, especially its impact on economic inactivity and on the comparative employment experience of Europe and the USA since 1973.

The basic labour market data set is for a sample of OECD countries, based on Maddison (1991), supplemented by estimates of the gender split of employment (Bairoch *et al.* 1968), and updated from OECD sources (see data Appendix). Maddison's data go back to 1870, and some of the charts include estimates for that year; but the 1870 data are particularly rough and the statistical analysis is confined to the three sub-periods 1913–50, 1950–73 and 1973–94, mostly with a restricted sample of eight countries (G7 plus the Netherlands) for which capital stock data are available. The Appendix provides a number of tables with country detail for sectoral employment shares for men and women separately.

1 AGRICULTURE, INDUSTRY AND SERVICES

1.1 Longer-run Trends in the Employment Structure, Men and Women

Analyses of economic development have typically regarded the decline in agriculture as moving labour from where its average productivity is very low to the 'modern sector' of industry and services where incomes per head are much higher. As late as 1960 agricultural incomes were typically less than one half those in industry and services. The ratio of value added per head in agriculture to that of the whole economy in 1960 was a third in the EEC and in Japan (OECD *Historical Statistics*). Thus agriculture still represented an important source of surplus labour which could move into the 'non-agricultural population' available for work in the modern sector.

The size of this reserve is not straightforward to calculate since countries have differed widely in the extent to which rural women were engaged in agriculture – in 1950 for example women made up 55 per cent of those recorded as working in agriculture in Germany but only 8 per cent in Sweden. Whilst demographic differences and farming practices might explain some part of such variations, the root cause was differing conventions about the employment status of rural women in the national statistics. Such variation makes employment a misleading indicator of reserves of labour in agriculture and also distorts comparisons of employment trends for women when agriculture declines.

Men's employment is a more consistent measure of the proportion of the population dependent on agriculture; this measure can be extended to include rural women by taking as the 'agricultural population' twice the number of men working in agriculture. Expressed as a percentage of the population of working age this gives an index of degree of involvement in agriculture. Whereas in 1913 around one third of the population of the advanced countries were still in the agricultural sector, by 1973 the proportion had shrunk to well under 10 per cent (Figure 3.1a). In Japan and Italy the decline was much greater; in the UK it occurred much earlier (Appendix Table A3.1). After 1973 with small numbers in agriculture its further decline was less important.

Surprisingly perhaps the decline in the importance of agriculture contributed little more to the growth of the non-agricultural population during the golden age after 1950 than it did during the 'trans-war' period 1913–1950 (Figure 3.1b). Although the percentage rate of decline of agriculture was faster after 1950, the agricultural population was so much larger in 1913 that even a more modest proportional exodus yielded a comparable number of recruits to the non-agricultural population. After 1973 the decline in agriculture continued, but from such a reduced level that it contributed far less to the growth rate of the urban population. In Japan, where the shrinkage in agriculture had been so spectacular in the golden age, its potential for supplying labour was much diminished after 1973 and non-agricultural population growth slowed from 3.3 per cent per year to 1.0 per cent per year (Appendix Table A3.2).

The phenomenon of deindustrialization – a declining share of industrial employment in total employment – began in the late 1960s and early 1970s.

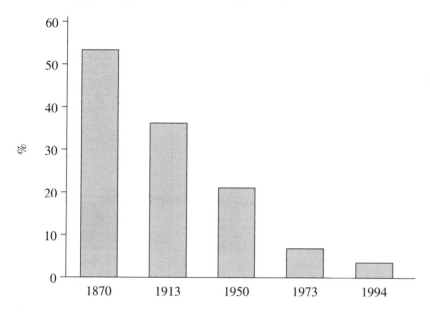

Figure 3.1a   Agricultural population: percentage of population aged 15–64

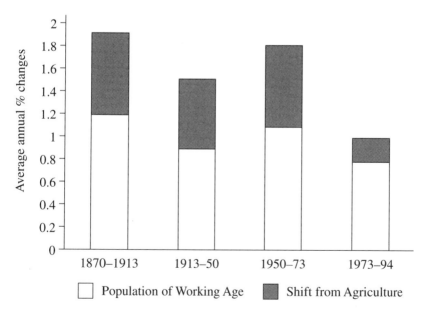

Figure 3.1b   Contributions to non-agricultural population growth

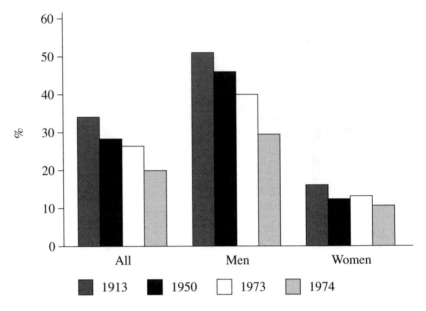

Figure 3.2   Industrial employment: percentage of non-agricultural population aged 15–64

But this measure is intertwined with the decline in agriculture; a better indicator of the importance of industry in the provision of jobs to the modern sector is given by the ratio of industrial employment to the non-agricultural population (the industrial employment rate). Figure 3.2 shows how industry has provided a consistently declining share of work for the non-agricultural population in the advanced countries as a whole. The rate of decline accelerated after 1973; the share falling by 7 percentage points as compared to only 2 percentage points over the previous 20 years. In Europe the decline became precipitate after 1973, bringing a fall of 10 percentage points by 1994 (see Appendix Table 3.3 for country detail).

The decline in industrial employment was particularly disastrous for men. Although the proportionate fall in European industrial employment was similar for men and women, male industrial jobs were much more important (in 1973 representing 48 per cent of total men's employment whilst only 28 per cent of employed women worked in industry). Industrial decline contributed 15 percentage points to the decline in the employment rate for men over the period 1973–94, whereas for women the contribution was less than 5 percentage points.

Services employment moved in line with the urban population until 1950 after which it provided an increasing proportion with jobs (Figure 3.3 and

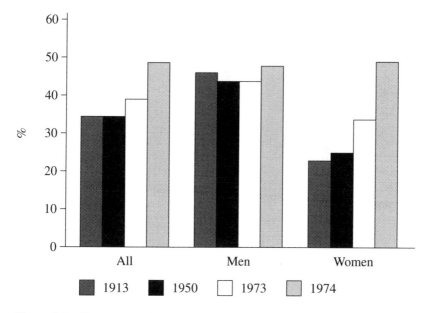

Figure 3.3   Services employment: percentage of non-agricultural population aged 15–64

Appendix Table A3.4). The increase of service employment accelerated after 1973, but the rise was greater in the USA (12 percentage points) than in Europe (7 percentage points) or Japan (8 percentage points). Women have been the main beneficiaries from the jobs created by the expansion of services. By 1994 women had more service jobs than men in both the USA (clearly) and Europe (just) in contrast to the position in 1913 when there were around twice as many men employed in services as women. After 1973 women's employment rate in services rose 18 percentage points in the USA, as compared to 12 percentage points in Europe and 11 percentage points in Japan. These increases far outweighed the declines in job opportunities for women in industry, leading to spectacular increases in the non-agricultural employment rate for women whilst the employment rate for men continued to drift down (Figure 3.4).

1.2   Capital Accumulation and Structural Change

The relationship between capital accumulation and structural change is complicated. In the neoclassical approach capital accumulation responds to the labour supply via flexible wages and capital–labour ratios. By contrast in the classical approach the limits placed on employment by the labour supply

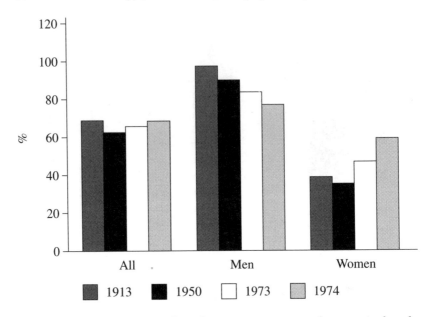

*Figure 3.4   Non-agricultural employment: percentage of non-agricultural
              population aged 15–64*

need not bind and employment trends in the modern sector depend on the
dynamism of accumulation. The growth rate of the capital stock is subject to
endogenous forces (unemployment bringing a higher profit share and investment – see Rowthorn 1999) but it may be affected by other influences in the
medium run and thus have an independent impact on employment trends.

Angus Maddison has provided data on the (non-residential) capital stock
covering the past century for eight countries (G7 and the Netherlands). This
shows the average growth rate of the capital stock rising from 1.9 per cent per
year between 1913 and 1950 to 5.3 per cent per year in the period up to 1973.
After 1973 the accumulation rate slipped back to 3.7 per cent per year. Partial
disaggregated data show that trends in capital stock growth in the golden age
were pretty similar in industry and services (see Glyn 1997). After 1973 they
diverged sharply in a number of countries with capital stock growth slacken-
ing in industry whilst being maintained in services. So accumulation in
industry and services is proxied by using the aggregate figure for both industry and services before 1973 and the sector figures for the post-1973 period.
For agriculture the hypothesis is that employment may be negatively affected
by the economy-wide accumulation rate, as investment in the modern sector
pulls workers off the land. The regression analysis reported in Table 3.1
examines how sectoral employment is influenced by capital stock growth.

Table 3.1 Sectoral employment, capital and labour supply, 1913–94

Employment by sector % change pa	Population of working age % pa	Agpopsh Initial year ratio	Nonag emp/Pop Initial year ratio	Capital stock (K) % pa	Const	Period dummies 1913–1950, 1950–1973	Country dummies	$\bar{R}^2$ (N)
(1) Agriculture (% pop)	-0.349 (.215) [.132]	-0.006 (.009) [.517]		-0.026 (.083) [.760]	0.048 (.037) [.168]	Insig	Insig	0.783 (24)
(2) Industry	0.376 (.526) [.492]	-0.010 (.017) [.587]	-0.045 (.017) [.023]	0.387 (.152) [.029]	0.0026 (.011) [.808]	0.021 (.005), insig	Insig	0.938 (24)
(3) Services	0.978 (.345) [.018]	0.030 (.012) [.031]	-0.057 (.014) [.002]	0.117 (.069) [.124]	0.040 (.011) [.004]	-0.009 (.004), insig	Insig	0.945 (24)

Notes:
Standard errors (Huber) in ( ): p-values in [ ].
Population of working age is instrumented using 'natural' population growth as explained in the text.

The regressions also examine how employment in the major sectors has responded to a number of aspects of labour supply. Firstly there is the population of working age. Immigration gives an endogenous twist to population growth, especially over the long periods considered here as migrants respond to job opportunities. Thus in the regressions the growth of the population of working age is instrumented using the 'natural' growth of population (that is, excluding migrants). Sectors which tend to absorb surplus labour would be expected to grow faster in countries and time periods when population growth was rapid. Secondly the share of employment in agriculture is included to capture labour reserves available for non-agricultural employment; the higher the initial share of population in agriculture (agpopsh), the greater is the potential for workers to move from the countryside into industry or services. Finally, in the equations representing employment growth in industry and services, the initial employment rate in the non-agricultural sector (Nonagemp/pop) is included; the higher the employment rate, the less is the scope for greater labour force participation or reduced unemployment. In the case of industry and services the dependent variable is the average annual percentage change in employment. In the case of agriculture however, the focus is on the extent to which the sector is providing labour for potential employment elsewhere; so the annual change in the ratio of male agricultural employment to population of working age is used as the dependent variable.

Equation 1 suggests a striking lack of systematic influences on the change in agricultural employment. Neither the speed of population growth, nor the size of the agricultural employment nor the growth rate of business capital stock is systematically related to the speed of run-down in agriculture. Neither are there persistent country effects nor systematic differences between the three time periods. This suggests that the decline in agriculture, and the parallel rise of urbanization, was a very idiosyncratic process, fluctuating over time and across countries in a way not closely tied to the kind of broad labour market influences considered here.

The growth of employment in the industrial sector (equation 2) was not significantly constrained by population growth or the extent of labour reserves in agriculture. The non-agricultural employment share is significant but it may be acting as a proxy for the level of development. However, industrial employment was strongly associated with capital accumulation within the industrial sector. The influences on services employment growth (equation 3) were rather different. All the labour supply variables are significant; population growth appears to have been translated proportionately into higher service employment. Services employment also grew faster where labour reserves were greater in both agriculture and in urban non-employment. However, services employment growth seems not to have been significantly affected by capital accumulation within services.

The broad picture, therefore, is that services employment growth is heavily influenced by labour supply and not by the capital stock, whereas industrial employment was sensitive to capital accumulation but not to the labour supply. This pattern for the impact of capital stock growth, first noted by Rowthorn (1995), can be confirmed analysing disaggregated data from the OECD's International Sectoral Database (11 industrial sub-groups and 6 services sub-groups for up to 14 countries and covering 1970–90). Labour supply influences are subsumed in the country dummies. For industry, the results suggest (Table 3.2) a very significant response of sub-group employment with respect to the sub-group capital stock (though the elasticity is lower than for the aggregate industry equation in Table 3.1). For the pool of service sub-groups, capital stock growth within the sub-group is not significant; however, capital stock growth in manufacturing appears to have a definite impact on services employment.

Table 3.2   Employment and capital stock – disaggregated results 1970–90

	Own capital stock %pa	Manufacturing K	Industry dummies	Country dummies	$\bar{R}^2$	N periods
(1) Industry emp	0.223 (.053) [.000]		Sig [.000]	Sig [.000]	0.534	241 2
(2) Service emp	0.110 (.088) [.214]	0.397 (.203) [.054]	Sig [.000]	Sig [.000]	0.704	138 2

Note:
Standard errors (Huber) in ( ); p-values in [ ].

1.3   Men and Women

The differing patterns for industry and services outlined above, together with the greater importance of industrial jobs for men and of services jobs for women, suggests that male and female employment will be subject to rather different influences. Table 3.3 summarizes the results of an analysis of factors affecting non-agricultural employment (industry plus services). For all workers together the results reflect those for industry and services in Table 3.1. All the labour supply influences and the capital stock are significant.[2] For women the capital stock plays no role, but the labour supply factors are very significant;

Table 3.3 Employment, capital and labour supply by gender, 1913–94

Non-agricultural employment % pa	Natural pop. of working age % pa	Capital stock (K) % pa	Agpopsh Initial year ratio	Nonag emp/pop Initial year ratio	Const	Period dummies	Country dummies	$\bar{R}^2$ (N)
(1) Total	0.739 (.313) [.040]	0.223 (.095) [.039]	0.024 (.028) [.069]	-0.056 (.013) [.001]	0.029 (.008) [.008]	Insig	Insig	0.956 (24)
(2) Women	0.934 (.278) [.007]	0.111 (.140) [.447]	-0.059 (.011) [.000]	-0.159 (.027) [.000]	0.108 (.021) [.000]	Insig	Sig [.032]	0.966 (24)
(3) Men	0.802 (.521) [.155]	0.266 (.137) [.081]	-0.028 (.017) [.108]	-0.058 (.023) [.029]	0.022 (.015) [.161]	0.011 (.005) Insig	Insig	0.930 (24)

Notes:
Standard errors (Huber) in ( ); p-values in [ ].
Population of working age is instrumented using 'natural' population growth as explained in the text.

for men capital stock is significant (at about the 8 per cent level), whilst the labour supply variables are much less important than for women.

2   STRUCTURAL CHANGE AND EMPLOYMENT PATTERNS

The role of structural change in the deterioration of Europe's employment performance after 1973, and its poor showing in relation to the USA, is highlighted in Table 3.4 which summarizes some of the patterns described in this chapter. The top rows record the decline in the growth rate of non-agricultural population in Europe after 1973 as the shift out of agriculture declined in importance; this meant a much slower growth rate of those requiring work outside agriculture. The core of the table analyses provision of jobs in industry and services. It splits changes in the non-agricultural employment rate in two ways. Firstly it shows the contributions of industry and services in providing jobs; then it shows how changes in the employment rate were reflected in changes in unemployment and in economic inactivity (labour force participation). These decompositions are shown first for all workers, and then for men and women separately. The performance of Europe after 1973 is compared first to its earlier record in the 1950s and 1960s (column 3) and then to the USA record after 1973 (column 5).

Services employment (in relation to the non-agricultural population) actually grew faster in Europe after 1973 than before. All the deterioration in employment performance (column 3) reflected the much sharper fall in industrial employment after 1973. This in turn meant that all the deterioration was suffered by men, with women gaining as much from the faster growth of service jobs as they lost from declining opportunities in industry. Compared with the USA, the steeper decline in industrial jobs and slower increase in services contributed almost equally to the relatively poor employment performance of Europe after 1973 (column 5). The faster decline in industry brought worse employment prospects for European men whilst the slower increase in service jobs accounts for slower employment growth for women in Europe.

The negative impact of deindustrialization after 1973 is brought out by contrasting it with declining agriculture after 1950. The decline in agriculture during the golden age was associated with a parallel increase in employment outside agriculture – see Figure 3.5. So, particularly for men, this was a 'positive' type of structural change (in the sense of Rowthorn and Wells 1987) reflecting changing patterns of demand in the economy. The deindustrialization of the post-1973 period has a quite different character – those countries where industrial employment declined most tended to have

Table 3.4   Employment trends in Europe and USA: 1950–94

All workers	Europe 1950–73	Europe 1973–94	Change	USA 1973–94	Europe– USA 1973–94
Average % pa changes					
Population of working age	0.57	0.54	–0.03	1.14	–0.60
Effect of agricultural decline	0.66	0.21	–0.45	0.06	0.15
Non-Ag Population	1.23	0.75	–0.48	1.20	–0.45
Non-Ag Employment	1.33	0.57	–0.77	1.79	–1.22
Average annual change in % points					
Non-Ag Emp/Non-ag Pop	0.07	–0.10	–0.17	0.40	–0.51
Industrial Emp/Non-ag Pop	–0.12	–0.46	–0.34	–0.19	–0.27
Services Emp/Non-ag Pop	0.19	0.34	0.15	0.60	–0.25
Inactivity/Non-ag Pop	0.02	–0.13	–0.15	–0.47	0.34
Unemployment/Non-ag Pop	–0.09	0.24	0.33	0.06	0.18
Men					
Average % pa changes					
Non-Ag Employment	1.06	0.03	–1.04	1.15	–1.13
Average annual change in % points					
Non-Ag Emp/Non-ag Pop	–0.30	–0.62	–0.33	–0.07	–0.55
Industrial Emp/Non-ag Pop	–0.31	–0.73	–0.41	–0.36	–0.37
Services Emp/Non-ag Pop	0.02	0.09	0.07	0.28	–0.19
Inactivity/Non-ag Pop	0.38	0.36	–0.02	0.01	0.35
Unemployment/Non-ag Pop	–0.08	0.26	0.34	0.06	0.20
Women					
Average % pa changes					
Non-Ag Employment	1.89	1.44	–0.45	2.66	–1.23
Average annual change in % points					
Non-Ag Emp/Non-ag Pop	0.33	0.37	0.04	0.86	–0.49
Industrial Emp/Non-ag Pop	0.01	–0.22	–0.22	–0.05	–0.17
Services Emp/Non-ag Pop	0.33	0.59	0.26	0.90	–0.31
Inactivity/Non-ag Pop	–0.24	–0.59	–0.35	–0.94	0.34
Unemployment/Non-ag Pop	–0.10	0.22	0.32	0.07	0.15

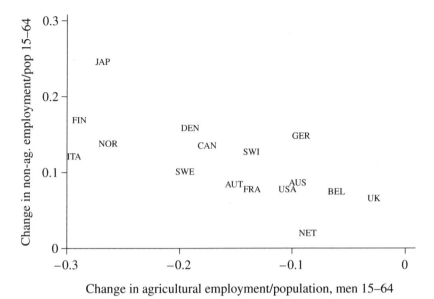

Figure 3.5   Agricultural and non-agricultural employment, 1950–73

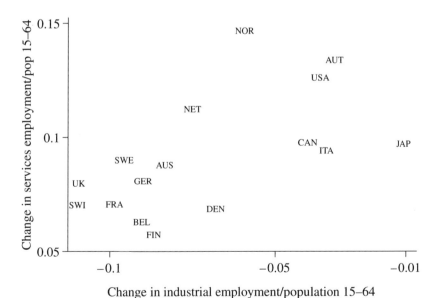

Figure 3.6   Industrial and services employment, 1973–94

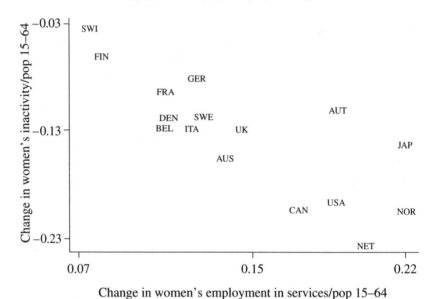

Figure 3.7   Women's inactivity and employment in services, 1973–94

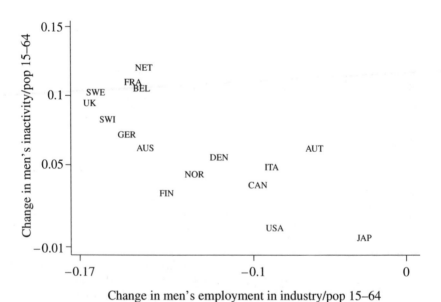

Figure 3.8   Men's inactivity and employment in industry, 1973–94

smaller increases in services employment (see Figure 3.6). This does not establish a directly causal role for the decline in industry – both sectors could be responding to common causes in terms of aggregate demand or in labour supply (though our earlier results seem to rule out this latter possibility). However, it is obvious that industrial expansion tends to raise employment in services by increasing demand for the output of services, either as inputs into manufacturing, or to supply final demand resulting from higher incomes in manufacturing. The evidence is at least consistent with deindustrialization, after 1973, restricting the growth of services rather than stimulating its growth by releasing labour.

This chapter has concentrated on employment trends without analysing how 'non-employment' was split into registered unemployment and economic inactivity. Table 3.4 shows that the deterioration in the European employment trend after 1973 (column 3) was entirely reflected in rising unemployment (for men and women); inactivity for women fell much faster after 1973 and rose no faster for men. In comparison to the USA, however, the European record on inactivity was also extremely poor after 1973. It rose much more than in the USA for men and fell much less for women and this accounts for about two thirds of the relatively slow employment growth in Europe. Inactivity trends seem more consistently related to structural change than does unemployment. The extent of the rise in women's participation is strongly connected to the rise in women's employment in services (Figure 3.7), though here the direction of causation can go both ways – rising labour force participation of women may have encouraged expansion of services as well as reflected it. More straightforward is the fact that increases in male inactivity were positively and closely related to the loss of industrial jobs (Figure 3.8); when industrial work disappeared men left the labour force to go on sickness benefit for example (see Gregg and Wadsworth 1999). This underlines just how important it is to analyse employment, and not just unemployment trends.

CONCLUSIONS

This chapter has analysed structural change in the advanced countries, focusing on the trends in eight countries since 1913. A number of broad conclusions may be drawn.

The decline in agricultural employment contributed very substantially to the growth of the urban labour force in the period before 1973, but much less subsequently. The decline of agricultural employment does not seem to be systematically related to broad characteristics of the employment structure (initial share in agriculture) or labour supply (population growth) or the rate of accumulation in the modern sector. Perhaps surprisingly, this suggests that the process of agricultural decline has been a rather idiosyncratic process, heavily dependent on the particular circumstances in individual countries in particular periods (for example agricultural policies).

Industry has provided a declining share of non-agricultural jobs over the long term, which has reduced the availability of work for men. Industrial employment does not appear to have been constrained by labour supply patterns, but was significantly increased by higher rates of capital accumulation.

Service sector employment expanded especially fast after 1973 and women have benefited most from this expansion. To some degree service sector employment appears to have acted as a sponge – it has persistently expanded more where labour supply has been plentiful, to an extent apparently not dependent on capital accumulation within the sector.

Whereas the decline in agriculture was associated with faster employment growth outside agriculture, countries where industrial employment declined faster tended to have a slower growth of services. This suggests limitations to the absorptive capacity of services.

In comparison to the USA, European employment performance since 1973 has suffered equally from faster decline of industry and slower growth of service jobs. Lack of industrial work has worsened employment prospects and brought economic inactivity for men; lack of service jobs has been associated with a relatively slow rise in women's labour force participation.

NOTES

1. Our thanks to Wendy Carlin, Bob Rowthorn and the editors and contributors to this volume for their suggestions.
2. The coefficient for population is somewhat less than 1 (but not significantly so). Krueger and Pischke(1997) obtain elasticities of 1 or more for various samples of OECD countries for the period 1959–95 but they use actual working age population rather than instrumenting it and they do not include a full set of country trends.

REFERENCES

Bairoch, P. and Associates (1968), *The Working Population and its Structure*, Brussels: Universite Libre de Bruxelles, Belgium.
Glyn, A. (1997) 'Does aggregate profitability *really* matter', *Cambridge Journal of Economics*, Sept, **21** (5), pp. 593–620.
Gregg, P. and J. Wadsworth (1999), 'Economic inactivity' in P. Gregg and J. Wadsworth (eds), *The State of Working Britain*, Manchester: Manchester University Press.

Krueger, A. and J.-S. Pischke (1997), 'Observations and conjectures on the US employment miracle', NBER Working Paper 6146.

Maddison, A. (1982), *Phases of Capitalist Development*, Oxford: Oxford University Press.

Maddison, A. (1991), *Dynamic Forces in Capitalist Development*, Oxford: Oxford University Press.

Maddison, A. (1995), *Monitoring the World Economy 1820–1992*, Paris: OECD.

Ramaswamy, R. and R. Rowthorn (1997), 'Deindustrialisation: Causes and Implications', IMF Working Paper, WP/97/42.

Rowthorn, R. (1995), 'Capital formation and unemployment', *Oxford Review of Economic Policy*, **11** (1), pp. 26–39.

Rowthorn, R. (1999), 'Unemployment, wage-bargaining and capital labour substitution', *Cambridge Journal of Economics*, July, **23** (4), 413–26.

Rowthorn, R. and J. Wells (1987), *Deindustrialisation and Foreign Trade*, Cambridge: Cambridge University Press.

DATA APPENDIX

Main Data Sources

Maddison (1991) and Bairoch *et al.* (1968) for 1870–1950 figures. These
were supplemented by Maddison (1995) for 1913 for the major countries. All
figures for 1973 and 1994 are from the *OECD Labour Force Statistics* unless
specified.

Population of working age and labour force by gender for 1950 are
from the *OECD Manpower Statistics* using 1950 or the first year for which
the breakdown was given, except for Germany and Japan where the figures
were taken from the ILO. These were then applied to the total figure provided
in Maddison (1991). The female proportion of the population of working age
before 1950 was assumed to be 50 per cent of the total.

Employment by Sector

1870–1950

For Denmark, Switzerland and Japan, no breakdown between industry and
services was provided for 1870 in Maddison (1991). For agriculture in Japan
the 1920 proportions provided in Bairoch *et al.* (1968) were used to estimate
the gender breakdown in 1870 and 1913.

Maddison (1991) did not have 1913 figures. These were taken from
Maddison (1995) Table 2-5 for the USA, France, Germany, Netherlands, UK
and Japan. For Finland an interpolation between the 1870 and 1950 figures
was made. In the rest of the cases the numbers for 1913 were taken from the
closest census results reported in Bairoch *et al.* (1968).

The 1950 figures are from Maddison (1991) except for the USA, France,
Germany, Netherlands, UK and Japan which were taken from Maddison
(1995) Table 2-5.

For 1870–1950 the gender breakdown of sectors is based on the proportions from the closest census results reported in Bairoch *et al.* (1968).
Obviously these estimates are very rough. For the USA for both 1870 and
1913 the gender breakdown in agriculture is taken from *Historical Statistics*
because none was available from Bairoch *et al.* (1968). For industry and
services a crude breakdown for 1913 could be calculated based on the 1950
breakdown in Bairoch and the change in the gender breakdown of manual
workers and (service + clerical + sales) workers from 1910 to 1950 as
provided by *Historical Statistics*.

1973–94

A number of specific country adjustments were made to the *OECD Labour Force Statistics* data for 1973 and 1994 where breaks in the series have been identified.

Capital Stock

Maddison actually compiled two sets of capital stock data, the first (1982) covering the G7 countries and based on national sources which used different asset lives and the second (1991), omitting Canada and Italy but including Netherlands, based on common assumptions as to asset lives. Some of the 1991 numbers are rather strange (for example rather high capital stock growth in the UK over 1950–73) and the sectoral data on capital stock from the OECD (1994) are based on national assumptions. So the data used here are from Maddison (1982), updated to 1990 from OECD (1994), plus the Netherlands from Maddison (1991).

Table A3.1   *Non-agricultural population as a share of population of working age (%)*

	1870	1913	1950	1973	1994
Austria	46	60	78	91	94.8
Belgium	62	77	90	96	98.0
Denmark		53	72	91	94.5
Finland	30	48	58	85	93.5
France	51	64	77	90	96.1
Germany	54	75	87	95	97.9
Italy	36	41	58	87	94.4
Netherlands	61	73	86	95	96.3
Norway	32	53	63	89	94.3
Sweden	42	47	73	92	96.4
Switzerland		68	78	91	94.3
UK	70	85	94	97	97.9
Canada	35	55	75	93	96.1
Australia	61	70	82	92	95.2
Japan	30	44	65	91	95.4
USA	42	69	85	96	96.8
Europe	52	67	79	92	96.5
All	47	64	79	93	96.4

Supply-side reasons for employment shifts

Table A3.2   *Non-agricultural population of working age: average % per annum growth rates*

	1870–1913	1913–50	1950–73	1973–94
Austria	1.6	0.9	0.7	0.9
Belgium	1.6	0.9	0.5	0.5
Denmark		2.0	1.7	0.6
Finland	2.3	1.5	2.6	0.8
France	0.7	0.5	1.4	1.0
Germany	2.0	1.1	1.1	0.7
Italy	0.9	1.8	2.4	1.0
Netherlands	1.6	1.9	1.7	1.1
Norway	2.0	1.6	2.1	0.8
Sweden	1.0	2.0	1.6	0.5
Switzerland		1.1	2.0	0.7
UK	1.5	0.8	0.3	0.4
Canada	3.1	2.4	3.1	1.8
Australia	3.2	1.9	2.6	1.8
Japan	1.8	2.4	3.3	1.0
USA	3.5	1.8	1.8	1.2
Europe	1.4	1.1	1.2	0.7
All	1.9	1.5	1.8	1.0

Table A3.3   *Industrial employment as a share of non-agricultural population of working age (%)*

	All workers					Men					Women				
	1870	1913	1950	1973	1994	1870	1913	1950	1973	1994	1870	1913	1950	1973	1994
Austria	31	29	32	28.8	24.2		44	55	44.0	37.0		14	13	14.7	11.0
Belgium	42	40	29	25.4	15.8		60	48	40.1	25.4		20	11	10.7	6.0
Denmark		32	33	28.5	20.3		50	52	41.1	29.5		14	14	15.7	10.8
Finland	40	34	37	28.8	17.0		51	55	41.8	24.7		17	21	16.3	9.0
France	38	36	32	28.2	16.2		46	49	41.8	24.6		26	17	14.3	7.7
Germany	36	37	31	33.5	23.5		60	55	50.5	34.4		13	12	17.1	12.1
Italy	50	51	30	24.1	18.5		70	50	38.8	28.3		32	13	10.2	8.8
Netherlands	30	29	30	23.3	15.1		51	54	39.3	24.6		8	7	6.9	5.2
Norway	44	34	35	25.3	17.7		51	58	41.3	27.7		17	12	8.9	7.4
Sweden	38	41	41	29.5	18.2		70	69	46.6	27.8		12	14	11.9	8.2
Switzerland		52	42	38.3	25.3		70	68	57.8	39.6		35	19	18.1	10.9
UK	43	35	32	30.8	19.3		52	49	46.9	29.5		18	15	15.0	9.0
Canada	49	33	28	20.5	15.8		58	47	33.2	24.2		8	9	7.8	7.2
Australia	37	30	29	26.1	16.5		51	46	41.3	25.8		10	11	10.4	7.0
Japan	39	33	25	29.1	26.5		47	40	41.0	36.6		19	11	17.7	16.3
USA	37	27	25	22.0	17.9		44	40	34.3	26.9		9	9	10.1	9.1
Europe	41	37	32	28.9	19.2	59	55	52	44.4	29.1	23	20	14	13.7	9.1
All	40	34	28	26.2	19.8		51	46	39.9	29.4		16	12	12.9	10.3

Table A3.4 Service employment as a share of non-agricultural population of working age (%)

	All workers					Men					Women				
	1870	1913	1950	1973	1994	1870	1913	1950	1973	1994	1870	1913	1950	1973	1994
Austria	25	23	27	30.6	43.5		27	35	33.4	40.2		18	22	28.0	46.9
Belgium	21	28	27	35.1	40.9		32	38	40.5	41.2		24	17	29.7	40.5
Denmark		45	41	47.4	52.9		46	43	47.1	48.0		45	40	47.6	57.8
Finland	46	35	35	39.5	42.1		40	36	34.1	34.7		29	34	44.7	49.7
France	32	29	34	37.1	42.0		37	41	40.0	40.6		21	27	34.1	43.4
Germany	27	22	25	33.2	40.6		31	33	37.0	39.7		12	19	29.6	41.6
Italy	33	34	27	28.0	35.7		50	40	39.6	42.9		18	16	16.9	28.6
Netherlands	35	34	34	37.5	48.5		43	45	47.2	48.8		26	24	27.6	48.2
Norway	59	45	39	41.9	55.3		43	46	42.6	48.4		47	32	41.1	62.5
Sweden	45	45	39	44.9	52.1		51	43	38.3	42.0		39	36	51.7	62.6
Switzerland		31	34	40.6	46.6		33	37	42.8	48.2		30	30	38.3	45.0
UK	36	35	35	41.0	48.6		43	44	43.5	44.3		28	28	38.5	52.9
Canada	33	38	33	42.7	51.6		55	42	47.5	48.5		21	23	37.9	54.7
Australia	42	38	39	43.0	50.6		51	50	47.9	50.2		24	26	37.9	51.1
Japan	50	43	32	38.6	46.8		64	45	46.8	50.8		21	21	30.7	42.8
USA	38	39	39	42.9	55.4		52	50	46.9	52.8		25	29	39.1	58.1
Europe	32	30	31	35.4	42.6	41	39	40	40.1	42.1	23	21	23	30.7	43.1
All	35	34	34	38.9	48.5		46	44	44.0	47.9		23	25	34.0	49.1

4. Technology and international skill demand[1]

Stephen Machin

1 INTRODUCTION

Across the industrialized world employers' demand for skilled workers has been rising. This has resulted in them being prepared to pay higher wages to workers with relevant skills, particularly to those with the aptitude and knowledge to utilize the new forms of technologies that are permeating into workplaces throughout the world. There has been much debate about what underpins this increased demand for skilled workers. A large (and still growing) academic literature has emerged which both documents trends in skill demand, and considers what are the key driving forces that lie behind the observed change. A lot of this work pays particular attention to the respective roles of technological change and globalization in shaping skill demand.

Technology-based explanations emphasize a skill bias that characterizes new technology. The skill-biased technological change (SBTC) view argues that this complementarity between skills and technology is the key factor that has generated the observed demand shifts in favour of skilled workers. On the other hand, the globalization view is predicated on the view that the opening up of markets to international competition, especially trade with low-wage southern hemisphere countries, has damaged the wage and employment position of less-skilled workers in the advanced world, and it is this which explains the relative demand shifts in favour of the skilled.

In this chapter I review the main findings from this literature, drawing on relevant empirical evidence along the way, with the chapter being structured in the following way. Section 2 describes the nature of shifts in skill demand that have occurred in recent years. Section 3 considers explanations of what lies behind the observed shifts. Section 4 focuses upon what is happening in the developing world. Finally, Section 5 concludes by briefly discussing some of the policy implications of the key findings of the research.

2   SHIFTS IN SKILL DEMAND

The US literature on demand for skills[2] begins with a stark finding: since the late 1970s real wages of young men with twelve or fewer years of education *have fallen* by one quarter. However, even though these less educated workers are cheaper to employ, their share in total employment has fallen massively. Put alternatively, they have lost out to their more skilled and educated counterparts in terms of wages, employment and unemployment. Demand has shifted against the less skilled and moved in favour of the more skilled who have won out in terms of labour market returns.

The international picture is also clear. In the developed world, less-skilled workers have fared worse in at least one of the dimensions of relative wages, employment or unemployment. Table 4.1 shows the nature of skill demand shifts for a number of countries based on the relative employment and wages of non-production *vis-à-vis* production workers (the only comparison possible for a reasonably large number of countries). The pattern is clear. The employment shares of the relatively skilled group of workers rose in all countries in the 1970s and 1980s. The pattern of wage shifts is more variable but seems to show increases in the 1980s at the same time as the relative employment increases. It is possible to combine the employment and wage changes into a single index of skill demand by looking at the wage bill share of non-production workers: this rises everywhere suggesting both that employers want more skilled workers and that their demand for them has increased as they are prepared to pay them relatively more.

Table 4.1 also reveals an important feature of the nature of shifts in skill demand. The table shows what happens if one breaks down the overall shifts into components that measure the extent of skill upgrading going on *within* industries as compared to *between* industries.[3] This is an important distinction as the extent to which the shifts are concentrated within specific industries is likely to reveal something about the importance of different explanations about what underpins the observed shifts in skill demand (this is discussed in Section 3 below).

The table makes it very clear that the bulk of the upgrading that has happened has occurred within, rather than between, industries. Put another way, some industries have experienced faster skill upgrading than others. Identification of which industries have had faster rates of upgrading, and their characteristics, can therefore shed light on what may underpin the improving relative labour market position of the more skilled.

Even more relevant is the fact that faster skill upgrading is observed in the same sorts of industries in different countries. Table 4.2 shows cross-country correlations of changes in non-production wage bill shares in the 1980–90

Table 4.1 Patterns of international skill upgrading

Country	1970–80			1980–90			Note
	Change in % non production (annualized)	% within	Change in wage ratio (%)	Change in % non production (annualized)	% within	Change in wage ratio (%)	
USA	0.20	81	-2	0.30	73	7	
Norway	0.34	81	-3	–	–	–	1970,80,n/a
Luxembourg	0.57	90	6	0.30	144	12	
Sweden	0.26	70	3	0.12	60	-3	
Australia	0.40	89	-17	0.36	92	2	1970,80,87
Japan	–	–	–	0.06	123	3	n/a,81,90
Denmark	0.44	86	-11	0.41	87	7	1973,80,89
Finland	0.42	83	-11	0.64	79	-2	
W. Germany	0.48	93	5	–	–	–	1970,79,n/a
Austria	0.46	89	7	0.16	68	7	1970,81,90
UK	0.41	91	-3	0.29	93	14	
Belgium	0.45	74	6	0.16	96	-5	1973,80,85
Average	0.40	84.3	-1.8	0.28	91.5	4.2	

Notes: From Berman, Bound and Machin (1998). The 'per cent within' column is based on comparing changes over time in the same 28 industries in each country (except for Belgium [24], W. Germany [22], Japan [27], Luxembourg [9 in 1970–80, 6 in 1980–90] and Norway [26]).

Table 4.2   Cross-country correlations changes in non-production wage bill shares: 1980–90

	USA	Sweden	Australia	Japan	Denmark	Finland	Austria	UK
Sweden	0.15							
Australia	0.35	0.16						
Japan	0.09	0.14	0.08					
Denmark	0.66*	0.06	0.11	0.14				
Finland	0.70*	0.12	0.37*	0.33	0.52*			
Austria	0.27	−0.44*	0.14	−0.11	0.31	0.29		
UK	0.64*	0.06	0.38*	0.01	0.53*	0.39*	0.47*	
Belgium	0.45*	−0.19	−0.28	−0.12	0.41	0.45*	0.51*	0.47*

Note: * = statistical significance at the 5 per cent level or better.

Source: Calculations based on the 28 industry data used in Berman, Bound and Machin (1998).

time period. There is indeed a cross-country correspondence: 31 out of 36 pairwise comparisons are positive and a sizeable number of the positive correlations are statistically significant (13 of them). This suggests that skill upgrading has a strong tendency to be clustered in the same sorts of industries across different countries.

3   WHAT LIES BEHIND THE DEMAND SHIFTS?

The basic facts outlined in Section 1 can be drawn upon to try to offer an explanation of what lies behind the declining demand for unskilled labour. The literature has identified several possible explanations of this decline, with the two main arguments being increased exposure to trade from the developing world and skill-biased (or unskilled labour-saving) technological change, SBTC. As we stand now, the combination of a number of research findings generates compelling evidence that increased demand for skill in the OECD is primarily due to SBTC. I will go through five sets of findings in turn to illustrate this.

1.   Despite the increase in the relative cost of skilled labour, the majority of industries in developed countries have had within-sector shifts in the composition of employment toward skilled labour. This is demonstrated by the numbers reported in Table 4.1.

2.   Employment shifts to skill-intensive sectors (the between-industry component of skill upgrading) seem too small to be consistent with

Table 4.3   Cross-country correlations in industry R&D intensity

	Denmark	France	Germany	Japan	Sweden	UK
France	0.68*					
Germany	0.79*	0.97*				
Japan	0.66*	0.95*	0.97*			
Sweden	0.73*	0.97*	0.97*	0.96*		
UK	0.73*	0.98*	0.95*	0.92*	0.98*	
USA	0.68*	0.90*	0.85*	0.91*	0.93*	0.94*

Notes:
The table reports are pairwise correlation coefficients based on 15 manufacturing industries (except for correlations for Denmark which are based on 14 industries due to missing data on the petroleum industry). They are weighted by the pairwise cross-country mean industry value-added share in total value-added.
* denotes statistical significance at the 5 per cent level or better.

Source: Machin and Van Reenen (1998).

explanations based on product demand shifts, such as those induced by increased international trade.

3.   Shifts in skill demand were concentrated in the same industries in different countries (see Table 4.2 above). Furthermore, there is a strong concentration of technological change in the same kinds of industries in different countries. Table 4.3 (reproduced from Machin and Van Reenen, 1998) shows that the more R&D-intensive industries are very much the same ones across countries. The same is true of UK–US comparisons of industry computer usage.[4]

4.   There appear to be strong, within-sector correlations between indicators of technological change (like computer usage and R&D intensity) and increased demand for skills. Figure 4.1 shows a strong correlation (always statistically significant) between skill upgrading and R&D intensity in six countries in the seventies and eighties.[5] Figure 4.2 shows no such relation between skill upgrading and increased import intensities for the same countries.[6]

5.   Case studies conducted by the US Bureau of Labor Statistics Office of Productivity and Technology that indicate the nature of innovations often mention innovations that lowered or are expected to lower production labour requirements. [7]

All this points to an important SBTC effect that has shaped the observed relative demand shifts. The fact that technology seems to have diffused across

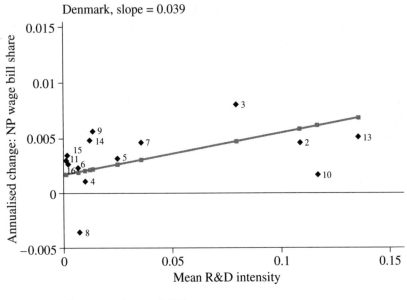

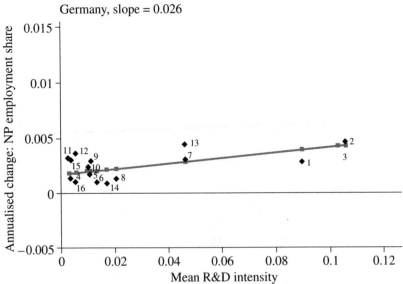

Figure 4.1   Regression estimates of the relationship between industry skill upgrading and R&D intensity

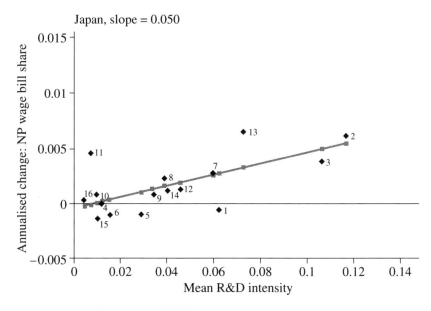

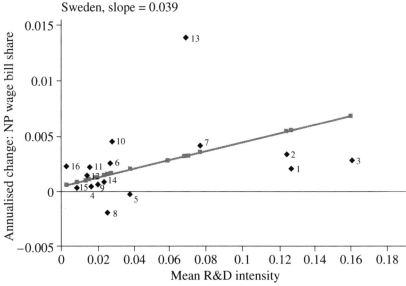

Notes: These are slopes from regressions of changes in non-production wage bill shares on R&D intensity controlling for changes in capital stock, changes in value added and time dummies. The industries are: 1 transport; 2 chemicals; 3 electrical machinery (including computers); 4 food, beverages and tobacco; 5 iron and steel; 6 metal products; 7 non-electrical machinery; 8 non-ferrous metal products; 9 non-ferrous mineral products; 10 other manufacturing; 11 paper products and printing; 12 petroleum; 13 professional goods; 14 rubber and plastics; 15 textiles; 16 wood products and furniture.

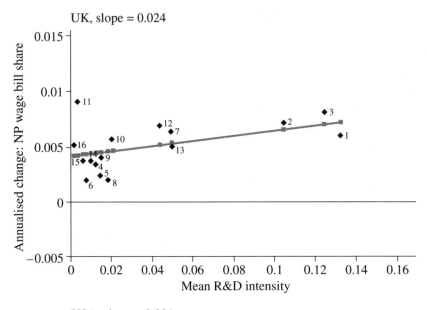

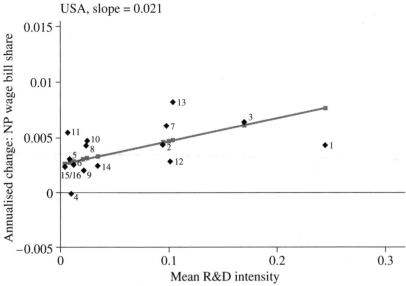

Figure 4.1   continued

Source: Machin and Van Reenen (1998)

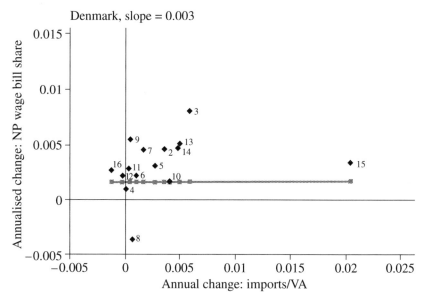

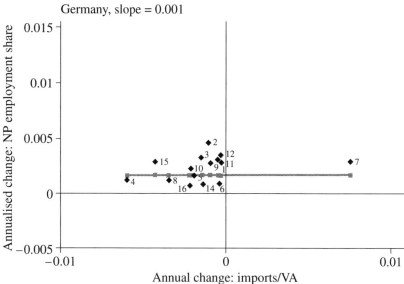

Figure 4.2   Regression estimates of the relationship between industry skill upgrading and changes in import intensity

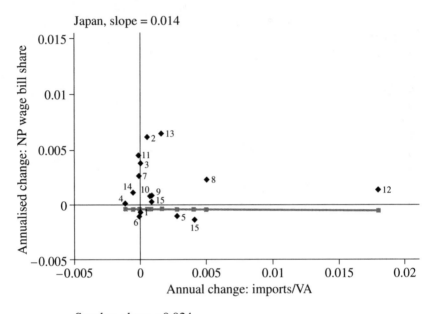

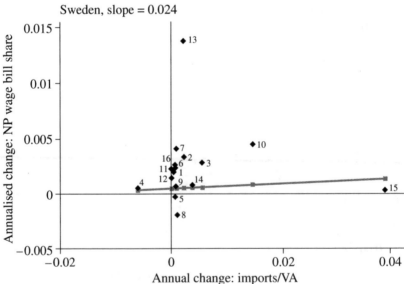

Figure 4.2   continued

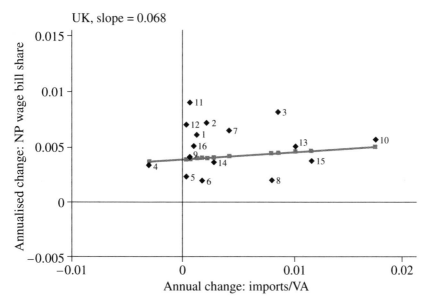

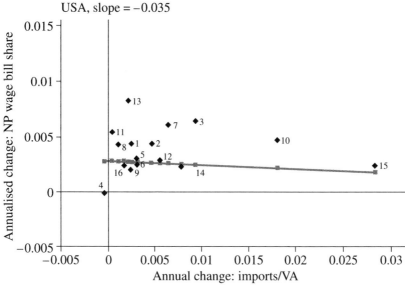

Notes: Based on the same regressions as those in Figure 4.1 but additionally including changes in industry import intensity. Industries are the same as for Figure 4.1.

Source: Machin and Van Reenan (1998)

international borders, and affected industries in different countries in similar ways, points to a global SBTC effect that has influenced wage and employment structure to the detriment of the less skilled in the advanced world.[8] It is much, much harder to find any direct evidence that increased international trade matters anywhere near as much for increased skill demand.

The case for SBTC being key to increased skill demand is further strengthened by work arguing that the recent experience continues a trend that has proceeded for most of this century. SBTC is present in US manufacturing dating back to the late 1950s (Berman, Bound and Griliches, 1994). Furthermore, Goldin and Katz (1996, 1998) document the role of electrification and the new production methods of continuous-process and batch processing in increasing demand for non-production workers in US manufacturing in the 1910s and 1920s. The trend SBTC hypothesis offers a simple explanation for the historical skill-premium. The skill premium has declined when supply outstripped demand (in the early 1900s as documented in Goldin and Katz, 1996, and in the 1970s) and has increased when the supply of more skilled and educated workers did not keep pace with demand.

4   SKILL DEMAND SHIFTS IN THE DEVELOPING WORLD

One can argue that extra 'degrees of freedom' can be obtained to evaluate the key hypotheses if the data range is expanded to cover the developing world. This is particularly poignant in the case of the globalization hypothesis as trade-based explanations argue strongly that one should see opposite patterns of skill shifts in the importing advanced countries (relative skill demand should rise as unskilled workers lose out) and in the exporting developing countries (where relative skill demand should fall as the demand for unskilled workers rises). The SBTC hypothesis, on the other hand, argues that developing countries should also be choosing from a menu of best practices that includes an ever-increasing proportion of skill-biased technology. One should also see increased demand for skills in the developing world as new technologies are diffused there (quite probably with a time lag) with the testable implication that technology absorption should be skill-biased in currently developing countries.

Data to compute industry demand shifts are much more sparse in the developing world. But what evidence exists also points to an increased demand for skilled workers that is consistent with a long-term global trend of SBTC. This is very hard to reconcile with the story that says the demise of the labour market position of less-skilled workers in advanced countries is down to the increased trade with low-wage, usually Southern hemisphere, countries.

So what evidence can be brought to bear here? First of all, several studies have found *increased* relative wages of skilled labour in several developing countries despite widespread trade liberalization in the 1980s which, if trade-based arguments were correct, would predict the opposite (see Feliciano, 1995, Hanson and Harrison, 1995 and Robbins, 1995).

Second, one can carry out exercises like those described in Section 2 for developing countries. Table 4.4 reports changes in the non-production wage bill share for three sets of countries: low, middle and high income countries (based on GDP per capita in 1985). The pattern is interesting and shows skill upgrading going on across the globe (for the developing countries and especially in the middle income range in the 1980's).

Table 4.4   Change in wagebill shares by income groups (weighted by wagebills)

	Low income	Middle income	High income
1970s mean change	0.23	–0.02	0.33
1980s mean change	0.05	0.45	0.42

Notes: The countries in each group are as follows. Low income: Ethiopia, Tanzania, India, Bangladesh, Pakistan, Egypt and the Philippines. Middle income: Guatemala, Turkey, Peru, Colombia, Korea, Malaysia, Czechoslovakia, Chile, Poland, Malta, Portugal, Hungary, Uruguay, Cyprus, Greece, Ireland, Spain, Venezuela. High income (as for Table 4.1 above): Japan, UK, Austria, Finland, Belgium, Denmark, Luxembourg, West Germany, Norway, Sweden, Australia, USA.

Source: Berman and Machin (2000).

Furthermore, the extent of skill upgrading in the developing world is positively correlated with what is going on in the developed world (see Berman and Machin, 2000, and Desjonqueres, Machin and Van Reenen, 1999). Table 4.5 reports correlations between skill upgrading across countries and US skill upgrading. The mapping is quite strong: in many low and middle income countries it seems that it is the same industries that have experienced faster skill upgrading. Furthermore, Table 4.6 reveals that these patterns of skill-upgrading in developing countries in the 1980s are well predicted by indicators of recent skill-biased technological change in the OECD (OECD R&D intensity and US computer usage), indicating skill-biased technology transfer into the middle and (to a lesser extent) the low income countries.[9] This rests well with the SBTC hypothesis but is very much contrary to the trade-based arguments of shifting skill demand.

Table 4.5   Correlations of country-specific industry skill upgrading with US skill upgrading

	Correlations of 1980s upgrading with US 1980s upgrading	Correlations of 1970s upgrading with US 1970s upgrading
High Income Group		
Countries	9	11
Positive	9	10
Significant positive	5	1
Significant negative	0	0
Middle Income Group		
Countries	12	8
Positives	11	7
Significant positives	2	0
Significant negatives	0	0
Low Income Group		
Countries	6	5
Positives	5	3
Significant positives	0	1
Significant negatives	0	0

Note: High, middle and low countries are defined in the notes to Table 4.4.

Source: Berman and Machin (2000).

5   CONCLUDING REMARKS

In this chapter I have considered recent empirical evidence on increases in the relative demand for skilled workers, both describing the key trends, and evaluating the explanations underpinning the observed changes. That the relatively skilled have done better in some (or all) dimensions of relative wages, employment and unemployment is very clear across a range of developed countries. The key factor underpinning the change seems to be technological change that is biased in favour of skilled workers and it is this, rather than increased international competition, that has boosted their relative labour demand. This finding is reinforced by looking at what is happening in the developing world (particularly in middle income countries),

Table 4.6   Correlations of country-specific industry skill upgrading with technology variables

	Correlations of 1980s upgrading with US computer usage	Correlations of 1980s upgrading with OECD R&D intensity (1980–90)	Correlations of 1970s upgrading with US computer usage	Correlations of 1970s upgrading with OECD R&D intensity (1973–80)
High Income Group				
Countries	10	10	12	12
Positive	10	8	10	10
Significant positive	5	4	6	4
Significant negative	0	0	1	1
Middle Income Group				
Countries	12	12	8	8
Positives	8	9	5	4
Significant positives	3	2	3	1
Significant negatives	0	0	1	2
Low Income Group				
Countries	6	6	5	5
Positives	3	3	4	2
Significant positives	1	1	0	0
Significant negatives	1	0	0	1

Note: High, middle and low countries are defined in the notes to Table 4.4.

Source: Berman and Machin (2000).

where skill demand is also increasing, probably due to the diffusion of SBTC across international borders across the world.

What these research findings suggest for policy is important at the national and international level. SBTC has had pervasive effects on labour market structure across the globe and this makes it clear that governments need to support education properly and to train workers to use the new technologies that are becoming central to the nature of work. The rapid pace of technological change, and its rapid diffusion across international borders, makes this a policy issue that will be central to the organization of work in the 21st century.

NOTES

1. This work draws heavily on some of my joint papers on the subject matter, especially Berman, Bound and Machin (1998), Machin and Van Reenen (1998) and Berman and Machin (2000). The work also draws on a paper presented at a UNIDO Conference in Vienna. I would like to thank my co-authors and other commentators on this work, without implicating them in any way for the views expressed in this piece.
2. In this work 'skill' is measured in a variety of ways and it should be acknowledged that the word is often used in a rather loose way. The skill measures used tend to be rather coarse and as such have their limitations. But the measures used do seem to display similar trends. For example, the two most commonly used measures (forced upon researchers by data availability constraints) are to define non-production workers and workers with a college degree as relatively skilled and production workers and non-graduates as relatively un-skilled. Trends in the wage and employment rates of non-production *vis-à-vis* production workers and graduates *vis-à-vis* non-graduates show very similar trends in the countries where they have been compared (see Berman, Bound and Griliches, 1994, for US comparisons and Machin and Van Reenen, 1998, for UK comparisons).
3. This involves computing the now well-known decomposition of the aggregate change in skill demand between two time periods, ΔS, for i (=1,...N) industries as $\Delta S = \Sigma \Delta S_i \overline{P}_i + \Sigma \Delta P_i \overline{S}_i$ where the first term is the within-industry component of skill upgrading and the second term is the between-industry component (P is a measure of the relative size of industry i, namely the share of industry i's wage bill of employment in the aggregate wage bill or employment, and a bar denotes a time mean).
4. Correlation coefficent for UK–US industry computer usage = 0.79 (from Machin and Van Reenen, 1998).
5. There are strong correlations between skill upgrading and industry computer usage in the UK and US as well (see Autor, Katz and Krueger, 1998, and Machin and Van Reenen, 1998).
6. All these results are derived from econometric models reported in Machin and Van Reenen (1998).
7. These studies are cited in more detail in Berman, Bound and Machin (1998).
8. Most of this evidence looks at industries. But SBTC is important in firm-level work as well. A good recent example is Siegel (1999).
9. This is based on the evidence in Berman and Machin (2000) showing positive correlations between industry skill upgrading in the developing world and US computer usage or OECD R&D intensity.

REFERENCES

Autor, David, Lawrence F. Katz and Alan Krueger (1998), 'Computing inequality: have computers changed the labor market?', *Quarterly Journal of Economics*, 113, 1169–214.

Berman, Eli and Stephen Machin (2000), 'Skill Biased Technology Transfer Around The World', *Oxford Review of Economic Policy*, **16** (3), 12–22, mimeo.

Berman, Eli, John Bound and Zvi Griliches (1994), 'Changes in the demand for skilled labor within US manufacturing industries: evidence from the Annual Survey of Manufacturing', *Quarterly Journal of Economics*, 109, 367–98.

Berman, Eli, John Bound and Stephen Machin (1998), 'Implications of skill-biased technological change: international evidence', *Quarterly Journal of Economics*, **113** (4), 1245–80.

Desjonqueres, T., S. Machin and J. Van Reenen (1999), 'Another nail in the coffin?

Or can the trade based explanation of changing skill structures be resurrected?', *Scandinavian Journal of Economics*, 101, 533–54.

Feliciano, Zadia (1995), 'Workers and trade liberalization: the impact of trade reforms in Mexico on wages and employment', Queen's College, mimeo, May.

Goldin, Claudia and Lawrence Katz (1996), 'Technology, Skill and the Wage Structure: Insights from the Past', *American Economic Review*, 136, 252–7.

Goldin, Claudia and Lawrence Katz (1998), 'The origins of technology-skill complementarity', *Quarterly Journal of Economics*, 113, 693–732.

Hanson, Gordon H. and Ann Harrison (1995), 'Trade, technology and wage inequality', National Bureau of Economic Research Working Paper 5110.

Machin, Stephen and John Van Reenen (1998), 'Technology and changes in skill structure: evidence from seven OECD countries', *Quarterly Journal of Economics*, 113, 1215–44.

Robbins, Donald J. (1995), 'Trade, trade liberalization and inequality in Latin America and East Asia – synthesis of seven country studies', Harvard, mimeo.

Siegel, Donald (1999), *Skill-Biased Technological Change: Evidence From a Firm-Level Survey*, W.E. UpJohn Institute for Employment Research, Kalamazoo, Michigan.

PART III

The cost disease of the services

5. Will the new information economy cure the cost disease in the USA?[1]

Joe P. Mattey

INTRODUCTION

As in other industrial countries, the sectoral structure of employment and nominal output in the USA has changed noticeably over the last several decades, and the nation appears to have 'fallen ill' with a 'cost disease' in the service sector. Productivity growth in the service sector has been quite weak, boosting production costs and prices of services. Despite this, the service sector's share of real output has trended upward, and the service sector's share of employment and nominal output has increased even faster. This chapter considers various possible explanations for the puzzle of why the US service sector has remained quite viable in terms of output shares – despite rapid increases in relative prices. The chapter focuses, in particular, on the possible past and future role of the growth in the information-orientedness of the economy in providing the 'cure' to the cost disease.

The next section of this chapter provides some of the basic statistics on the structure of employment, output, costs, and prices in the USA, thereby identifying the extent to which symptoms of the 'cost disease' have been present. The third section reviews various other potential explanations of the maintenance of real service sector shares that have been offered in the literature. The fourth and final section of the chapter turns to the issue of how the increasing information-orientedness of the economy might be affecting these trends.

EVIDENCE OF THE COST DISEASE IN THE USA

Sectoral Labour Productivity, Costs, and Prices

More than thirty years have passed since William Baumol and William Bowen (1965), in a famous commentary on the outlook for the performing arts,

Table 5.1   Growth of labour productivity, unit labour costs, and prices by major industry group in the USA

	Per cent change at an annual rate 1977–96		
Industry group	Output per employee	Unit labour cost	Price
All sectors	0.7	4.5	4.5
Agriculture, forestry, and fishing	2.4	3.5	1.4
Mining	3.0	2.5	2.8
Construction	–0.7	5.2	5.2
Manufacturing	3.1	2.4	2.9
Transportation	0.4	3.5	3.6
Communications	3.8	1.7	3.0
Electric, gas and sanitary services	1.5	4.3	5.0
Wholesale trade	3.1	2.3	2.1
Retail trade	0.7	3.6	3.6
Finance, insurance and real estate	0.6	6.4	6.0
Services	–0.5	6.9	6.3
Private households	2.1	3.7	3.7
Government	0.0	5.6	5.5

Notes:
Output per employee is the ratio of the quantity index for gross domestic product by industry to the number of full-time and part-time employees.
Unit labour cost is the ratio of total compensation of employees to the quantity index for gross domestic product by industry.
Price is the implicit price deflator for gross domestic product.

Source: Author's calculations using the US Bureau of Economic Analysis' estimates of Gross Product by Industry.

noted that services which are 'stagnant', in the sense that labour productivity is stable, are likely to suffer from an increase in relative costs if labour productivity in other sectors of the economy is rising.[2] Indeed, the US services sector appears to have suffered from Baumol's 'cost disease'.[3] Between 1977 and 1996, output per employee in the services sector edged down at about 0.5 per cent at an annual rate, whereas labour productivity has posted notable gains in most other major sectors of the US economy (Table 5.1). Accordingly, over this period unit labour costs in the services sector increased 6.9 per cent at an annual rate, about 2.5 percentage points faster than the overall rate of increase in unit labour costs in the US economy. Most of this cost differential showed through to a faster rate of increase in prices of

Table 5.2 Growth of labour productivity, unit labour costs, and prices in selected service industries in the USA

Industry	Output per employee	Unit labour cost	Price
	Per cent change at an annual rate 1977–96		
Total services	−0.5	6.9	6.3
Hotels and lodging	−1.3	7.0	6.9
Personal services	−1.1	5.9	6.3
Auto repair, services, and parking	−1.8	6.7	6.2
Miscellaneous repair services	−2.0	7.2	7.2
Motion pictures	0.2	5.7	5.0
Amusement and recreation services	0.2	5.3	4.7
Legal services	−3.1	10.8	8.2
Educational services	−0.8	6.2	6.1
Social services	0.6	4.8	4.8
Membership organizations	0.3	5.1	5.1
Health services	−1.9	8.3	7.6
Business services and other	−0.2	6.0	5.2

Notes:
Output per employee is the ratio of the quantity index for gross domestic product by industry to the number of full-time and part-time employees.
Unit labour cost is the ratio of total compensation of employees to the quantity index for gross domestic product by industry.
Price is the implicit price deflator for gross domestic product.

Source: Author's calculations using the US Bureau of Economic Analysis' estimates of Gross Product by Industry.

services relative to other commodities. Services prices increased 6.3 per cent at an annual rate over these two decades, almost 2 percentage points faster than the overall rate of price increase.

More detailed information on labour productivity trends for individual service industries shows that this weakness in measured productivity growth and fast rate of increase in costs is broad-based (Table 5.2).[4] In all of the major service industries, labour productivity growth fell short of the economy-wide average of a 0.7 per cent annual growth rate. The productivity growth shortfalls were most noticeable in auto and other repair services, legal services, and health services. Accordingly, the rates of increase in unit labour cost and in price were particularly rapid in these industries.

Sectoral Composition of Output and Employment

Unbalanced labour productivity growth has consequences for the sectoral composition of output and employment in the economy. As noted by Baumol (1967a) (proposition 3), if there are two sectors, a 'progressive' and an 'unprogressive' or stagnant sector, and the ratio of real outputs of the two sectors is held constant, then as time progresses, an increasing fraction of the labour force will be employed in the unprogressive sector. Also, given that the prices of the output of the stagnant sector will tend to increase faster than the prices of the output of the progressive sector, the former will account for an increasing share of the economy's nominal output.

The US economy has exhibited these types of characteristics. The service sector share of real output has been flat to slightly up over the last two decades; at 19 per cent in 1996, the service sector share of real output was a bit higher than in 1977 (Table 5.3). Given the weaker labour productivity

Table 5.3   Shares of output and employment by major industry group in the USA

	Per cent of total					
	Real output		Nominal output		Employment	
Industry group	1977	1996	1977	1996	1977	1996
All sectors	100	100	100	100	100	100
Agriculture, forestry and fishing	1	2	3	2	2	2
Mining	2	1	3	1	1	0
Construction	5	4	5	4	4	4
Manufacturing	19	19	23	17	22	15
Transportation	3	3	4	3	3	3
Communications	2	3	2	3	1	1
Electric, gas and sanitary services	3	3	3	3	1	1
Wholesale trade	5	7	7	7	5	5
Retail trade	9	9	9	9	16	17
Finance, insurance and real estate	17	18	14	19	5	6
Services	17	19	13	20	19	29
Private households	0	0	0	0	2	1
Government	17	13	14	13	20	17

Notes:
Real output is real gross domestic product in chained 1992 dollars.
Employment is the number of full-time and part-time employees.

Source: Author's calculations using the US Bureau of Economic Analysis' estimates of Gross Product by Industry.

growth there, the service sector's share of employment has increased sharply
from about 19 per cent in 1977 to 29 per cent in 1996. The service sector's
share of nominal output also has increased, from about 13 per cent in 1977 to
20 per cent in 1996.

*Table 5.4   Shares of output and employment in selected service industries
in the USA*

| | Per cent of total | | | | | |
| | Real output | | Nominal output | | Employment | |
Industry group	1977	1996	1977	1996	1977	1996
Total services	17	19	13	20	19	29
Hotels and lodging	1	1	1	1	1	1
Personal services	1	1	1	1	1	1
Auto repair, services and parking	1	1	1	1	1	1
Miscellaneous repair services	0	0	0	0	0	0
Motion pictures	0	0	0	0	0	0
Amusement and recreation services	1	1	1	1	1	1
Legal services	1	1	1	1	0	1
Educational services	1	1	1	1	1	2
Social services	0	1	0	1	1	2
Membership organizations	1	1	1	1	2	2
Health services	6	5	4	6	5	8
Business services and other	4	7	3	7	4	8

Notes:
Real output is real gross domestic product in chained 1992 dollars.
Employment is the number of full-time and part-time employees.

Source: Author's calculations using the US Bureau of Economic Analysis' estimates of Gross
Product by Industry.

Among the service industries, the upward trend in employment shares was
broad-based (Table 5.4). There was about a 1 percentage point increase in
employment in several smaller industries, including legal, educational and
social services. However, two industry groups – health services and business
services – accounted for the bulk of the increase in service sector employment. The employment share of health services increased from 5 per cent in
1977 to 8 per cent in 1996, and the employment share of business services
increased from about 4 per cent in 1977 to 8 per cent in 1996.[5]

POSSIBLE RESOLUTIONS OF THE PARADOX

The vibrancy of the service sector, in terms of its growing share of output and employment in the economy, and stagnancy of the service sector, in terms of its rate of labour productivity growth, is a paradox that we want to explain. In particular, we want to understand why the increasing relative price of services has not led to a decline in their real output share through the workings of a substitution effect.

The economics literature on this subject has offered several possible explanations. First, it is possible that the dominance of a substitution effect has led to a decline in real service shares in terms of the final demand commodity bundle, only not in terms of the domestic economy's sectoral composition of value-added. Such a drop in the final demand share is possible without leading to a drop in the value-added share if either services have been increasingly used as an intermediate input to domestic production or the foreign trade balance has shifted in such a way as to more than offset the effects of this final demand substitution effect on domestic production of services. Second, it is possible that the negative substitution effect in private consumption has been offset by a positive income effect. Third, the appearance of an increase in the relative price of services could be misleading; there might be mismeasurement of this type.

Commodity Composition of Final Demand

The available data on the commodity composition of final demand in the United States undermine assertions that the paradox of the vitality of services is present only in terms of sectoral value-added. For example, similar to the services sectoral share of value-added, in real terms personal consumption of services also has been flat to slightly up over the past two decades (Table 5.5). In 1977, real consumption of services was 36 per cent of overall final demand; this share drifted up to 38 per cent by 1997. In nominal terms the increase was even larger, from a 30 per cent share in 1977 to a 40 per cent share in 1997.

Our discussion of the 'cost disease' so far has made no mention of the flow of services from the housing stock, which is a substantial portion of overall consumption expenditures. However, housing service consumption is not a straightforward object of study with respect to the cost disease, as the output of this service depends on a stock, not on current period labour efforts. Our assessment of the overall trend in services consumption is not altered by the excluding of housing. The additional detail shown in Table 5.5 indicates that most of the increase in the personal consumption services share was in services other than housing. Indeed, medical care services accounted for a full 4 percentage points of the increase in the PCE services nominal expendi-

Table 5.5   Shares of final demand in the USA by selected types of expenditure

| | Per cent of total expenditures | | | |
| | Real | | Nominal | |
Category	1977	1997	1977	1997
Total expenditures	100	100	100	100
Personal Consumption	66	68	63	68
Goods	31	30	33	28
Services	36	38	30	40
Housing	10	10	9	10
Services ex. housing	25	28	21	29
Medical care	9	10	6	10
Other services	17	18	15	19
Investment	15	17	18	15
Government	21	18	21	18
Exports	6	16	8	14
Goods	4	13	6	11
Services	2	3	2	3
Imports	7	15	9	13
Goods	6	13	8	11
Services	1	2	1	2

Source: Author's calculations using the US Bureau of Economic Analysis' estimates of Gross Domestic Product by type of expenditure.

ture share. Outside of housing, the increase in the PCE services share of nominal expenditures was broad-based, as the share for PCE services other than housing and medical care also increased by about 4 percentage points over the past two decades.

The data on US foreign trade activity also fail to support any claim that the services paradox only exists in terms of domestic sectoral value added. Although exports of services have increased somewhat over the past two decades, they account for only a small share of overall service-producing activity in the US economy. The services exports share of overall expenditures stood at 3 per cent in 1997, up from 2 per cent in 1977. Also, imports of services have not declined, as would have been necessary for this channel to have caused a large wedge between domestic value-added from the services sector and domestic absorption of services.

That said, there is some merit to the observation that services might have been increasingly used as an intermediate input. The output of the business services sector is primarily used as an intermediate to domestic production, and as noted above, there has been a large increase over the past two decades in the business services sector's share of real and nominal value-added in the US economy.[6]

Strength of the Income Effect

Another possible resolution of the paradox of the vibrancy of the service sector, in the presence of relatively weak productivity growth, relies on the assumption that the income elasticity of demand for services is higher than the income elasticity of demand for goods. In this case, as illustrated in Schettkat and Appelbaum (1997), the income effect on real output shares might be strong enough to offset the substitution effect.

Empirically, evidence on the relative strengths of the income elasticities for goods and services is mixed. International comparisons of the relationship between real output shares for specific services and income per capita suggest that demand has an income elasticity in excess of unity for some services, such as housing and medical care, but not for many other types of services (Falvey and Gemmell 1996). Estimates from other types of datasets, such as cross-sections of individual households, also yield mixed results on the income elasticity of various services.[7]

Even if the results unanimously showed that the demands for services were highly income elastic, a major difficulty would arise in deriving the implications of the differing income elasticities for the long-run evolution of demand for services. In modelling household demand, the models generally ignore the amount of time that needs to be spent in consuming alternative commodities. As noted by Baumol (1967b) in his modification of the Linder Theorem, many services are particularly time-intensive in consumption, and the shadow value of this time tends to increase as income rises. Thus, a second substitution effect – away from time-intensive service consumption – is likely to crowd out some of the conventional income-elasticity effect.

Possible Mismeasurement

We complete this section of the chapter by reviewing one last tactic that has been employed in the literature to explain the service sector labour-productivity/output-share paradox; some have claimed that the rate of service price inflation has been systematically overstated and to a degree that exceeds the rate at which goods price inflation might have been overstated.[8] Before reviewing some of the merits of this argument, we note that it only potentially explains the productivity part of the paradox, not the fact that the service sector share of nominal output and of employment has been growing rapidly. Rather, revelation of a differential degree of mismeasurement would remove the appearance of a large shift in relative prices of services versus goods, eliminating the prima facie evidence that we might have expected to see some substitution away from services towards goods, in terms of real output shares.

Certainly, the potential exists for a high degree of mismeasurement of service price deflators. For the most part, the Bureau of Economic Analysis uses particular consumer price indices (CPIs) as deflators of the output of specific service industries in the estimation of gross product by industry.[9] Substantial evidence exists that, for many components of the CPI, these indices are biased upwards as measures of changes in the cost of living.[10] Some of the largest biases appear to have arisen in the CPI for medical care services and other components of the deflator of gross product originating in the health services industry.[11] It is likely that these biases in the medical services deflators have led to substantial understatement of the rate of labour productivity growth in the health care industry and an overstatement of the increase in the relative price of (quality-adjusted) medical care services.

The deflator for the business service industry also appears to be subject to a high degree of measurement error that is likely to overstate the rate of increase in the relative price of business services and understate the rate of labour productivity growth in the industry. In the case of business services, the BEA does not actually use any price indices in the construction of the implicit deflator, but rather directly estimates changes in real output based on employment growth rates, using the assumption of no change in labour productivity for individual business service industries.[12] In this sense, the productivity paradox arises by assumption in the business service industry.

Although it is clear that there are severe measurement problems for these two key industries (health care and business services), not enough evidence exists about the extent of bias in each of the goods and service industry deflators for definitive conclusions to be reached about how much price index mismeasurement has contributed to the appearance of the broader service sector productivity paradox. That said, various authors have explained particularly difficult measurement issues that arise in the service industries.[13]

THE IMPACT OF GROWTH OF THE INFORMATION ECONOMY

We now turn to the issue of how growth in the information-orientedness of the economy might be affecting these trends in output, employment, costs and prices. To shed some light on recent historical developments, we review some of the extant research on the information economy and the productivity paradox. Then, we discuss the sense in which the rising costs of commodities produced in stagnant productivity sectors are a 'disease', and we discuss what types of structural changes in the economy would constitute 'cures' for this malady.

Extant Research on the Information Economy and the Productivity Paradox

A few other authors have explored the possibility that the growth of the information economy is an important aspect of the cost disease/productivity paradox. One strand of thought is that information workers, like, say, barbers, do not have very many opportunities to increase their labour productivity by increasing inputs of other factors (capital, materials) or by taking advantage of technological progress. After all, manipulating information to produce knowledge is a cognitive process, and even the most advanced 'artificial intelligence' machines are far from mastering the capabilities of the human mind. Another strand of thought de-emphasizes the cognitive aspect and emphasizes creative, artistic aspects of human efforts as fundamental. Under this latter view, rapid overall productivity gains are likely to be realized from the adoption of advancing information technologies, and this will afford society the opportunity to shift employment towards more creative, essentially human activities.

In various writings, William Baumol has provided some support for both of these views. For example, Baumol and Baumol (1984) emphasize that creative, artistic aspects of human efforts are fundamental and ultimately will be a source of stagnancy for labour productivity in the entertainment industry, despite the development of mass media distribution systems. In contrast, Baumol and Blackman (1983) emphasize that an information-oriented cognitive activity (software maintenance and development) is likely to dominate the long-run cost trend for library operations.

For the US economy as a whole, Baumol, Blackman and Wolff (1989, chapter 7) provide some useful quantitative evidence on trends in output and employment from an information content perspective. By introducing a distinction between workers engaged in 'data processing' and 'knowledge production', they are able to discriminate among information workers with respect to capital–labour substitution possibilities. In particular, they show that trend employment growth from 1960 to 1980 was faster for knowledge workers, for whom substitution possibilities are limited, than data processors – who have been supplanted to a larger degree by information processing equipment. Wolff (1996) shows that this trend continued from 1980 to 1990. In both studies, they also provide evidence against the possibility that the source of rapid knowledge worker employment growth is a large increase in the effective final demand for commodities with a high knowledge content.

Wolff (1997) extends this line of analysis in several dimensions, and, along the way, admits the possibility that measurement error might be behind the finding that there was not a large increase in the final demand for commodities with a high knowledge content. He notes that a major puzzle is why productivity growth in service-producing industries failed to recover in the 1977–87 period. This was an era of accelerated computerization and much employment restructuring in the service-producing sectors. Among other interesting results, he shows that variables measuring the degree of computerization and the share of information worker (particularly, professional worker) employment both have significant negative coefficients in regressions explaining rates of productivity growth across service industries. He concludes that this and other assembled evidence '... provide strong circumstantial evidence of mismeasurement of service output. It does seem that brainpower – whether human or artificial – is associated with a more heterogeneous output (or a greater variety of output), making output harder to measure' (p. 23).

Owing to limitations on the availability of detailed sectoral estimates of real output, the analyses of Wolff (1996, 1997) and Baumol, Blackman, and Wolff (1989) proceed at relatively high levels of sectoral aggregation. To provide some link between their evidence on information worker employment growth, the possibility of output mismeasurement, and the detailed sectoral information shown elsewhere in this chapter, Table 5.6 provides a more detailed look at trends in nominal output and employment within the business and professional service industry groups. As noted earlier, much of the large increase in the employment share of the service sector in the US was the result of an increase in the 'business services and other' component, which includes professional services except legal services (Table 5.4). Within the business and professional services group, most of the growth in employment has taken place in the personnel supply services and computer programming and data processing industries. Based on the occupational mix within these industries, the increase in personnel supply employment does not appear to account for much of the increase in knowledge worker employment, although it is consistent with the upward trend in data worker employment. In contrast, a large proportion of the employees in the computer services industry are 'knowledge workers'; strong growth in this industry has resulted in large increases in its shares of nominal output and employment. These trends suggest that we might be better able to understand the link between the information economy and the cost disease/unbalanced growth phenomenon by closer scrutiny of developments within the computer programming and data processing industry.

Table 5.6   Shares of gross output and employment in selected business and professional service industries in the USA

Industry group	Per cent of total			
	Nominal output		Employment	
	1972	1992	1972	1992
Business and professional services	100	100	100	100
Advertising	19	4	5	2
Consumer credit reporting	1	1	3	1
Mailing, reproduction, commercial art	3	4	4	3
Services to dwellings and other buildings	4	4	14	10
Misc. equipment rental and leasing	4	4	3	3
Personnel supply services	4	7	12	25
Computer programming and data processing	6	20	5	11
Misc. business services	15	10	24	14
Management and public relations services	8	11	6	8
Engineering, architectural, and surveying services	13	15	13	10
Legal services	19	20	12	12

Note: Nominal gross output is estimated receipts at establishments in these industries.

Source: Author's calculations using the 1972 and 1992 Censuses of Service Industries.

Productivity Stagnancy as a 'Disease'

This paper is entitled 'Will the new information economy cure the cost disease in the US?' We use the term 'disease' consistently with the earlier literature, but we have not yet indicated here any sense in which the unbalanced employment growth and cost inflation trends we have described actually pose social or economic problems. In and of themselves, unbalanced growth and widening cost differentials are not necessarily indicative of reduced social welfare; although the large shifts in relative prices implied by such cost differentials may elicit some notional substitution away from commodities produced by stagnant sectors, the overall production possibilities of the economy can still expand, affording the representative consumer the opportunity to purchase more of all commodities (Bradford 1969, Keren 1972).

That said, unbalanced growth is not necessarily free of negative social implications. The real world is heterogeneous; rather than being occupied by a representative consumer, our economy and society are comprised of people with varied talents, skills, income levels, ambitions and tastes. Unbalanced growth has the potential to bring about large societal changes in the distribution of individual, and hence aggregate, welfare.

Many of the various writings on the social implications of unbalanced growth have an undertone of lament. Authors have addressed such questions as whether unbalanced growth will lead to the extinction of some types of performing arts or whether it will be responsible for a continuing decline in the quality of municipal government services or a decline in the quality-of-life in urban areas more generally. As noted above, in Baumol, Blackman, and Wolff (1989) the concern shifted to the effects of growing information worker employment. Reich (1991) pursued similar ideas and promulgated the term 'symbolic analysts' to describe a class of occupations, basically those referred to elsewhere as knowledge-workers, that have been accounting for an increasing share of overall income. His subsequent writings and speeches given as Secretary of Labor bemoan a widening of disparities in wealth, income, and opportunity in the USA that partly owes to increased economic power of society's most fortunate, including the 'symbolic analysts'.[14] In considering types of possible 'cures' for the cost disease, we suggest focusing the discussion on these three issues, the tendency of society to support creative/artistic pursuits, the evolution of the spatial distribution of a broader set of amenities, including government services, and the evolution of the distribution of income, wealth, and opportunity across individuals.

The New Information Economy as a 'Cure'

The main purpose of this chapter has been to compile some of the evidence on the degree to which symptoms of the 'cost disease' have been present in the USA and to review the literature that offers some useful perspective on these trends. No attempt is made to develop new theories or to test earlier-offered explanations. In part, this reflects the fact that so much careful work has been done on the subject by others that we would probably not have much new to add to the assessment of the trends through the mid-1990s.

We make here some final remarks on a development that has not yet been well-studied in the literature on unbalanced growth and the cost disease: the rapid growth of new information markets which use the Internet and World Wide Web. By new information economy, we mean the recent development of the rapidly growing use of the Internet to conduct business and personal activities.[15]

We cannot know, in advance, how recent and impending breakthroughs in information and telecommunication technologies actually will affect the economy and society.[16] The academic economics literature has developed a framework useful for envisaging the possibilities.[17]

In partial view of the academic framework for understanding these fundamental market forces, information industry analysts have begun to document how the recent growth of the Internet is affecting the economy and society

and have speculated about the future. For example, three of the major themes
in British Telecommunications (1998) are 'The way we learn', 'The way we
work', and 'The emergence of a have and have not society'. In this report, the
advances in information-communication technologies are seen as increasing
the geographic scope of labour markets and many product markets, including
that for educational services. Concerns about the potential for widening
income inequality centre around the possibility that lower-income individuals
cannot afford minimal threshold levels of investments in human capital (for
example, education) and physical capital (for example, internet-connected
computers) needed to take advantage of the information-economy productivity gains.

The US Department of Commerce (1998) has elucidated similar themes.
Also, in a chapter on 'Workers in the digital age', the report puts forth the
argument that labour demand will shift towards skills useful in designing,
programming, and maintaining the computing and communications infrastructure. Additionally, they note that demand for workers able to create
useful or entertaining information content is likely to increase.

The group studying these issues for the Organisation for Economic Cooperation and Development (OECD) concurs with these basic themes and
offers some supporting evidence. For example, on the issue of universal
access to key enabling information technologies, OECD (1998a) points out
that the percentage of households with computers is highly positively correlated with household income and that internet access rates show a similar
correlation. Other than active governmental efforts to promote universal access, the one ray of hope they offer to the less affluent is that rapid technological
change may eventually drive the costs of enabling technologies low enough
to facilitate broader-based participation. The logic of the unbalanced growth
model also implies that if productivity gains are rapid enough in the progressive sectors, overall societal income levels might increase enough to make the
enabling technologies affordable to virtually all members of society.

This chapter's review of historical trends in the USA offers grounds for
optimism that the new information economy will allow society to deal well
with unbalanced growth. The increases in overall societal income levels that
are accompanying rapid technological change may themselves contain the
medicine needed to cure the cost disease.

NOTES

1. The ideas expressed in this chapter, which was originally prepared for the October 1998
    Tilburg University/Utrecht University workshop on Structural Change and Employment in
    Amsterdam, are solely those of the author and do not reflect official views of the Federal
    Reserve System.

2. Baumol and Bowen (1965) note that Scitovsky and Scitovsky (1959) are among those with even earlier discussions of the effects of differential rates of productivity change on costs and prices.

3. This basic malady, that in a world with unbalanced growth, the differential rates of productivity change would lead to ever-increasing costs, has come to be known as Baumol's cost disease, owing to his original work with Bowen, the formalization of some of these ideas in Baumol (1967a), and his many subsequent writings on the subject. See Baumol (1997) for a compendium.

4. The discussion here focuses on the services sector of the US economy, which is a subset of the service-producing sectors of economy. The latter group includes, in addition to the services sector, the transportation, communication, electric, gas, and sanitary services (utilities), wholesale and retail trade, finance, insurance, and real estate (FIRE), household, and government sectors. Among service-producing sectors, the transportation, FIRE, services, and government sectors have relatively stagnant measured labour productivity. However, the communications, utilities and trade sectors are relatively 'progressive' (exhibit a moderate uptrend in labour productivity), consistent with the dichotomy of service-producing sectors developed by Baumol, Blackman, and Wolff (1989), chapter 6, which was based on data from 1947 to 1976.

5. The figures discussed here and shown in Tables 5.2 and 5.4 pertain to a 'business services and other' group that includes what is known in the current industry classification system as 'business services' and 'other services' and what was known in the former (1977) industry classification system as 'business services' and 'miscellaneous professional services'.

6. See ten Raa and Wolff (1996) for a discussion of how increased outsourcing of business services probably helped lead to a resurgence of total factor productivity growth in the US manufacturing sector in the late 1970s and early to mid-1980s.

7. For example, Marquis and Long (1995) find a relatively small income elasticity of demand for non-group health insurance. Branch (1993) finds a small income elasticity of the demand for electricity.

8. See, for example, Slifman and Corrado (1996).

9. See Yuskavage (1996) for some documentation of BEA's gross product by industry deflation method.

10. See Boskin *et al.* (1996) for a summary of potential CPI biases and Baker (1998) for some alternative views.

11. As explained in Yuskavage (1996), BEA's estimates of real gross product originating in the health services industry are constructed by a double-deflation method. Nominal gross output is deflated by various health care CPIs, Health Care Financing Administration (HCFA) input price indices, and (beginning in 1993 or 1994) Producer Price Indices (PPIs) for health care, particularly physicians' services. As explained by Boskin *et al.* (1996, p. 58), the major deficiency of these deflators is that they do not attempt to measure the changes in the prices of health care 'outcomes' but rather focus on the costs of obtaining various health care 'inputs'. Separate statistical research by Cutler *et al.* (1996) and Shapiro and Wilcox (1996) compares quality-adjusted output (that is, outcome-based) price indices to CPI-type input price indices for particular medical services (heart attack treatments and cataracts) and finds an upward bias in the health care service CPI on the order of 4 percentage points per annum. This is much larger than the Boskin *et al.* (1996) estimates of the extent of bias in the goods components of the CPI, as a group.

12. Specifically, business service sector gross product originating (GPO) is constructed by equating the rate of real output growth to the rate of employment growth in individual business service industries and then aggregating these implied real output growth rates with shifting weights, based on the nominal gross output shares of the industries. Accordingly, estimated aggregate labour productivity growth can deviate from zero slightly; for example, if nominal output shares shift within the business service sector towards constituent industries with higher estimated labour productivity levels, then aggregate labour productivity will be estimated to have increased.

13. See Sherwood (1994) for a useful summary of the difficulties in the measurement of service outputs.
14. See, for example, Reich (1997).
15. Usage of the Internet is large and growing very fast. Zakon (1998) estimates that the number of Internet hosts was about 30 million in early 1998, up from about 5 million at the beginning of 1995. British Telecommunications (1998) reports estimates of 53 million internet users worldwide as of September, 1997 (citing International Data Corporation as the source of this estimate), and notes that Nielsen Media Research shows that 70 per cent of US corporations have an on-line presence.
16. More quantitative research would be useful for understanding the prospective impact of the new information economy on the structure of employment, output, income, and opportunity. To date, the lack of data on the specific character of Internet-related activity has hampered research on the likely impact of the growth of the Internet. However, OECD (1998b) presents some interesting techniques for trying to circumvent the difficult measurement issues. Attempts to measure activity usually either focus on categorizing and counting the stock of web page content or the flows of the transmission of this content, so-called 'hits'. The OECD report develops an additional indicator, the categorization and counting of the links among the stock of web pages. This technique allows some indirect measurement of the geographic scope of the product markets served by various types of information providers. To discriminate among competing predictions of how radically the growth of the Internet is likely to transform the economy, it would be useful to measure and better understand these geographic scopes.
17. The academic economics literature has characterized information commodities and information markets. Information is usually defined as anything that can be digitized. When traded in a market, information is a commodity. Information commodities differ from other commodities in several respects (Varian 1998). First, information is an experience good; its quality is ascertained in the act of consuming information. Second, the costs of initial information production tend to be high, but the marginal costs of reproduction and dissemination tend to be low; in this sense, information goods tend to exhibit significant increasing returns to scale. Third, information commodities are typically non-rivalrous in consumption; that is, in many circumstances, multiple parties may consume the information without diminishing the value of the information. This can create problems with the excludability of the commodity, particularly if intellectual property rights are weak or difficult to enforce.

     These characteristics of information commodities interact with the characteristics of information technologies in the evolution of market structures and products. Information production and dissemination technologies tend to be comprised of multiple components organized into systems. For efficient functionality, the components must meet the compatibility standards of the systems. Hence, the costs of switching any individual components to an alternative with imperfect compatibility are likely to be high. This tends to result in the lock-in of components.

     In the academic economics literature, analysis of the returns to scale issue in the software industry has largely focused on the fact that lock-in effects can result in a winner-take-all characteristic of the market structure. In US communications markets, ownership of the components tends to be more decentralized than in the software market. The literature on the communications market has pursued the idea that when the information production and dissemination apparatus is organized as a network, there are significant network externalities; that is, the value of the information services increases with the number of participants in the network.

     Another key strand of the literature argues that some information markets naturally have a monopolistically competitive market structure. Advertising and other means of establishing superior reputations tend to be used to establish product differentiation within the market, owing to the experience good characteristic of information (that its quality cannot be fully ascertained outside the act of consumption).

REFERENCES

Baker, Dean (1998), *Getting Prices Right: The Debate over the Consumer Price Index*, Armonk, NY: M.E. Sharpe for the Economic Policy Institute.

Baumol, William J. (1967a), 'Macroeconomics of unbalanced growth: the anatomy of urban crisis', *American Economic Review*, June, **57**, 415–26.

Baumol, William J. (1967b), 'Income and substitution effects in the Linder theorem', *Quarterly Journal of Economics*, November, **87** (4), 629–33.

Baumol, William J. and Ruth Towse (eds) (1997), 'Baumol's Cost Disease: The Arts and other Victims', Cheltenham, UK and Lyme, US: Edward Elgar.

Baumol, Hilda and William J. Baumol (1984), 'The mass media and the cost disease', in William S. Hendon, Douglas V. Shaw and Nancy K. Grant (eds), *Economics of Cultural Industries*, Association for Cultural Economics, 109–123.

Baumol, William J. and Sue Anne Batey Blackman (1983), 'Electronics, the cost disease, and the operation of libraries', *Journal of the American Society for Information Science*, **34** (3), 181–91.

Baumol, William J. and William G. Bowen (1965), 'On the performing arts: the anatomy of their economic problems', *American Economic Review*, **50** (2), May, 495–502.

Baumol, William J., Sue Anne Batey Blackman and Edward N. Wolff (1989), *Productivity and American Leadership: The Long View*, Cambridge, MA: MIT Press.

Boskin, Michael J., Ellen R. Dulberger, Robert J. Gordon, Zvi Griliches and Dale Jorgenson (1996), 'Toward a more accurate measure of the cost of living', Final Report to the US Senate Finance Committee from the Advisory Commission to Study the Consumer Price Index, December.

Bradford, David F. (1969), 'Balance on unbalanced growth', *Zeitschrift für Nationalökonomie*, 29, 291–304, reprinted in Ruth Towse (ed.), *Baumol's Cost Disease: The Arts and other Victims*, Cheltenham, UK and Northampton, US: Edward Elgar.

Branch, Raphael E. (1993), 'Short run income elasticity of demand for residential electricity using consumer expenditure survey data', *Energy Journal*, **14** (4), 111–21.

British Telecommunications (1998), [online] 'BT World Communications Report 1998/9', http://www.bt.com/global_reports/1998–99.

Cutler, David M., Mark McClellan, Joseph P. Newhouse and Dahlia Remler (1996), 'Are medical prices declining?', NBER Working Paper 5750, September.

Falvey, Rodney E. and Norman Gemmell (1996), 'Are services income-elastic? Some new evidence', The Review of Income and Wealth, **42** (3), September, 257–69.

Keren, Michael (1972), 'Macroeconomics of unbalanced growth: comment', *American Economic Review*, **62** (1), March, 149.

Marquis, Susan M. and Stephen H. Long (1995), 'Worker demand for health insurance in the non-group market', *Journal of Health Economics*, **14** (1), May, 47–63.

Organisation for Economic Co-operation and Development (OECD) (1998a), 'The economic and social impact of electronic commerce: preliminary findings and research agenda', DSTI/ICCP(98)15/REV2, September.

Organisation for Economic Co-operation and Development (OECD) (1998b), 'Internet infrastructure indicators', DSTI/ICCP(98)7/Final, October.

Reich, Robert B. (1991), *The Work of Nations: Preparing Ourselves for 21st Century Capitalism*, New York: Alfred Knopf.

Reich, Robert B. (1997), 'The Unfinished Agenda', Secretary of Labors speech given to the Council of Excellence in Government, Washington, DC, January 9.

Schettkat, Ronald and Eileen Appelbaum (1997), 'Are Prices Unimportant? The Changing Structure of Industrialized Economies', working paper 97–10, Onderzoekschool AWSB, Universiteit Utrecht, the Netherlands.

Scitovsky, Tibor and Ann Scitovsky (1959), 'What price economic progress?', *Yale Review*, Autumn.

Shapiro, Matthew D. and David W. Wilcox (1996), 'Mismeasurement in the consumer price index: an evaluation', in Ben Bernanke and Julio Rotemberg (eds), *NBER Macroeconomics Annual*, Cambridge, MA: MIT Press, pp. 93–142.

Sherwood, Mark K. (1994), 'Difficulties in the measurement of service outputs', *Monthly Labor Review*, March.

Slifman, L. and C. Corrado (1996), 'Decomposition of productivity and unit costs', Board of Governors of Federal Reserve System, Occasional Staff Studies, November.

ten Raa, Thijs and Edward N. Wolff (1996), 'Outsourcing of services and the productivity recovery in US manufacturing in the 1980s', Discussion paper No. 9689, Tilburg University Center for Economic Research.

US Department of Commerce (1998), [online] 'The emerging digital economy', http://www.ecommerce.gov/emerging.htm.

Varian, Hal R. (1998), 'Markets for information goods', paper presented at Bank of Japan conference, April (revised in October).

Wolff, Edward N. (1996), 'The growth of information workers in the US economy, 1950–1990: the role of technological change, computerization, and structural change', Research Report 96–41, C.V. Starr Center for Applied Economics, New York University, November.

Wolff, Edward N. (1997), 'The productivity paradox: evidence from indirect indicators of service sector productivity growth', paper presented at the CSLS conference on Service Sector Productivity and the Productivity Paradox, Ottawa, Canada, April.

Yuskavage, Robert E. (1996), 'Improved estimates of gross product by industry, 1959–94', *Survey of Current Business*, **76** (8), August, 133–55.

Zakon, Robert H. (1998), [online] 'Hobbes' Internet Timeline', http://www.isoc.org/zakon/Internet/History/HIT.html.

6. Productivity trends and employment across industries in Canada

Pierre Mohnen and Thijs ten Raa[1]

1 INTRODUCTION

In a famous article of 1967, William Baumol predicted that services would price themselves out of the market, given their lower productivity growth and the consequent rise of their relative price, compared to non-service goods. Twenty years later, we observe that measured productivity growth in services is indeed relatively low, but that at the same time the modern economy is based less on manufacturing and more on service. Economic activity has substantially shifted away from manufacturing towards services, as it had moved from the primary sector to manufacturing in the first half of the last century. How to reconcile these observations?

In this chapter we examine the apparent paradox in the light of the Canadian experience. We first look at the facts. In section 2, we trace productivity trends and employment shifts for the Canadian economy over the period 1962–91. Second, we review a list of potential explanations. Labour productivity growth provides only a partial picture of productivity performance since it ignores the role of capital accumulation, so we look at total factor productivity growth. In section 3, we distinguish between value-added and final demand. Their macro identity breaks down at the sectoral level and this has implications on the issue. Value-added might be more concentrated in services than before, reflecting a crowding-out of services from manufacturing, and yet final demand composition has barely changed. We then examine shifts in final demand composition at both the commodity and final demand category levels. In section 4, we explore the hypothesis that Canadian services may have gained a comparative advantage in international trade. Last, but not least, production and final demand for services may have gained ground as a result of technical change. The verdict on the latter mechanism is provided in section 5. We conclude in section 6 by summarizing the results of our analysis of the Canadian experience.

2   LABOUR EMPLOYMENT AND PRODUCTIVITY

To assess the extent to which economic activity has shifted towards services and to examine the sluggishness of productivity in services, we use the input–output data of the Canadian economy at the medium level of aggregation (50 sectors and 92 commodities) and the KLEMS database (Johnson, 1994 and Statistics Canada, various issues). We report results for ten groups of sectors: the primary sector, manufacturing, construction, transportation, communication, wholesale trade, retail trade, FIRE (finance, insurance and real estate), business services and personal services.[2] We compare three periods, the 1960s, 1970s and 1980s, which are not exactly decades, but cover the periods 1962–74, 1975–81 and 1982–91. The two years separating the periods are slump years. This choice enables us to compare productivity and employment as much as possible over comparable phases of the business cycles. Table 6.1 reveals the changing pattern of labour employment by sector. The big losers are the primary sector and manufacturing. Their combined employment share has dwindled by 11.7 percentage points. Employment in services has gone up, except for construction and transportation. The big winners are business and personal services with a surge in total employment share of 9.2 percentage points.

Table 6.1   Labour distribution (sectoral shares in per cent)

Groups of sectors	1960s	1970s	1980s	80s–60s
Primary	15.4	11.8	9.8	−5.6
Manufacturing	27.7	24.4	21.6	−6.1
Construction	9.8	9.3	8.6	−1.2
Transportation	6.4	6.3	5.8	−0.6
Communication	3.1	3.6	3.5	0.4
Wholesale trade	5.7	6.2	7.0	1.3
Retail trade	14.3	15.2	14.9	0.6
FIRE	5.0	6.3	7.0	2.0
Business services	4.2	6.8	9.6	5.4
Personal services	8.4	10.1	12.2	3.8
Total economy	100	100	100	0

Notes:
1. The 1960s correspond to the period 1962–74, the 1970s to 1975–81, and the 1980s to 1982–91.
2. At the M-level of disaggregation, primary regroups sectors 1–7 and 39, manufacturing 8–28, construction 29, transportation 30–32, communications 33–34, wholesale trade 35, retail trade 36, FIRE 37, 38 and 40, business services 41, 47–50, and personal services 42–46.

Table 6.2   Value-added/labour (1986 $C per hour)

Groups of sectors	1960s	1970s	1980s	80s–60s
Primary	15.66	19.32	23.96	+53%
Manufacturing	17.37	22.63	26.47	+52%
Construction	17.60	21.90	25.83	+47%
Transportation	15.42	19.11	23.11	+50%
Communication	26.52	39.81	53.87	+103%
Wholesale trade	16.32	19.01	22.32	+37%
Retail trade	10.62	11.86	12.82	+21%
FIRE	58.52	64.08	70.30	+20%
Business services	13.28	14.95	16.23	+22%
Personal services	15.72	17.86	16.27	+3%
Total economy	17.92	22.30	25.41	+42%

Note: See Table 6.1 for the definitions of periods and sectors.

The shift of employment towards the services can to some extent reflect the stagnant productivity in services. The story is usually cast in terms of labour productivity. Table 6.2 shows real value-added per unit of labour for the ten groups of sectors and the three time-periods. Value-added is the value of the net output vector of commodities for a group of sectors. The figures are in 1986 $C(anadian) per hour worked. Table 6.2 reveals the Baumol disease. The top five groups of sectors, the 'nuts-and-bolts' chamber of the Canadian economy, all show dramatic increases in real value-added per hour from the 1960s to the 1980s, ranging from 47 per cent (in construction) to 103 per cent (in communication). The bottom five groups of sectors, the 'soft' chamber of the economy (wholesale and retail trade, FIRE, and business and personal services), depict increases in real value-added per hour below the total economy's average over the same period, with personal services trailing at 3 per cent. At the M-level of aggregation, labour productivity growth is thus negatively correlated with employment growth. Services, except for construction and communication, display the greatest growth in employment but also the lowest growth in labour productivity.

Now, we know that labour productivity is not the ideal way to measure productivity since it relates output only to the labour input. A stagnant labour productivity is not a problem if labour substitutes for capital and the factor savings are just on another input. Table 6.3 reports the capital/labour ratios, also in 1986 $C per person-hour. All sectors but wholesale trade have increased their capital intensity. The question is whether the 'soft' part of the economy has done so at a lower pace and thereby compensated for its poorer

Table 6.3   Capital–labour ratios (1986 $C per hour)

Groups of sectors	1960s	1970s	1980s	80s–60s
Primary	55.81	93.36	128.99	+131%
Manufacturing	31.75	43.48	58.41	+84%
Construction	5.71	7.90	11.41	+100%
Transportation	106.54	107.00	121.90	+14%
Communication	253.51	309.64	424.04	+67%
Wholesale trade	12.33	11.92	11.76	−5%
Retail trade	9.01	8.94	9.85	+9%
FIRE	35.45	52.52	86.17	+143%
Business services	13.41	10.60	15.42	+15%
Personal services	22.65	22.39	26.57	+17%
Total economy	38.69	48.62	61.26	+58%

Note: See Table 6.1 for the definition of periods and sectors.

labour productivity performance. The answer is 'yes' for retail trade and for business and personal services, but 'no' for FIRE. Because of the relative capital savings in at least four of these five sectors, the Baumol disease may be less severe if we measure the performance of sectors in terms of total factor productivity (TFP) instead of labour productivity. It can be shown that, under constant returns to scale, TFP growth is equal to labour productivity growth minus the growth in the capital/labour ratio multiplied by the cost share of capital.

Table 6.4 reports annualized TFP-growth rates for our ten groups of sectors over the three periods. The Canadian economy was healthy in all periods. In fact, the aggregate Solow residual, that is, the Domar weighted averages of the sectoral Solow residuals, are 1.41, 0.47 and 0.17 respectively for the three periods. Notice the pervasive TFP slowdown between the 1960s and the 1980s, except for the primary sector, which went through a tremendous recovery in the 1980s. It is interesting to see that, with the exception of personal services, the weak services sectors that we have identified so far did not perform worse than manufacturing. In fact, Canadian manufacturing TFP-growth declined throughout the three periods. It even became negative in the 1980s. Personal services match this downward trend, but wholesale and retail trade, business services and FIRE outperformed manufacturing. As we suspected, the Baumol disease is more localized when measured in terms of total factor productivity growth. It mainly applies to personal services. Now that we have clarified the symptom, let us turn to some of the possible explanations.

Table 6.4   TFP-growth rates (annualized percentages)

Groups of sectors	1960s	1970s	1980s	80s–60s
Primary	–0.83	–2.11	1.10	+1.93
Manufacturing	0.94	0.16	–0.20	–1.14
Construction	–0.17	1.92	–0.39	–0.22
Transportation	2.82	0.08	1.03	–1.79
Communication	3.91	1.50	0.64	–3.27
Wholesale trade	2.04	1.39	0.98	–1.06
Retail trade	1.58	–0.16	0.81	–0.77
FIRE	1.09	1.31	0.40	–0.69
Business services	0.48	0.62	–0.12	–0.60
Personal services	–0.12	–1.02	–1.87	–1.75
Total economy	1.41	0.47	0.17	–1.24

Note: See Table 6.1 for the definition of periods and sectors.

3   VALUE-ADDED VERSUS FINAL DEMAND

Perhaps the clue in understanding the persistence of services is the presence of intermediate inputs. Most economic models treat sectors as production units that map factor inputs, labour and capital, into 'output'. Summation of these 'outputs' over the sectors yields national product. In such a framework, national product and income are equal, not only in the aggregate, but also sector by sector. The presence of intermediate inputs preserves the macro-identity between national product and national income, but invalidates it at the sectoral level. The contributions of services to the national product and national income differ.

To obtain a concise understanding of the issue, let

$$(u_{ij})$$
$$i = 1, \ldots, n$$
$$j = 1, \ldots, m$$

be the use table, where n is the number of commodities and m the number of sectors. Here u_{ij} is the amount of commodity i used by sector j. Similarly, let

$$(v_{ji})$$
$$j = 1, \ldots, m$$
$$i = 1, \ldots, n$$

be the make table, where v_{ji} is sector j's output of commodity i. The use and make tables are the heart of the System of National Accounts. Subtracting the use table from the transposed make table one obtains the net output table, where the typical element is

$$(w_{ji}) = (v_{ji} - u_{ij})$$
$$i = 1, \ldots, n \qquad\qquad i = 1, \ldots, n$$
$$j = 1, \ldots, m \qquad\qquad j = 1, \ldots, m$$

The dimension is commodity by sector. Column totals yield value-added by sector, while row totals yield final demand by commodity. Total value-added equals total final demand, as the sum of the column totals must be equal to the sum of the row totals. This is the identity between national income and national product, but there is no need for an equality between any column total and any row total. In particular, the contributions of the services to value-added and final demand may differ. This is particularly true of the business services. Although value-added is high (a large column total), final demand may be negligible (a small row total). Many sectors outsource their service activities to the business service sector. As a result, much activity is carried out in the business service sector, creating value-added. However, this sector does not produce many commodities for final demand. As said, most studies measure the contribution of services in terms of value-added, so it is

Table 6.5   Real value-added distribution (sectoral shares, 1986 $C in per cent)

Groups of sectors	1960s	1970s	1980s	80s–60s
Primary	13.1	10.2	9.2	–3.9
Manufacturing	26.8	24.7	22.4	–4.4
Construction	9.6	9.1	8.7	–0.9
Transportation	5.6	5.4	5.2	–0.4
Communication	4.7	6.5	7.4	+2.7
Wholesale trade	5.2	5.3	6.2	+1.0
Retail trade	8.5	8.1	7.5	–1.0
FIRE	16.2	18.1	19.4	+3.2
Business services	3.1	4.6	6.2	+3.1
Personal services	7.3	8.0	7.8	+0.5
Total economy	100	100	100	0

Note: The 1960s correspond to the period 1962–74, the 1970s to 1974–81, and the 1980s to 1981–91. For the groups of sectors see Table 6.1.

of interest to contrast the latter with the contribution of services to final demand. Tables 6.5 and 6.6 show the shares of services in value-added and in final demand, respectively.

Table 6.5 confirms the growing importance of services as sources of earning. The primary sector and manufacturing saw their shares of real value-added substantially and continuously decline. Between the 1960s and the 1980s, roughly 8.3 per cent of real value-added moved from agriculture and manufacturing towards the services. A continuous but less severe relative loss of activity also took place in construction, transportation and retail trade. Whereas personal services saw their relative value-added share increase only slightly, all other services, in particular FIRE and business services, became much more important in relative terms.

Table 6.6 shows the final demand shares for the commodity groups roughly corresponding to our ten groups of sectors. The correspondence is not exact, as sectors may be active in more than one line of product, but it is sufficiently close for comparison. The pattern is basically the same as for value-added, that is manufacturing shrinks and services expand. The shift of final demand towards services amounts to 5.3 per cent, which is three percentage points less than the shift of value-added. So indeed, the rise of the services in terms of commodities is not as dramatic as in terms of value-added. Among the services, construction, transportation, retail trade and personal services are

Table 6.6   Final demand distribution (commodity shares, 1986 $C in per cent)

Groups of commodities	1960s	1970s	1980s	80s–60s
Primary	2.7	1.6	3.1	+0.4
Manufacturing	29.9	27.8	24.1	−5.8
Construction	19.5	18.6	16.7	−2.8
Transportation	2.5	2.4	2.3	−0.2
Communication	2.5	3.5	4.1	+1.6
Wholesale trade	3.4	4.0	5.0	+1.6
Retail trade	8.4	8.7	8.5	+0.1
FIRE	15.5	16.9	18.7	+3.2
Business services	5.4	5.7	6.7	+1.3
Personal services	10.2	10.9	10.7	+0.5
Total economy	100	100	100	0

Note: At the M-level of disaggregation, primary corresponds to commodities 1–13 and 93–94, manufacturing to 14–69, construction to 70–72, transportation to 73–74, communication to 75–79, wholesale trade to 80, retail trade 81, FIRE to 82–83, business services to 84, part of 89, 90–92, and personal services 85–88, part of 89. For the definition of periods, see Table 6.1.

*Table 6.7   Final demand distribution by categories of final demand
(category shares, 1986 $C in per cent)*

Categories of final demand	1960s	1970s	1980s	80s–60s
Goods	40.6	38.9	35.5	–5.1
Housing	11.3	12.3	14.1	2.8
Services other than housing	17.8	17.9	18.6	0.8
Investment	27.8	28.2	26.8	–1.0
Government	5.0	6.6	7.5	+2.5
Net trade	–2.4	–3.9	–2.5	–0.1

Note: At the M-level of disaggregation, goods correspond to final demand categories 1–9, housing to 10, services other than housing to 11 and 13, investment to 14–23, government to 27 and 28, and net trade to 12, 24–26. For the definition of periods, see Table 6.1.

the weakest growth performers. The increase in final demand for services is less pronounced when expressed in terms of the categories of final demand.

In Table 6.7, consumption can be split into goods, housing and other services. Housing and other services together explain 3.6 percentage points of the shift in final demand towards services. Investment and government expenditures are not broken down into goods and services, which could in part explain the lower increase in services when analysed in terms of catego-

*Table 6.8   Domestic final demand distribution (commodity shares, 1986 $C
in per cent)*

Groups of commodities	1960s	1970s	1980s	80s–60s
Primary	2.3	2.3	2.2	–0.1
Manufacturing	32.9	31.3	28.6	–4.3
Construction	19.1	17.6	16.2	–2.9
Transportation	1.9	1.9	2.0	+0.1
Communication	2.4	3.1	3.8	+1.4
Wholesale trade	2.7	3.2	4.0	+1.3
Retail trade	8.2	8.3	8.2	0
FIRE	15.5	16.5	18.7	+3.2
Business services	5.1	5.5	5.8	+0.7
Personal services	10.0	10.4	10.5	+0.5
Total economy	100	100	100	0

Note: For the definition of commodities and periods, see Table 6.6.

ries of final demand. If we compare our results with those reported by Joe Mattey (Chapter 5 in this volume), the apparent shift towards services in final demand is even less pronounced in the USA than in Canada.

However modest, it remains a fascinating challenge to explain the increase of the real share of services in final demand. As a first step towards solving the mystery of increasing demand for services, we must distinguish between domestic final demand and net exports. Table 6.8 shows the domestic final demand share for the ten commodity groupings. Compared to Table 6.6, it includes all final demand categories but net exports. The shift from the primary and secondary sectors of activity towards services is down to 4.4 per cent only. This further reduction prompts us to explore the possibility that the Baumol disease in Canada has been countered by a shift in comparative advantage towards services.

4   A SHIFT IN COMPARATIVE ADVANTAGE?

Canada is a small, open economy. The output of services is determined not only by preference and technology, but also by the terms of trade. In other words, even when productivity developments are relatively unfavourable to services and when shifts in the preferences of consumers are insufficient to counter this trend, the output of services may still be strong if the Canadian comparative advantage has shifted towards the production of services.

It is not easy to determine the comparative advantage of a national economy. The standard approach is to compare costs across countries, but there are two problems with this line of analysis. First, the observed costs reflect not only technology, but also market distortions, such as monopoly power, tariffs and rents resulting from barriers to entry or to trade. Second, the abundance of factor inputs co-determines the comparative advantage. Ricardian technology and Heckscher–Ohlin factor abundance effects are equally crucial in the determination of comparative advantage (Trefler, 1995). Leamer and Levinsohn (1995) note that empirical testing of comparative advantage along the lines of the Heckscher–Ohlin–Vanek theory of the factor content of trade, requires independent data on endowments, technology and trade, but that one ingredient, usually technology, is missing in applied work. Instead, we have analysed the optimal allocation of activity across sectors for the Canadian economy, given real input–output data describing the structure of domestic absorption and technology, given data on factor availabilities from Statistics Canada KLEM's database, and finally given proxies for world prices.

Formally, we maximize the level of domestic final demand (given the observed proportions across commodities), subject to the material balance, the labour, capital, and the balance of payment constraints. The latter constraint is evaluated at world prices. We equate the world prices with the US prices, given that Canada is a small and open economy, and that most of Canadian trade is with the USA. The maximization of the level of domestic final absorption subject to the aforementioned constraints constitutes a linear programme. The shadow prices of the tradeable commodities can be shown to be proportional to the US prices. The shadow prices of the factor inputs measure their productivities. The shadow prices of the non-tradeable commodities are equal to their costs. The primal variables, the activity levels of the sectors, reveal the comparative advantages. They signal which sectors would expand or contract under perfectly competitive conditions and free trade. We have run the linear programme for every year in the period 1962–91. A shift of comparative advantage is indicated by (dis)activation of sectors. A fuller presentation of the model is contained in ten Raa and Mohnen (1998).

The pattern of comparative advantage is surprisingly stable, even at the medium level of aggregation comprising 50 sectors. Crude petroleum or pipeline transport enjoys a comparative advantage for all years but one. The industry of fabricated metal products enjoys a comparative advantage through 1988. Tobacco products and printing and publishing do so from 1981 onwards. All these primary and manufacturing sectors share the comparative advantage with essentially one service sector each year: first FIRE (the 1962–72 period), then health services (the 1973–80 period, except for 1976 when it is amusement and recreational services), and lastly travel, advertising and promotion (the 1981–91 period), accompanied by accommodation and food services through 1988. There is no shift from the primary sectors and manufacturing towards services. We can therefore conclude that international trade cannot explain the persistence of Canadian activity in services.

5   TECHNOLOGICAL CHANGE

Another potential explanation for the shift of value-added and final demand towards the service sectors is technological change. First, new products appear at a much faster rate than before and at affordable prices: videos, CD-roms, laser disks, cellular phones, roller-blades, notebooks, scanners, and so on. Second, with these new products, entirely new services emerge. Think of video stores, computer stores, cybercafes, internet server providers, software companies, internet search companies, central alarm systems, new telecommunication companies and so on. Third, Information and Communication Technologies (ICT) have changed the way of doing business. Many tasks along the product value chain are now outsourced: advertising, programming, after-sales service, and so on. New business units specialize in these tasks, which partially explains the rise in value-added in business services. Because of the pressure of competition and innovation in business services, companies specialize in their core activities and tend to outsource secondary activities, which they used to perform in-house. Even households switch from non-business services to market services. Time is devoted to earning money and letting the personal services sector perform part of the household chores, such as housekeeping, babysitting, financial planning and so on. Fourth, new products and services often carry higher value-added, because of customer snobbishness, low competition at the beginning of the product life-cycle, product differentiation, tied-in sales, high income elasticities, and low substitution possibilities. Demand for old, but especially for new, services have a higher income elasticity than demand for traditional manufactured goods. Competition shifts value creation from the manufacturing stages towards the various stages of servicing, for example providing life-time service plans, product-life insurance contracts, purchase on credit options, car-leasing instead of car-selling. There might also be a saturation effect for manufactured goods, whereas demand for services can be boundless. For example, a household's demand for cars is pretty dry after owning two or three cars, but demand for health services, leisure, or travel can increase by much more than a factor of two or three. Fifth, some companies producing manufactured goods have diversified into offering new services connected with their manufactured product. The service arm of the company may have grown so much that the whole company becomes classified into services.[3]

Table 6.9   R&D stock distribution (sectoral shares, 1986 $C in per cent)

Groups of sectors	1960s	1970s	1980s	80s–60s
Primary	4.6	5.9	5.3	+0.7
Manufacturing	91.1	84.3	75.2	−15.9
Construction	0.1	0.1	0.2	+0.1
Transportation	0.6	1.2	0.8	+0.2
Communication	1.8	5.0	7.2	+5.4
Wholesale trade	0.1	0.2	0.8	+0.7
Retail trade	0.1	0.2	0.8	+0.7
FIRE	0.4	0.7	2.3	+1.9
Business services	0.6	1.2	3.8	+3.2
Personal services	0.6	1.2	3.8	+3.2
Total economy	100	100	100	0

Note: For a definition of sectors and periods, see Table 6.1.

To give some substance to the hypothesis of technological change, we examine in Table 6.9 the sectoral evolution of R&D stocks. Those stocks represent not yet obsolete stocks of knowledge accumulated from past R&D expenditures. Although R&D is only an input in the generation of technological change, it is one of the most revealing indicators of innovation. Table 6.9 shows that the proportion of total R&D stock residing in manufacturing has dropped sharply from 91.1 per cent in the 1960s to 75.2 per cent in the 1980s. Manufacturing still remains the sector where most R&D is done, but services are rapidly gaining ground, especially in communication and in business and personal services. Since, as a first approximation, we can assume that the efficiency of converting R&D into new products is the same in all industries, differential growth in R&D stocks across sectors implies differential growth in economic activity across sectors.

6 CONCLUSION

In the period spanning the three decades from 1961 to 1992, the Canadian service sectors accounted for an ever greater share of employment in the economy, even though their productivity growth was lower than in the primary sector and in manufacturing. To reconcile this apparent contradiction with the so-called Baumol disease, which predicts a decline in the share of services given their relative poor productivity performance and ensuing rising relative price, we have explored four potential explanations. First, the incorporation of capital in productivity analysis makes the disease less acute. Indeed, over this period annualized TFP growth rates were not worse in the two most expanding service sectors (FIRE and business services) than in manufacturing. Second, the proper accounting of intermediate inputs drives a wedge between the income and product shares of the services, rendering them less buoyant in terms of product share: for all service sectors combined, the real value-added share rose by 8.3 percentage points, whereas the commodity output share rose by only 5.3 percentage points. Third, limitation to domestic final demand shares makes the role of services become even more modest: an increase of only 4.4 percentage points. Fourth, and related to this, we found no validity to the argument that a shift in comparative advantage towards services may have countered the decline of services due to their higher relative prices. In short, Canadian services suffer little from the Baumol disease when capital is taken into account. However, their share of domestic final demand does not keep pace with their employment and value-added shares. Yet the service shares of domestic final demand do rise and this remains a puzzle to be explained. One explanation could be a shift of innovation towards services and, related to this, a shift of consumer preferences towards these new services. If R&D figures are anything to go by, they tend to bolster this explanation.

One final remark is in order. The very figures of labour productivity or total factor productivity in services might be seriously mismeasured. Services are hard to measure and, for some of them, accurate estimates of output are not even available. Moreover, in the presence of technological change, quality improvements in services and the prices of entirely new services are even harder to measure correctly. It is very likely that services are undervalued, as their output is often measured by their cost of production, given the lack of reliable price data and a proper definition of what services are actually supposed to measure. Hence it may well be that there is no real Baumol disease in services, as prices are rising by less and total factor productivity by more than what is actually measured in the official statistics.

NOTES

1. We thank the participants of the Amsterdam conference and an anonymous referee for helpful comments.
2. Sectors 41 to 50 were allocated to business or to personal services according to their ratio of shipments to domestic intermediate and final demand. Business services are characterized by a preponderance of deliveries to intermediate domestic demand.
3. For more documentation on some of these dimensions of technological change and their impact on productivity and activity in services, see Neef (1998), Coyle (1999), and Shapiro and Varian (1999).

REFERENCES

Baumol, William (1967), 'Macroeconomics of unbalanced growth: the anatomy of urban crisis', *American Economic Review*, **57**, 415–26.
Coyle, Diane (1999), *The Weightless World*, Cambridge: MIT Press.
Leamer, E.E. and J. Levinsohn (1995), 'International trade theory: the evidence', in G. Grossman and K. Rogoff (eds), *Handbook of International Economics*, Vol. III, Amsterdam: North-Holland.
Johnson, J. (1994), 'Une base de données KLEMS décrivant la structure des entrées de l'industrie canadienne', Statistique Canada, Division des Entrées-Sorties, Cahier Technique #73F.
Mattey, Joe (2001), 'Will the new information economy cure the cost disease in the US?', chapter 5 in this volume.
Neef, Dale (ed.) (1998), *The Knowledge Economy*, Boston: Butterworth-Heinemann.
Shapiro, Carl and Hal Varian (1999), *Information Rules*, Boston: Harvard Business School Press.
Statistics Canada (various issues), System of National Accounts – The Input–Output Structure of the Canadian Economy, Minister of Supply and Services, Ottawa.
ten Raa, Thijs and Pierre Mohnen (1998), 'Sources of productivity growth: technology, terms of trade, and preference shifts', CentER discussion paper #98105.

Trefler, Daniel (1995), 'The case of missing trade and other mysteries,' *American Economic Review*, **85**, 1029–45.

PART IV

Demand-side reasons for services persistence

7. Are prices unimportant? The changing structure of the industrialized economies*

Eileen Appelbaum and Ronald Schettkat

1 INTRODUCTION

The distribution of employment among economic sectors in the industrialized economies has changed dramatically. One popular explanation for these shifts relies on the assumption of a hierarchy of needs that distinguishes among basic needs for food and shelter, needs for other material goods, and more sophisticated needs for non-material goods, including services (Maslow, 1970). According to this theory, income elasticities of demand are functions of per capita income and differ by sector. In particular, the income elasticity of demand for services increases with rising income as the hierarchy of needs favours the fulfilment of more sophisticated desires at higher levels of income. This pattern of sectoral income elasticities, in combination with rising income and a slower productivity growth in the service sector compared with manufacturing, leads to an increase in the output and employment shares of services in industrialized economies as income increases – that is, to post-industrial society (Clark, 1940; Fourastie, 1963 [1949]; Bell, 1973; Cornwall and Cornwall, 1994). In this approach, however, demand depends solely on income and on a psychologically based hierarchy of needs. No role is ascribed to prices in the discussion of changes in industrial structure.

In contrast, many economists, while noting the rising share of services in nominal output and the shift of employment to service industries, find that the share of services in real output remained constant as per capita income increased. (See, for example, Baumol, Blackman and Wolff (1989) for the USA over the period 1947 to 1976; Ramaswamy and Rowthorn (1997) for the economies of the USA, Japan and the European Union taken as a whole from 1960 to 1994; Fuchs[1] (1968) even found a decline in the share of real

* This paper has first been published in the *Journal of Post Keynesian Economics (JPKE)*, Spring 1995, **21**(3), 387–98. With thanks to the publisher M.E. Sharpe, Inc. and the Editor Paul Davidson for the kind permission for reprint.

service output in real non-agricultural output.) The increase in the share of services in nominal output is due to the effect of unbalanced productivity growth in manufacturing and services on relative prices. Low productivity growth in services leads to rising relative prices in this sector, and thus to a higher share of services in nominal output (Baumol, 1967). In real terms, however, many researchers have observed that the shares of manufacturing and service output are essentially unchanged, an empirical result that appears to undermine the psychological explanation for changing economic structures. Rather than being caused by shifts in demand for real output, the steady decline in the share of employment of the goods sector and the rise in the employment share of services is the result of constant real output shares in each sector, in combination with higher productivity growth in goods production compared with services. Thus price developments affect the share of services in nominal output, but relative prices appear to have no effect on their share of real output. Real output grows at the same rate in both the goods and service sectors of the economy, independent of the trend in relative prices of these two sectors.

This is a rather surprising outcome, since it is a central tenet of demand theory that trends in relative prices affect quantity demanded. Indeed, Salter (1960) found a strong role for changes in relative prices in explaining changes in the British industrial structure in the period 1924 to 1950.

The circumstances in which real output shares can remain constant as prices change are fairly restrictive. There are two cases:

1. Income elasticities are positive and equal to one in both sectors while price elasticities in both sectors are equal to zero. In this case, only real income developments are important; price trends have no effect.
2. Income elasticities are positive, but differ between the sectors (for example, the income elasticity of demand is less than one for manufactured goods, greater than one for services). However, the differential effects of increases in real income on the growth of output in each sector are just exactly offset by differences in price elasticities in each sector and the trend in relative prices. In this case, both income and price developments influence the behaviour of relative output shares.

Case (1) is highly unlikely, since price elasticities equal to zero require vertical demand curves in both sectors. Moreover, ignoring trends in relative prices can lead to incorrect conclusions about future developments in output and employment shares of the sectors.

In this chapter, we develop a simple formal model that allows us to examine the effects of income and price elasticities and of trends in income and relative prices on output and employment shares. The model suggests that rapid increases in real per capita income and slow changes in relative prices in the past may have contributed to constant real output shares. This may now be changing. In the USA, per capita income stagnated in the 1970s and grew slowly in the 1980s while the pace of the decline in the price of manufactured goods relative to the price of services accelerated.[2] The model allows us to examine the changes in price elasticities of demand for goods and services that are required to keep output shares constant. The analysis also suggests that, over some future time period, changes in relative output shares may plausibly be expected to occur.

Finally, both the 'hierarchy of needs' approach and the 'constant real output shares' approach suggest that low productivity growth is required for the relative expansion of service employment. One important result of our analysis is that we are able to show that, under reasonable assumptions, an increase in productivity in services not only raises overall productivity growth in the economy, it increases the share of services in real output and hastens the shift to service sector employment.

2 A FORMAL MODEL OF CHANGES IN EMPLOYMENT AND OUTPUT SHARES

2.1 Prices in a Sectoral Model

Models used to explain changes in sectoral employment and output shares generally ignore prices (see, for example, Ramaswamy and Rowthorn, 1997, Appendix I; Cornwall and Cornwall, 1994; Sundrum, 1990).[3] The basic sectoral model can be described as follows. Let Y = real output of the economy; L = total employment; $1/\beta$ = the labour force participation rate (assumed constant); $POP = \beta L$ = population; y = per capita income; R = average labour productivity in the economy; λ_i = share of labour force employed in the ith sector; $\Sigma\lambda_i = 1$; $k_i = \lambda_i R_i / R$, sectoral output share; ε_i = income elasticity of demand for the ith good. The subscript i indicates sector-specific variables, and a '·' above a variable indicates growth rates. We extend this model by adding price variables as follows. P = overall price level;[4] $\pi_i = P_i / P$, relative price of output of the ith sector; w = wage rate; ε_{ii} = own (relative) price elasticity of demand, ith sector, $\varepsilon_{ii} < 0$; ε_{ik} = cross (relative) price elasticity of demand, ith good, kth price $(i \neq k)$; $y_i = g_i(\pi_i, \pi_k, y)$ relates per capita consumption of the output of the ith sector to per capita income and relative prices where π_k is a vector of prices of all goods k $\neq i$.

Assuming cost-based pricing, a uniform wage, w, and a uniform mark-up, γ, we have $P_i = \gamma w / R_i$, $P = \gamma w / R$, and $\pi_i = P_i / P = R / R_i$. The growth rate of relative prices is $\dot{\pi}_i = \dot{R} - \dot{R}_i$. That is, the percentage change in the relative price of the output of the ith sector is given by the difference between the overall rate of productivity growth and the rate of productivity growth in the sector. The relative price of the sector's output falls when sectoral productivity growth is above overall productivity growth and rises when it is below.

2.2   Changes in Employment Shares

We can now derive changes in the employment share of the ith sector as a function of the sector's productivity growth rate and of its own- and cross-price elasticities as well as its income elasticity. From the definitions above it follows that

$$d(\lambda_i R_i) = d(L_i/L \cdot Y_i/L_i) = d(Y_i/L) = 1/L \cdot dY_i - Y_i/L^2 \cdot dL.$$

Recall that

$$Y_i = \beta L y_i \text{ and } y_i = g_i(\pi_i, \pi_k, y).$$

Substituting, we have

$$d(\lambda_i R_i) = \beta dy_i = \beta[(\delta y_i/\delta y)dy + (\delta y_i/\delta \pi_i)d\pi_i + \sum(\delta y_i/\delta \pi_k)d\pi_k]$$

Algebraic manipulation leads to

$$d(\lambda_i R_i) = \lambda_i R_i[\varepsilon_i \dot{R} + \varepsilon_{ii}(\dot{R} - \dot{R}_i) + \sum \varepsilon_{ik}(\dot{R} - \dot{R}_k)] = \lambda_i dR_i + R_i d\lambda_i.$$

Then,

$$d\lambda_i = \lambda_i[\varepsilon_i \dot{R} + \varepsilon_{ii}(\dot{R} - \dot{R}_i) + \sum \varepsilon_{ik}(\dot{R} - \dot{R}_k)] - \lambda_i \dot{R}_i$$

and

$$\dot{\lambda}_i = d\lambda_i/\lambda_i = [(\varepsilon_i \dot{R} - \dot{R}_i) + \varepsilon_{ii}(\dot{R} - \dot{R}_i) + \sum \varepsilon_{ik}(\dot{R} - \dot{R}_k)] \qquad (7.1)$$

The change in the employment share of the ith sector depends on income and price elasticities and on the rate of growth of productivity in the sector relative to overall productivity. Recall that $\dot{R} - \dot{R}_i$ is the growth rate of the price of the ith good relative to the overall price level. Thus, price elasticities and price trends, as well as the income elasticity and growth in overall productivity, affect the change in the sector's employment share. It may clarify this result if we consider the familiar case of a Cobb–Douglas utility function. In this case, $\varepsilon_i = 1$, $\varepsilon_{ii} = -1$, and $\varepsilon_{ik} = 0$ for i not equal to k. In equation 7.1, we see that the first term shows the effect of the income elasticity of demand as per capita income rises. The unit income elasticity of demand implies that changes in real income leave the output share of sector i unchanged. If, moreover, there is an above-average rate of productivity growth in sector i, this implies a falling employment share as real income increases. However, as the second term shows, when the price elasticity of demand is -1, this effect on the employment share is just exactly offset by the increase in demand for output as a result of the decrease in relative prices due to the above-average productivity growth in this sector. We have the familiar result that $d\lambda_i / \lambda_i = 0$.

Alternatively, we can rearrange the terms of equation 7.1 to yield

$$\dot{\lambda}_i = \dot{R}(\varepsilon_i + \varepsilon_{ii}) - \dot{R}_i(\varepsilon_{ii} + 1) + \sum \varepsilon_{ik}(\dot{R} - \dot{R}_k) \tag{7.2}$$

The second term of equation 7.2 shows the tendency of the employment share of the ith sector to shrink when demand for the output of the sector is price inelastic ($|\varepsilon_{ii}| < 1$). If, in addition, productivity growth is above average in the ith sector and the income elasticity of demand is approximately 1 (or less), the employment share of the sector can be expected to decline even if the relative price of the sector is declining.[5] As we argue below, these parameters have characterized the manufacturing sector of the advanced industrialized economies since the mid 1970s (see also Appelbaum and Schettkat 1995).

Equation 7.2 can be rewritten to show the determinants of employment growth in a sector:

$$\dot{\lambda}_i = \dot{L}_i - \dot{L} = \dot{L}_i - (P\dot{O}P)$$

$$\dot{L}_i = (P\dot{O}P) + \dot{R}(\varepsilon_i + \varepsilon_{ii}) - \dot{R}_i(\varepsilon_{ii} + 1) + \sum \varepsilon_{ik}(\dot{R} - \dot{R}_k) \tag{7.3}$$

Thus, employment growth in a sector in absolute terms is affected by the sector's price and income elasticities, its productivity growth, and overall productivity growth in the economy (see also Boyer 1988, Appendix 9.1). It is also favourably affected by increases in population, and negatively by decreases.

2.3 Changes in Output Shares

The change in the output share of the ith sector is $(Y_i / Y) = \dot{y}_i - \dot{y}$. We make use of

$$\dot{y}_i = \varepsilon_i \cdot dy/y + \varepsilon_{ii} \cdot d\pi_i / \pi_i + \sum \varepsilon_{ik} \cdot d\pi_k / \pi_k$$

to obtain

$$\dot{y}_i - \dot{y} = (\varepsilon_i - 1)\dot{R} + \varepsilon_{ii}(\dot{R} - \dot{R}_i) + \sum \varepsilon_{ik}(\dot{R} - \dot{R}_k)$$

Assuming that the sum of cross price elasticities is relatively small and can be ignored,

$$(\dot{Y}_i / Y) = (\varepsilon_i - 1)\dot{R} + \varepsilon_{ii}(\dot{R} - \dot{R}_i) \qquad (7.4)$$

Constant output shares require

1. $\varepsilon_i = 1$, and either $\varepsilon_{ii} = 0$ or productivity growth is the same in every sector; or
2. the effect of income growth, due to the income elasticity of demand and rising real income as overall productivity increases, is exactly offset by the price elasticity of demand and the trend in the relative price of the sector $(\dot{R} - \dot{R}_i)$.

These possibilities are summarized in Table 7.1 for the case of two sectors, goods and services, with higher productivity growth in goods production.

3   PRICE EFFECTS AND OUTPUT SHARES: IMPLICATIONS

We begin by observing that output shares can be constant even if the psychological theory that there is a hierarchy of needs is accepted and we assume, in line with that theory, that the income elasticity of demand is less than one for industrial products and more than one for services in the advanced economies. The constant real output shares of goods and services for the period of the 1950s and 1960s found by Baumol, Blackman and Wolff (1989) can be explained as follows. Strong overall productivity (and real per capita income) growth during those decades would have increased consumption of both goods and services. Assuming an income elasticity less than one for industrial products and greater than one for services,[6] this would have led, however, to a less than proportional increase in the output of goods and a more than proportional increase in the output of services. These tendencies toward a declining output share of industrial output and a rising output share of services were offset, however, by the effects of price elastic demand on the output of each sector. Above average productivity growth in goods production and below average productivity growth in services led to a decline in the price of goods relative to the price of services.

Table 7.1 Predictions of changes in real output shares under different assumptions of price and income elasticities and productivity trends

	A price elasticity = 0 income elasticity = 1		B Price elasticity < 0 income elasticities unequal, ≠ 1	
	Goods	Services	Goods	Services
Productivity growth in goods production higher than in services $(R_i \neq R)$				
Income effect on share in real output	↑ (proportional, because $\varepsilon_i = 1$)	↑ (proportional, because $\varepsilon_i = 1$)	↓ (less than proportional, because $\varepsilon_i < 1$)	↑ (more than proportional, because $\varepsilon_I > 1$)
Price effect on share in real output	0 ($\varepsilon_{ii} = 0$)	0 ($\varepsilon_{ii} = 0$)	↑ (falling prices and $\varepsilon_{ii} > 0$)	↓ (rising prices and $\varepsilon_{ii} > 0$)
Net effect on share in real output	0	0	0	0
Net effect on share in employment	↓ (because $\dot{R}_i > \dot{R}$)	↑ (because $\dot{R}_i < \dot{R}$)	↓ (because $\dot{R}_i > \dot{R}$)	↑ (because $\dot{R}_i < \dot{R}$)
Productivity growth in goods and services equal $(R_i = R)$				
Income effect on share in real output	↑ (proportional, because $\varepsilon_i = 1$)	↑ (proportional, because $\varepsilon_i = 1$)	↓ (less than proportional, because $\varepsilon_i < 1$)	↑ (more than proportional, because $\varepsilon_I > 1$)
Price effect on share in real output	0 ($\varepsilon_{ii} = 0$)	0 ($\varepsilon_{ii} = 0$)	0 (because no relative decline in price)	0 (because no relative decline in price)
Net effect on share in real output	0	0	↓	↑
Net effect on share in employment	0 (because $\dot{R}_i = \dot{R}$)	0 (because $\dot{R}_i = \dot{R}$)	↓ (because $\dot{R}_i = \dot{R}$)	↑ (because $\dot{R}_i = \dot{R}$)

With demand price elastic in each sector, the change in relative prices led to a more than proportional increase in the output of goods and a more than proportional decrease in the output of services. Thus the price effects approximately offset the income effects.

It is more difficult to explain why the goods share of real output did not increase in the 1970s, when overall productivity growth slowed in the industrialized economies, most notably in the USA, weakening the effect of growing income on demand for services; and even more so in the 1980s, when the differential in sectoral rates of productivity growth increased sharply[7] and the relative price of industrial products appears to have declined more precipitously than in earlier periods.[8] Clearly, if the demand for goods remained price elastic in the later as well as the earlier period, the share of goods production in real output should have increased in the 1970s and 1980s. In fact, the share of goods production in real output has remained constant (Rowthorn and Ramaswamy, 1997) or even declined (see Figure 7.1). This empirical result requires an explanation.

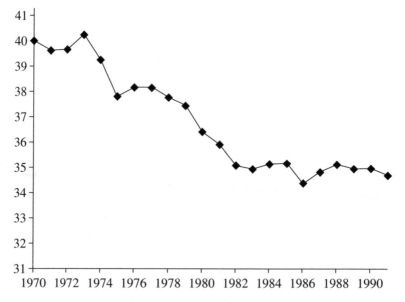

Source: Computations based on the OECD International Structural Database; aggregation of countries with 1985 PPPs in US $; Industry includes: Mining (ISIC 2), Manufacturing (ISIC 3), Energy (ISIC 4), and Construction (ISIC 5); GDP does not include Agriculture.

Figure 7.1   The share of real industry output in total non-agricultural output (in per cent)

We have argued elsewhere (Appelbaum and Schettkat, 1994, 1995, see also Möller in this volume) that the price elasticity of demand for goods has declined over the last several decades in the industrialized economies as a result of economic development and rising per capita income. Briefly, the core of the argument is that over time, as rising incomes lead to the accumulation of household wealth and the stock of consumer durables increases, the price elasticity of demand for many consumer durables can be expected to decline. This is a familiar phenomenon in marketing (Pine 1993). Furthermore, price elasticities of demand, like income elasticities, depend on levels of consumption previously achieved. As per capita income increases and the demand curve for a sector's output shifts outward, the absolute value of the elasticity of demand at any price declines, a relationship sometimes referred to as Harrod's Law.[9] Moreover, current relative prices reflect past productivity growth in the various industries and therefore tend to be lower in industries that have experienced more rapid productivity growth. If, in addition, the income elasticity of goods is less than services once food and other basic material needs have been met, then the income effect of a decline in the price of goods must be smaller than the income effect of the same percentage change in the price of services. As a result, the price elasticity of the demand for goods must also be smaller than for services. For all of these reasons, the price elasticity of demand for goods can be expected to decline. Eventually, as productivity growth continues to raise per capita income and households accumulate stocks of durable goods, the price elasticities of demand for many goods become inelastic.[10] In these circumstances, increases in productivity and reductions in relative price of manufactured goods lead to increases in the quantity demanded that are smaller than the increase in productivity.[11]

The constant output share of manufactured goods suggests, in light of equation 7.4, that demand for manufactured goods has become more price inelastic in the last two decades than it was in earlier decades. Otherwise, the much more rapid decline in relative price of this sector in the recent period would have led to an increase in the real output share of manufactured goods.

Finally, with income elasticities of many services greater than one, and demand for these services price elastic, equation 7.4 reveals the surprising conclusion that an increase in productivity in service industries that brings productivity growth in line with or above overall productivity growth in the economy will accelerate the growth in demand for these services and increase their real output share. With the absolute value of the price elasticity greater than one, equation 7.3 shows that employment in these service industries will also increase (provided that this effect is not offset by a decline in population). Thus, improvements in productivity in services emerge as the key not only to raising per capita incomes in the industrialized economies but also to expanding employment.

NOTES

1. Fuchs found that the share of real intermediate services increased, which together with the declining share of real service output in total output implies a shrinking of the share of real final service consumption.
2. For example, Lawrence and Slaughter (1993) point to the following as indicators of the decline in the relative prices of goods in the USA: the GNP deflator for goods declined relative to the overall GNP deflator by 5.0 per cent in the 1960s, by 5.7 per cent in the 1970s, and by 13.1 per cent in the 1980s; the commodity price component of the CPI declined relative to the services component by 16.2 per cent in the 1950s, by 13.3 per cent in the 1970s, and by 23.9 per cent in the 1980s.
3. While the formal model employed by Ramaswamy and Rowthorn omits price variables, the effect of prices is acknowledged in a footnote (1997, footnote 9): 'The observed stability of the real output share of manufacturing is likely to be the outcome of offsetting income and price effects on demand. The income elasticity of demand for manufactures may be somewhat less than unity, but real expenditure on such goods is stimulated by falling relative prices due to relatively rapid productivity growth in the manufacturing sector. This chapter does not seek to disentangle such effects, but takes their combined effect as given.'
4. P is a weighted average of sectoral prices, where the weights are sectoral output shares.
5. A sharp increase in prices of services relative to goods can also, through the effect on cross price elasticities, lead to a substitution of self-service activities and manufactured goods for the purchase of services, for example, substituting the purchase of frozen dinners, microwaves and home preparation for the purchase of fast food restaurant meals. However, these effects are likely to be small in relation to the own price and income effects.
6. Estimates for income and price elasticities vary substantially. Fuchs (1968) reports demand elasticities for services of 1.12 and for goods of 0.93, mainly caused, however, by low elasticities for food at home and for tobacco. The difficulty of estimating price and income elasticities is apparent in Houthakker and Taylor (1966, chapter 4). The authors assume that price and income elasticities are unchanged over the entire period 1929 to 1961 and estimate equations that predict consumption in 84 categories of personal consumption expenditure. Prices are dropped from the equation in 40 per cent of the cases because the authors judged the results to be untenable, and numerous other decisions about variables to retain and specifications of equations are made in order to obtain a good fit in the various categories and predict consumption in 1970. As the authors observe in the introduction, '... the sobering test of common sense was applied at nearly every step of the empirical research ....'.
7. The ratio of productivity growth in services to productivity growth in manufacturing in the industrialized countries was: 1960–70: 0.652; 1971–94: 0.355 (OECD Historical Statistics 1960–1994).
8. See Lawrence and Slaughter 1993, footnote 2; also Krugman and Lawrence 1994.
9. Theil, Chung and Seale (1989) show empirically that the price elasticity of demand for food decreases as income increases and the share of income spent on food decreases. The price elasticity is about 0.80 in India where 56 per cent of income is spent on food, but it is only 0.15 in the USA where 12 per cent of income is spent on food.
10. Marketing specialists refer to markets in which demand for goods is price inelastic as 'saturated' markets. Markets are completely unsaturated if all sales are to customers who are entirely new to the product and completely saturated if all possibilities of sales are replacements of or additions to existing products (Pine 1993: 269).
11. Note, however, that the reaction to price increases will be different. The quantity response to a price increase may actually be stronger (that is, may be price elastic) at least in the short run in saturated markets. This is because, in more saturated markets, the share of consumption that replaces goods already owned by consumers is higher. As a result, the

purchase of new goods can more easily be postponed in response to a price increase, at least in the short run or when price increases are not expected to be permanent.

REFERENCES

Appelbaum, E. and R. Schettkat (1994), 'The End of Full Employment? Economic Developments in Industrialized Economies', *Intereconomics*, Vol. 57 (May/June): 122–130.

Appelbaum, E. and R. Schettkat (1995), 'Employment and Productivity in Industrialized Economies', *International Labor Review*, **134**, (4–5) (Special Issue): 605–23.

Baumol, W. (1967), 'Macroeconomics of unbalanced growth: the anatomy of the urban crisis', *American Economic Review*, Vol. 57 (June): 415–26.

Baumol, W., S. Blackman and E.N. Wolff (1989), *Productivity and American Leadership: The Long View*, Cambridge, MA: MIT Press.

Bell, D. (1973), *The Coming of Post-Industrial Society: A Venture in Social Forecasting*, New York: Basic Books.

Boyer, R. (1988), 'New technologies and employment in the 1980s: from science and technology to macroeconomic modeling', in J.A. Kregel, E. Matzner and A. Roncaglia (eds), *Barriers to Full Employment*, New York: St. Martin's Press.

Clark, C. (1940), *The Conditions of Economic Progress*, London: Macmillan.

Cornwall, J. and W. Cornwall (1994), 'Growth theory and economic structure', *Economica*, **61** (242) (May): 237–51.

Fourastie, J. (1963), *Le Grand Espoir du XXe Siècle*, definitive edition, Paris: Gallimard; first published 1949.

Fuchs, V.R. (1968), *The Service Economy*, New York: NBER; distributed by Columbia University Press.

Houthakker, H.S. and L.D. Taylor (1966), *Consumer Demand in the United States, 1929–1970: Analyses and Projections*, Cambridge, MA: Harvard University Press.

Krugman, P. and R.Z. Lawrence (1994), 'Trade, jobs and wages', *Scientific American*, **270** (4) (April): 44–56.

Lawrence, R.Z. and M.J. Slaughter (1993), 'International trade and American wages in the 1980s: giant sucking sound or small hiccup', *Brookings Papers on Economic Activity: Microeconomics 2*, pp. 161–210.

Maslow, A.H. (1970), *Motivation and Personality*, New York: Harper and Row.

Möller, J. (2001), *Income and price elasticities in different sectors of the economy* (this volume).

Pine, Joseph (1993), *Mass Customization*, Boston: Harvard Business School Press.

Ramaswamy, R. and R. Rowthorn (1997), 'Deindustrialization: causes and implications', IMF Working Paper, Washington, DC (April).

Salter, W.E.G. (1960), *Productivity and Technical Change*, Cambridge: Cambridge University Press; 2nd edition with addendum by W.B. Reddaway (1966).

Sundrum, R.M. (1990), *Economic Growth in Theory and Practice*, London: Macmillan.

Theil, H., C.F. Chung and J.L. Seal (1989), *Advances in Econometrics, Supplement I, International Evidence on Consumption Patterns*, Greenwich, CT: JAI Press.

8. Structural economic dynamics and the final product concept[1]

Giovanni Russo and Ronald Schettkat

1   INTRODUCTION

The structure of employment and nominal GDP in the USA, Europe and other highly industrialized countries has changed dramatically over the last decades. During this period, manufacturing industries have declined and service industries have expanded. This structural shift is often described as de-industrialization or post-industrial society. All authors agree that both the share of services in nominal GDP and the share of services in employment has increased, but there is surprising disagreement about the nature of these changes these days. Many economists found a constant share of real service output in real GDP (Baumol, Blackman and Wolff 1989, for the USA over the period 1947 to 1976, Ramaswamy and Rowthorn 1997 for the economies of the USA, Japan, and the European Union from 1960 to 1994). Fuchs (1968) even found a decline in the share of real services in real GDP. The indisputable increase in the share of services in nominal GDP and employment is thus the effect of a constant relative demand pattern in combination with unbalanced productivity growth. Low productivity growth rates in services alongside high productivity growth rates in manufacturing led to the growth of the service industries in relative terms.[2] However, for recent decades Appelbaum and Schettkat (1997) found evidence for a rising share of services in real GDP.

Most of the empirical analyses are based on National Accounts Statistics, which use an institutional division of the economy. Changes in the inter-industry division of labour can therefore cause changes in the inter-industry composition of GDP or employment even if the structure of final demand remains unchanged. For example, it is argued that the shift in relative real output from manufacturing to service industries is a statistical artefact. Outsourcing of service activities from manufacturing leads service industries to grow but this is simply the result of a reorganization of the production chain rather than reflecting changes in final demand. By the same argument, Europe–USA differences in industry composition reflect different degrees of specialization rather than a diverging composition of final demand. According to this argument, specialization, inter-firm and hence inter-industry division of labour are more advanced in the USA and therefore the service sector as measured in National Accounts statistics appears to be larger in the USA than in Europe (for example, DIW 1996). In short, there are two lines of arguments explaining changes in the structure of industrialized economies observed in National Account Statistics: the first states that changes are nominal but not real (unbalanced productivity growth). The second one posits that different structures reflect changes in the inter-industry division of labour rather than changes in final demand. One may say that, according to these arguments,[3] structural economic dynamics and structural differences between countries are a myth. They are measurement error.

Whatever the trends in real shares are, they are based on National Accounts Statistics, which use an institutional decomposition of the economy, and they reflect indeed a mixture of final-demand and reorganization variables. It is impossible to derive a clear relationship between final product demand and production from conventional National Accounts Statistics. Investigating changes in Final Product Demand (FPD) and its effect on the structure of production requires the analysis of vertically integrated sectors (Pasinetti 1983) as can be derived from Input–Output statistics.

Similarly, industry-specific labour productivity (calculated as value-added to labour input) and related industry-specific employment trends are difficult to interpret because such a productivity measure may rise (and employment may fall) if less productive activities are outsourced to other industries. Conclusions derived from such measures may thus be very misleading (see ten Raa and Wolff 1996 who investigate the importance of outsourcing for US manufacturing).

In the present study outsourcing is denoted as an increase of value added purchased from other industries in final demand for a product.[4] Outsourcing is the result of replacement of in-house services (that is, advertising, accounting, and business-related services) with services purchased from outside the firm (and the industry).

The present chapter assesses the importance of outsourcing as the cause for the increased importance of the service industries and its impact on productivity measures (see also Momigliano and Siniscalco 1982). We first develop employment and productivity measures for vertically integrated sectors, which accounts for direct (within industry) and indirect (intermediate goods bought from the rest of the economy) inputs needed to produce a certain amount of products. Employment necessary to satisfy a certain demand for a product will be called Final Product Employment (FPE). The productivity over the integrated production process will be called Final Product Productivity (FPP). We contrast changes in FPE and FPP with changes in the conventional industry-specific measures (industry-specific employment and industry-specific productivity in the institutional definition of National Account Statistics). We then decompose changes in FPE and FPP into industry-specific components and inter-industry components in order to investigate the sources of change. The empirical analysis is based on an international comparable Input–Output database provided by OECD, matched with the OECD International Structural Data Base (ISDB), and on conventional data drawn from National Accounts Statistics (see the appendix for details). All the variables used in the calculations are expressed at constant prices (except employment expressed in number of workers).

The structure of the chapter is as follows: section 2 introduces the definition of final product productivity and final product employment (employment and productivity in the vertically integrated sector), section 3 links the final product concept to structural change in the economy. Section 4 contains the results of the decomposition of changes in final product productivity in the period 1970–90 for Japan, Germany, France and the USA. Section 5 offers an analysis of the results. The conclusions are presented in section 6.

2   THE FINAL PRODUCT CONCEPT: FINAL PRODUCT EMPLOYMENT AND FINAL PRODUCT PRODUCTIVITY

Labour productivity in an industry may rise for various reasons: 1) technological progress (including work organization), 2) substitution of labour through capital, 3) increasing skills of labour, 4) outsourcing of less productive tasks to other industries. The latter may be facilitated by information and communication technologies, and it is the number-one explanation for declining manufacturing employment. What we measure as more efficient production in manufacturing, however, may be a misperception if the efficiency of the whole production process is at stake. What we observe as industry specific productivity growth can, in the extreme, be entirely caused by a shift of less productive activities to other (service) industries.

To identify outsourcing effects, we construct a productivity measure which relates the final product demand to overall labour input in the vertically integrated production chain, that is including the labour input into intermediate production. This measure we call final product productivity (FPP). The final demand for the product that is mainly produced in industry h can be written as:

$$FPD_h = VA_{hh} + \sum_{i \neq h} VA_{ih} \qquad (8.1)$$

where FPD_h represents final demand for product h (h is the typical product of industry h), VA_{hh} represents value-added created in industry h incorporated in final demand for product h, and VA_{ih} denotes value-added created in other industries of the vertically integrated product sector but incorporated into final demand for product h (intermediate goods produced in industries i and delivered to industry h). Using the concept of vertically integrated sectors we define the final product productivity (*FPP*) as final product demand divided by employment in the vertically integrated sector (final product employment, *FPE*).

$$FPP_h = \frac{FPD_h}{FPE_h} \qquad (8.2)$$

For the empirical specification we make use of two assumptions:

(i)   the amount of labour needed to produce one unit of product is inde-
       pendent of the destination of the product;
(ii) the amount of value-added incorporated in one unit of product is inde-
       pendent of the destination of the product.

In other words, (i) and (ii) state that the product of a specific industry is produced with the same productivity (industry's average productivity) independent of its destination (final demand or intermediate goods).
   We can then write:

$$VA_{ih} = \pi_i E_{ih}; \forall h \qquad (8.3)$$

where π_i is industry i's productivity (value-added/employment), h is the subscript for the destination of industry i's product, and E_{ih} is the indirect employment in industry i generated by final demand for product h. Indirect employment is defined as follows:

$$E_{ih} = \frac{x_{ih}}{GO_i} \frac{FPD_h}{GO_h} E_i \qquad (8.4)$$

where E_i is employment in industry i, GO_i is the gross output (final demand plus intermediate goods minus imports) of industry i and x_{ih} (the entry in the input–output table corresponding to row i and column h) is the amount of intermediate goods that industry h purchases from industry i. The ratio FPD_h / GO_h represents the proportion of purchased goods incorporated in final demand for product h. Thus, E_{ih} is employment in industry i induced by final demand for product h (indirect employment). Moreover, direct employment in industry h $E_{hh} = E_h^*(FD_h/GO_h)$ and FPE_h is thus the sum of direct and indirect employment:

$$FPE_h = E_{hh} + \sum_{i \neq h} E_{ih} \tag{8.5}$$

The final product productivity can be written as follows:

$$FPP_h = \pi_h \frac{E_{hh}}{FPE_h} + \sum_{i \neq h} \pi_i \frac{E_{ih}}{FPE_h} \tag{8.6}$$

The final product productivity of the vertically integrated sector h is given by the weighted average of the productivity of all industries contributing to production of product h. The weights are the employment shares of individual industries in overall employment in the vertically integrated product sector.

Changes in FPP can be decomposed into a pure productivity effect (due to changes in industry-specific productivity in the industries of the vertically integrated product sector), a structural effect (due to changes in the employment structure of the vertically integrated product sector), and an interaction term:

$$\Delta FPP_h = \sum_i \Delta\pi_i a_{ih} + \sum_i \pi_i \Delta a_{ih} + \sum_i \Delta\pi_i \Delta a_{ih}$$

$$a_{ih} = \frac{E_{ih}}{FPE_h} \tag{8.7}$$

where a_{ih} is industry i's employment share in final product employment of product h. The productivity effect tells us how much variation in final product productivity is due to changes in industry-specific productivity keeping the employment structure of the vertically integrated product sector unchanged. The structural effect indicates how much variation in final product productivity is due to changes in the employment structure of the vertically integrated product sector keeping industry-specific productivity levels unchanged. Clearly, the structural effect is an indicator of the importance of employment reallocation (outsourcing) within a vertically integrated product sector.

The structural and productivity effects can be further decomposed into an own (initiated in industry h) and an imported (initiated in delivering industries) component:

$$\Delta FPP_h = \Delta\pi_h a_{hh} + \sum_{i \neq h} \Delta\pi_i a_i + \pi_h \Delta a_{hh} + \sum_{i \neq h} \pi_i \Delta a_{ih} + \sum_i \Delta\pi_i \Delta a_{ih} \tag{8.8}$$

where the first and third factors on the right-hand side (outside summation) are the own components of the productivity and structural effect, respectively.

To illustrate how the above decomposition can be used for the analysis of the outsourcing process the third term $(\pi_h \Delta a_{hh})$ indicates the presence of outsourcing whenever it is negative (relative employment in industry h declines in the vertically integrated product sector). If outsourcing is apparent, the first component, if positive, tells us that low productivity activities have been outsourced. Moreover, if the fourth component in equation (8.8) (that is, the weighted sum of other industries' productivity) is negative it indicates outsourcing of low productive activities from industry h to other low productivity industries. Industry-specific productivity increases in this case, but FPP may not change. The fourth term can also be positive if productive activities are outsourced to highly productive industries. FPP will rise. Reorganizing production in the latter case improves productivity of the integrated production process.

3   DYNAMICS IN THE FINAL PRODUCT CONCEPT

3.1   The Effect of Outsourcing on Structural Change

The growth of the service sector[5] and the relative (but in Europe also the absolute) decline of manufacturing industries have been explained by the reorganization of the production process. According to this argument, manufacturing industries outsourced part of their service activities into specialized firms that are then counted as part of the service sector. Thus, as measured in the National Account Statistics, the service sector grows and manufacturing declines (Appelbaum and Schettkat 1990). By the same reason USA–Europe differences in industry composition are said to be a statistical artifact. In Europe as compared to the USA the production process is according to this argument less specialized, that is, a higher share of service activities are performed within manufacturing firms rather than being outsourced to specialized service firms. In National Accounts, however, industry definition follows the institutional criteria of the main economic activity. Thus, similar service activities are counted as manufacturing in Europe but as services in the USA. In other words, USA–Europe differences are not real but rather a statistical artefact.

Given these arguments one expects an increasing share of intermediate products to flow from service industries to manufacturing. The share of intermediate products delivered from the service to manufacturing in manufacturing's gross output should have increased and it should be higher in the

Table 8.1 *Percentage of intermediate products and own value-added in gross output in manufacturing and in services, constant prices*

Year	Intermediate products in gross output		Own value-added in gross output		Intermediate products to value-added ratio	
	Services in manufacturing 1	Manufacturing in services 2	Manufacturing 3	Services 4	Services in manufacturing 5	Manufacturing in services 6
JAPAN						
1970	14.22	9.51	20.19	70.09	70.43	13.56
1980	14.06	8.82	26.71	68.03	52.72	12.97
1990	14.93	10.03	31.00	64.83	48.17	15.48
USA						
1972	11.91	7.66	34.31	71.05	34.71	10.77
1977	12.65	7.18	31.71	70.45	39.91	10.2
1990	13.19	6.85	38.32	67.54	34.42	10.15
GERMANY						
1978	12.98	9.65	33.18	69.46	39.12	13.9
1990	16.73	8.24	30.96	66.75	54.05	12.35
FRANCE						
1972	10.82	6.55	33.46	78.06	32.33	8.39
1977	11.77	6.54	34.66	77.78	33.97	8.41
1990	16.77	5.84	32.19	69.79	52.09	8.36

CANADA							
1971	11.35	13.55	26.53	57.41	42.8	23.61
1976	11.50	11.85	27.90	59.52	41.21	19.9
1990	9.32	15.91	32.65	58.57	40.58	15.91
DENMARK							
1972	10.35	9.51	30.16	74.08	34.31	12.84
1977	11.05	9.19	30.82	74.35	35.86	12.36
1990	11.86	9.10	30.12	71.58	39.37	12.71
UK							
1968	9.16	9.99	35.94	79.02	27.79	11.6
1979	10.22	16.03	30.97	72.92	51.76	14.02
1990	13.14	16.09	26.96	54.27	59.38	24.21

Notes:
Services: Wholesale and Retail Trade, Restaurants and Hotels [ISIC 6];
    Transport Storage and Communication [ISIC 7];
    Financial, Insurance, Real Estate, and Business Services [ISIC 8];
    Community, Social and Personal Services [ISIC 9].
Manufacturing: Manufacturing [ISIC 3].

Source: Computation based on OECD input–output database.

USA than in less specialized Europe. The OECD input–output database allows us to investigate these hypotheses directly. Table 8.1 shows the share of intermediate products purchased from all service industries in gross output of all manufacturing industries. First of all, it is striking how stable the shares are and how little they vary across countries. Over two decades the share of intermediate services in manufacturing's gross output has not changed at all in Japan and has risen only modestly in the USA and Denmark (it has declined in Canada). In Germany, France and the UK, the share has increased more but it is far from anything like the explosion we might have expected from popular and economic discussion. Most important, in the USA, which is usually classified as the economy with the highest degree of specialization, the share of intermediate services in manufacturing's gross output is lower than in France and Germany, which are usually examples for backward economies. Not only is the share in the USA lower but also the increase is much less than in the European economies.

The Europe–USA comparison does not produce different results if one investigates the relations from the other side, that is if one asks how much of the gross output is value-added produced within the sector itself. These figures are displayed in columns 3 and 4 of Table 8.1. Over time there is, if anything, evidence for insourcing by manufacturing and outsourcing by the service sector (with respect of both gross output and value-added). An exceptional case with respect to the trend in the ratio own value added to gross output is manufacturing in Japan. Here the share of own value-added increased substantially from 1979 to 1990. This may reflect the dramatic catching up process in which Japan moved from a low quality producer to a top quality producer and it may reflect the higher share of innovative products in Japan (see Petit *et al.* 1997).

3.2   The Final Product Demand Approach versus the Institutional Approach

Additional information on the causes of structural change can be obtained by contrasting the economic structure as obtained from the institutional classification (National Accounts Statistics) with the one obtained from the final product approach. Figures based on the conventional, that is the institutional division of the economy are shown in the upper panel of Table 8.2. The ratio of value-added in services to value-added in manufacturing rose everywhere, except for Japan where it was actually falling, which reflects the rising share of own value-added created in manufacturing mentioned above (Table 8.1). But the differences in the level of these ratios are remarkable with values of about 210 in Germany and Japan but values around 300 in the remaining countries. Trends and levels are even more exaggerated if one uses employment (number

Table 8.2   *Ratios of services over manufacturing, in the institutional division and in the final product concept (ratios * 100)*

Years	USA	Canada	Japan	France	Germany	Denmark	UK
			Institutional Approach				
			value added				
1968–72	242	228	303	227	–	329	154
1976–80	282	238	253	230	172	352	235
1990	281	277	207	315	211	386	282
			employment				
1968–72	277	178	155	188	–	236	150
1976–80	302	232	201	211	149	292	203
1990	444	448	162	323	181	333	338
			Final Product Approach				
			final demand				
1968–72	164	105	138	111	–	128	98
1976–80	171	92	148	110	89	131	107
1990	174	116	130	114	83	129	112
			consumption				
1968–72	199	155	218	129	–	162	136
1976–80	221	164	260	138	121	179	154
1990	299	239	247	169	147	230	167
			exports				
1968–72	50	17	38	23	–	49	31
1976–80	66	17	24	21	15	48	38
1990	31	23	17	31	14	48	19
			gross output				
1968–72	117	105	87	97	–	134	70
1976–80	127	112	99	103	82	146	100
1990	159	155	99	145	98	162	147

Notes:
Exact Years: USA 1972, 1977; Canada 1971, 1976; Japan 1970, 1980; France 1972, 1977; Germany 1978; Denmark 1972, 1977; UK 1968, 1979.
Services: Wholesale and Retail Trade, Restaurants and Hotels [ISIC 6];
        Transport Storage and Communication [ISIC 7];
        Financial, Insurance, Real Estate, and Business Services [ISIC 8];
        Community, Social and Personal Services [ISIC 9].
Manufacturing: Manufacturing [ISIC 3].

Source: Computations based on OECD, ISBD for Institutional approach; and on OECD and input–output database for the final product approach.

of persons), which is of course influenced by intersectoral productivity differences but also by differences in the average number of hours worked. For gross output (the value of all products produced in a sector; that is, final demand plus intermediate goods minus imports) the levels of the services-to-manufacturing ratios are much lower which reflects the lower share of own value-added in manufacturing industries (compare Table 8.1). In other words manufacturing is more integrated into the rest of the economy than services, but trends remain similar: service industries are gaining importance.

Gross output ratios are the same whether measured with the institutional division or in the Final Product Approach but with the latter concept final demand can be further decomposed into subcategories (lower panel of Table 8.2). Probably surprising on the background of the discussion on increasing trade of services in the world economy, there is no uniform picture in service-to-manufacturing ratios in exports. Some countries (Canada, France, and the UK) show increasing ratios whereas others (the USA and Japan) show a clearly declining trend and Germany's ratio remains at a very low level. Most importantly industrialized economies appear to move towards service industries in consumption. Here a uniform trend toward the services industry occurs but the European countries show low levels of the service-to-manufacturing ratios in private consumption compared to the USA, Canada and Japan.

To conclude, actual outsourcing appears to be very different from the common view. It has not increased dramatically and thus can hardly have caused the observed trend in manufacturing employment. National economies appear to be very similar with respect to the division of production between manufacturing and services. Furthermore, the USA–Europe difference in the share of service input in manufacturing gross output needs to be revised in light of the statistical evidence presented.

4   FINAL PRODUCT PRODUCTIVITY (FPP)

Final product productivity, that is the productivity of the vertically integrated product sector, accounts for changes in the structure of the production chain. Outsourcing improves FPP if the change in the division of labour creates efficiency gains. FPP remains constant if activities are simply reshuffled between industries without creating any efficiency gain.

Annual compound growth rates of FPP, industry specific productivity, FPE, industry specific employment for the USA, Japan, Germany and France are presented (and confronted) in Table 8.3. We find a strong positive correlation between industry-specific employment growth and employment growth in the vertically integrated product sector [FPE] ($\rho_{US} = 0.57^*$, $\rho_{Ger} = 0.66^*$, $\rho_{Fr} = 0.45^*$, $\rho_{Jpn} = 0.78^*$).[6] Thus employment dynamics at the industry level and in the vertically integrated product sector seem to be determined by the same economic variables. Furthermore, industry-specific productivity growth and productivity growth in the vertically integrated product sector positively correlate ($\rho_{US} = 0.90^*$, $\rho_{Ger} = 0.93^*$, $\rho_{Fr} = 0.96^*$, $\rho_{Jpn} = 0.24$).

One way to look on outsourcing is to investigate the ratio of direct employment (industry's h employment to produce product h) to indirect employment (employment necessary in the rest of the economy to produce product h). These ratios are displayed in Table 8.4, which shows that they range in most cases between 2 and 3. That is, direct employment is still the most important part in final product employment, although it is declining in most manufacturing industries. Furthermore, the structures of the four economies appear to converge, the correlation between the direct to indirect ratio across countries increasing during the last two decades.

To quantify the importance of outsourcing for productivity gains we decompose changes in FPP into a structural component (reshuffling of employment among industries belonging to the vertically integrated product sector) and a productivity component that measures the effects of changes in industry-specific productivity. The source of change for industry-specific productivity may or may not be outsourcing itself but in addition technical progress may also play an important role. For example, industry-specific productivity may increase if an industry outsources low productive activities into another industry. This would not only increase productivity in the industry considered but it would also increase the employment share of those industries of the vertically integrated product sector delivering intermediate goods (see equation (8.6)). In the case of pure outsourcing without efficiency gains these components would cancel out in the vertically integrated product sector; that is, ΔFPP would be equal to zero. The results of the decomposition of the variation in final product productivity (see equation (8.7)) are presented in Figures 8.1 to 8.4 for the USA, Germany, Japan, and France. A positive structural effect implies that employment shifts to high productivity industries within the vertically integrated product sector outweigh employment shifts to low productivity industries. Positive productivity effects show that weighted productivity gains offset weighted productivity losses, and that therefore, overall productivity in the vertically integrated product sector increases.[7] A positive interaction effect signals either increasing indirect employment shares in industries with increasing productivity or declining indirect employment shares in industries with declining productivity.

What clearly emerges from the analysis of the four figures is that variations in final product productivity are mainly due to productivity effects (France may be an exception though). Structural effects are present, but they are generally much smaller. Thus while outsourcing certainly takes place, the impact on FPP is limited and the main effect is related to productivity growth

Table 8.3 *Productivity and employment growth rates in the institutional and final product approaches*

	Compound annual growth rate of:				Differences (growth rates)	
	1	2	3	4	5	6
INDUSTRY	FPP	PROD	FPE	EMP	FPP–PROD	FPE–EMP
	Germany 1978–90					
Agriculture, forestry & fishing	3.06	6.98	-1.93	-3.32	-3.92	1.39
Mining & quarrying	-1.85	-2.36	-8.70	-2.15	0.51	-6.55
Food, beverages & tobacco	0.56	-0.10	0.28	-0.78	0.67	1.06
Textiles, apparel & leather	1.42	1.21	-0.96	-3.47	0.21	2.50
Wood products & furniture	0.42	-0.94	1.18	-0.83	1.37	2.02
Paper, paper products & printing	0.71	0.62	4.54	0.71	0.08	3.83
Industrial chemicals	1.28	2.23	1.25	1.08	-0.95	0.16
Non-metallic mineral products	1.33	1.88	0.39	-1.46	-0.55	1.85
Basic metal Industries	2.44	5.71	2.22	-1.11	-3.26	3.33
Metal products machinery equipments	1.20	1.20	2.22	0.84	0.00	1.37
Other manufacturing	1.91	2.16	-0.41	-1.18	-0.24	0.76
Electricity, gas & water	-1.51	-1.06	2.38	0.93	-0.45	1.45
Construction	1.02	0.37	-0.35	-0.43	0.64	0.07
Wholesale & retail trade	1.36	1.58	0.97	0.73	-0.22	0.23
Restaurants & hotels	-0.86	-1.74	2.33	2.21	0.87	0.12
Transport & storage	2.33	3.21	1.16	0.55	-0.88	0.60
Communication	4.86	5.68	1.05	0.29	-0.81	0.75
Finance & insurance	2.24	2.45	2.57	1.77	-0.20	0.79
Real estate & business services	–	–	–	–	–	–
Community, social & personal services	-0.09	-1.44	3.23	3.65	1.35	-0.42
Producers of government services	-0.05	-0.05	1.08	1.12	0	-0.04
Other producers	0.96	1.43	3.32	3.24	-0.47	0.07

USA 1972–90

Agriculture, forestry & fishing	1.26	2.75	0.93	-0.10	-1.49	1.04
Mining & quarrying	-1.16	-0.92	9.25	0.72	-0.24	8.52
Food, beverages & tobacco	0.96	1.07	0.15	-0.24	-0.10	0.39
Textiles, apparel & leather	2.42	4.79	0.19	-1.66	-2.36	1.85
Wood products & furniture	1.49	2.28	1.80	0.25	-0.78	1.55
Paper, paper products & printing	0.31	0.42	1.96	1.46	-0.11	0.50
Industrial chemicals	-0.30	1.80	0.99	0.81	-2.11	0.18
Non-metallic mineral products	0.63	0.98	0.94	-0.75	-0.35	1.69
Basic metal Industries	-0.25	-0.82	-0.10	-2.17	0.56	2.06
Metal products machinery equipments	2.26	3.22	1.52	0.43	-0.95	1.08
Other manufacturing	1.03	1.66	1.52	-0.19	-0.63	1.72
Electricity, gas & water	-1.56	-1.79	3.25	1.50	0.23	1.75
Construction	-0.41	-1.23	1.67	1.85	0.81	-0.17
Wholesale & retail trade	0.46	1.74	2.56	2.30	-1.28	0.26
Restaurants & hotels	-0.56	-0.75	3.43	3.01	0.19	0.41
Transport & storage	0.91	1.59	1.47	1.36	-0.68	0.11
Communication	2.99	3.91	0.17	0.57	-0.91	-0.40
Finance & insurance	0.23	0.97	3.82	2.94	-0.74	0.88
Real estate & business services	-2.47	-2.69	5.56	5.46	0.21	0.09
Community, social & personal services	0.09	0.20	3.64	2.98	-0.11	0.65
Producers of government services	0.38	0.38	1.34	1.20	-1.1E-05	0.13
Other producers	–	7.22	–	1.22	–	–

Notes:

FPP: Final Product Productivity (thousands of 1985 DM, thousands of 1982 US $)

PROD: Productivity in the industry (thousands of 1985 DM, thousands of 1982 US $)

FPE: Final Product Employment (number of persons)

EMP: Employment in industry (number of persons)

Differences: Refers to differences in annual compound growth rates of the variables indicated

Growth: Annual compound growth rate of the ratio of direct employment to indirect employment.

145

Table 8.3 (*continued*)

INDUSTRY	Compound annual growth rate of:				Differences (growth rates)	
	1	2	3	4	5	6
	FPP	PROD	FPE	EMP	PP-PRO	FPE-EMP
		Japan 1970–90				
Agriculture, forestry & fishing	4.66	1.34	-2.57	-1.10	3.32	-1.46
Mining & quarrying	2.68	-1.61	-6.65	-1.95	4.30	-4.69
Food, beverages & tobacco	3.11	-0.09	1.41	0.61	3.21	0.80
Textiles, apparel & leather	3.83	0.10	-0.35	-0.37	3.73	0.01
Wood products & furniture	2.38	0.32	2.43	-0.80	2.06	3.23
Paper, paper products & printing	4.30	3.00	-0.07	0.535	1.30	-0.61
Industrial chemicals	5.61	6.12	-0.21	-0.28	-0.51	0.07
Non-metallic mineral products	3.24	2.81	-0.68	-0.77	0.42	0.08
Basic metal Industries	16.54	1.85	-1.94	0.36	14.69	-2.31
Metal products machinery equipments	5.89	2.56	0.33	0.82	3.33	-0.49
Other manufacturing	5.03	0.93	-0.10	0.24	4.10	-0.34
Electricity, gas & water	2.00	1.87	2.85	0.39	0.12	2.45
Construction	3.22	1.66	1.58	0.08	1.55	1.49
Wholesale & retail trade	2.09	1.72	1.72	0.57	0.37	1.14
Restaurants & hotels	0.78	-0.03	2.80	0.55	0.82	2.25
Transport & storage	3.07	2.25	0.15	0.51	0.82	-0.35
Communication	1.92	0.94	8.22	2.75	0.98	5.46
Finance & insurance	0.66	0.56	1.13	2.46	0.09	-1.32
Real estate & business services	1.18	-0.11	3.85	1.45	1.29	2.40
Community, social & personal services	4.02	-0.08	4.38	1.94	4.10	2.44
Producers of government services	2.86	1.11	1.13	0.03	1.75	1.09
Other producers	7.28	-0.34	4.03	1.24	7.62	2.78

France 1972–90

	FPP	PROD	FPE	EMP	Differences	Growth
Agriculture, forestry & fishing	3.08	5.50	-2.59	-3.72	-2.42	1.13
Mining & quarrying	5.07	7.20	-3.41	-3.23	-2.12	-0.17
Food, beverages & tobacco	1.23	1.11	0.78	0.04	0.12	0.73
Textiles, apparel & leather	1.40	2.67	-1.68	-3.77	-1.26	2.09
Wood products & furniture	2.11	3.20	-0.01	-1.03	-1.09	1.01
Paper, paper products & printing	1.23	1.91	0.72	0.02	-0.67	0.69
Industrial chemicals	2.86	2.82	0.89	-0.33	0.03	1.22
Non-metallic mineral products	-0.19	-1.72	3.32	-2.29	1.52	5.61
Basic metal Industries	3.95	4.41	-0.11	-2.38	-0.46	2.26
Metal products machinery equipments	1.47	2.96	0.58	-0.93	-1.49	1.52
Other manufacturing	1.25	2.45	1.14	-0.16	-1.19	1.30
Electricity, gas & water	3.16	3.71	1.66	1.32	-0.55	0.34
Construction	0.30	2.02	-1.09	-1.10	-1.71	0.01
Wholesale & retail trade	0.40	1.62	0.69	0.57	-1.21	0.12
Restaurants & hotels	-0.09	-0.15	1.98	1.68	0.05	0.30
Transport & storage	0.98	2.12	0.94	0.86	-1.14	0.07
Communication	4.68	7.31	1.64	1.37	-2.63	0.27
Finance & insurance	-5.81	-6.42	-3.30	2.04	0.60	-5.34
Real estate & business services	0	0	0	4.37	0	-4.37
Community, social & personal services	0.45	1.08	3.39	3.43	-0.62	-0.04
Producers of government services	0.75	0.75	1.84	1.84	0	0
Other producers	0	0	0	0	0	0

Notes:
FPP: Final Product Productivity (millions of 1985 Yen, millions of 1985 FF)
PROD: Productivity in the industry (millions of 1985 Yen, millions of 1985 FF)
FPE: Final product Employment (number of persons)
EMP: Employment in industry (number of persons)
Differences: Refers to differences in annual compound growth rates of the variables indicated
Growth: Annual compound growth rate of the ratio of direct employment to indirect employment.

Table 8.4 Direct to indirect employment ratio per country

	Direct to indirect employment ratio							
	Germany		Japan		USA		France	
INDUSTRY	1978 1	1990 2	1970 3	1990 4	1972 5	1990 6	1972 7	1990 8
Agriculture, forestry & fishing	1.95	2.30	4.01	3.08	2.71	3.15	3.30	2.96
Mining & quarrying	3.23	2.24	2.17	1.85	8.31	5.22	4.34	3.13
Food, beverages & tobacco	2.05	1.81	5.11	3.51	1.87	1.76	1.74	1.64
Textiles, apparel & leather	3.41	2.66	3.31	2.89	2.81	3.39	3.42	3.07
Wood products & furniture	2.36	1.94	3.88	2.77	2.14	2.12	2.22	2.42
Paper, paper products & printing	3.14	2.77	4.07	3.36	3.17	2.744	4.13	3.14
Industrial chemicals	2.38	2.84	2.25	2.88	1.76	2.02	1.85	2.34
Non-metallic mineral products	2.37	2.20	2.03	2.14	2.30	2.21	2.52	1.94
Basic metal Industries	3.50	3.28	1.94	3.55	2.79	2.01	3.32	2.78
Metal products machinery equipments	3.22	2.89	2.07	2.96	2.79	3.73	2.72	2.54
Other manufacturing	1.97	1.79	1.75	1.70	1.92	1.99	1.69	1.68
Electricity, gas & water	2.67	1.98	3.33	2.38	3.12	2.06	2.43	3.38
Construction	1.98	1.79	1.68	1.69	2.01	1.86	1.91	1.82
Wholesale & retail trade	2.92	2.86	2.96	3.54	3.86	3.95	4.34	3.62
Restaurants & hotels	1.70	1.59	2.60	2.02	1.99	1.92	2.78	2.44
Transport & storage	2.53	2.63	3.18	2.63	2.90	3.33	3.43	3.35
Communication	6.26	7.00	5.19	6.31	4.39	4.76	5.57	9.43
Finance & insurance	4.30	4.04	6.42	4.63	3.88	3.96	8.09	5.20
Real estate & business services	–	–	4.80	4.17	6.34	5.95	0	4.81

	Base year				1990			
	Germany	Japan	USA	France	Germany	Japan	USA	France
Community, social & personal services	2.53	2.40	3.85	2.60	2.84	2.51	4.45	4.47
Producers of government services	0	0	0	0	0	0	0	0
Other producers	3.57	3.52	8.15	2.45	0	0	0	0
Correlation between years within countries	0.95*		0.60*		0.90*		0.66*	

Correlation between countries	Base year				1990			
	Germany	Japan	USA	France	Germany	Japan	USA	France
Germany	1				1			
Japan	0.57*	1			0.90*	1		
USA	0.48*	0.05	1		0.53*	0.60*	1	
France	0.64*	0.21	0.43*	1	0.80*	0.82*	0.73*	1

Note: * significant at 10 per cent confidence level.

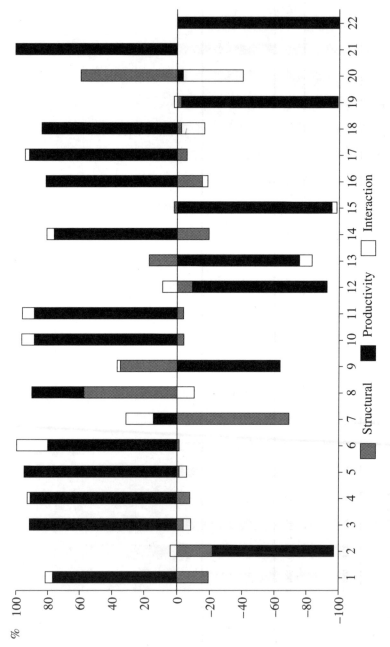

Figure 8.1   Decomposition of variation in FPP, period 1972–90, USA

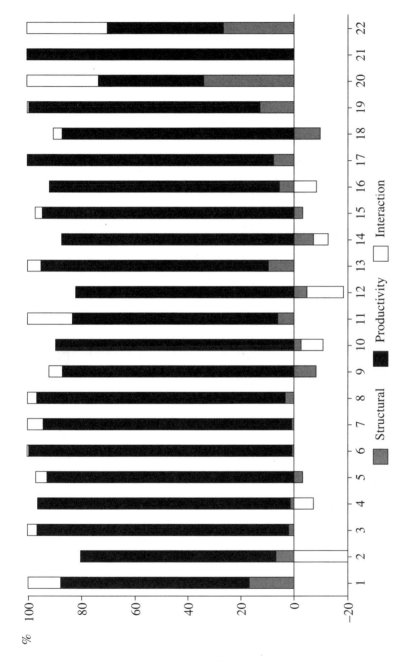

Figure 8.2 Decomposition of variation in FPP, period 1970–90, Japan

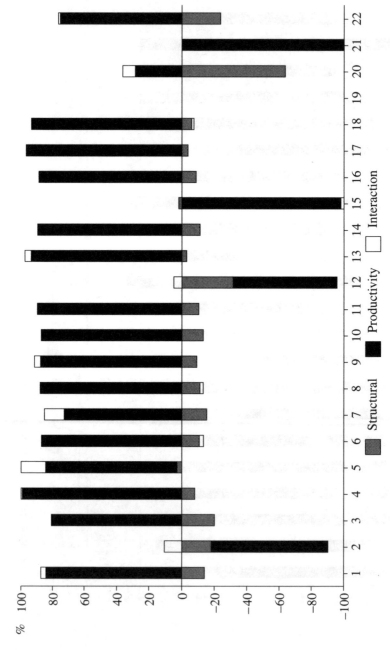

Figure 8.3   Decomposition of variation in FPP, period 1978–90, Germany

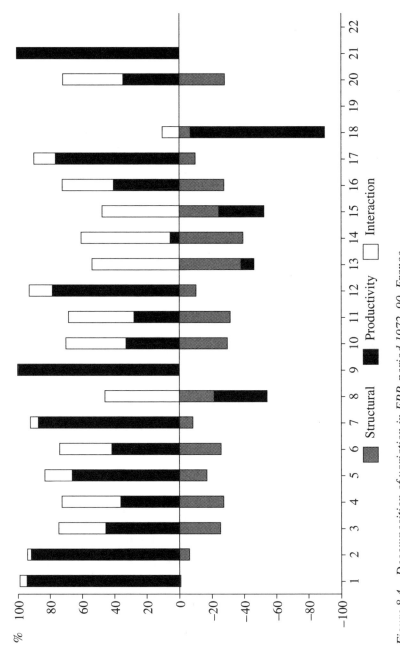

Figure 8.4 Decomposition of variation in FPP, period 1972–90, France

Table 8.5   Decomposition of the structural and productivity effect into industry own and imported components

INDUSTRY	Structural effect			Productivity effect		
	Total	own	imported	Total	own	imported
	Germany					
Agriculture, forestry & fishing	-0.07	0.01	-0.09	0.49	0.39	0.09
Mining & quarrying	-0.04	-0.07	0.02	-0.18	-0.19	0.01
Food, beverages & tobacco	-0.02	-0.03	0.01	0.09	-0.00	0.10
Textiles, apparel & leather	0.00	-0.04	0.04	0.18	0.10	0.07
Wood products & furniture	0.00	-0.03	0.04	0.04	-0.06	0.10
Paper, paper products & printing	-0.01	-0.02	0.01	0.10	0.05	0.04
Industrial chemicals	-0.03	0.03	-0.06	0.17	0.20	-0.03
Non-metallic mineral products	-0.02	-0.01	-0.01	0.20	0.16	0.03
Basic metal Industries	-0.03	-0.00	-0.03	0.35	0.38	-0.02
Metal products machinery equipments	-0.02	-0.01	-0.00	0.18	0.11	0.06
Other manufacturing	-0.02	-0.03	0.00	0.29	0.26	0.02
Electricity, gas & water	-0.05	-0.07	0.01	-0.11	-0.10	-0.01
Construction	-0.00	-0.02	0.01	0.12	0.02	0.09
Wholesale & retail trade	-0.02	-0.00	-0.01	0.20	0.15	0.05
Restaurants & hotels	-0.05	-0.02	-0.02	-0.04	-0.09	0.05
Transport & storage	-0.04	0.00	-0.05	0.36	0.29	0.06
Communication	-0.02	0.01	-0.03	0.79	0.74	0.04
Finance & insurance	-0.01	-0.01	-0.00	0.32	0.32	0.00
Real estate & business services	0	0	0	0	0	0
Community, social & personal services	-0.02	-0.00	-0.01	0.01	-0.08	0.09
Producers of government services	0	0	0	-0.00	-0.00	0
Other producers	-0.05	-0.00	-0.04	0.17	0.12	0.04

	Japan					
Agriculture, forestry & fishing	0.25	-0.01	0.27	1.04	0.20	0.84
Mining & quarrying	0.07	-0.02	0.10	0.85	0.09	0.75
Food, beverages & tobacco	0.01	-0.04	0.06	0.76	0.49	0.27
Textiles, apparel & leather	0.02	-0.01	0.03	1.19	0.40	0.79
Wood products & furniture	-0.02	-0.05	0.03	0.59	0.34	0.24
Paper, paper products & printing	0.01	-0.03	0.04	1.30	1.13	0.16
Industrial chemicals	0.02	0.05	-0.03	1.84	1.76	0.08
Non-metallic mineral products	0.03	0.00	0.02	0.83	0.39	0.43
Basic metal Industries	-1.96	-0.69	-1.26	21.13	16.32	4.80
Metal products machinery equipments	-0.07	0.03	-0.11	2.44	1.23	1.20
Other manufacturing	0.10	-0.00	0.10	1.28	0.04	1.24
Electricity, gas & water	-0.04	-0.07	0.02	0.62	0.46	0.15
Construction	0.09	0.00	0.09	0.75	0.23	0.51
Wholesale & retail trade	-0.04	0.01	-0.06	0.60	0.30	0.29
Restaurants & hotels	-0.00	-0.06	0.05	0.17	0.08	0.08
Transport & storage	0.05	-0.02	0.08	0.85	0.35	0.50
Communication	0.03	0.02	0.00	0.42	0.38	0.04
Finance & insurance	-0.01	-0.04	0.02	0.15	0.12	0.03
Real estate & business services	0.03	-0.02	0.05	0.22	0.18	0.04
Community, social & personal services	0.40	-0.04	0.45	0.46	-0.02	0.48
Producers of government services	0	0	0	0.76	0.76	0
Other producers	0.81	-0.09	0.91	1.33	0.97	0.35

Table 8.5 (continued)

INDUSTRY	Structural effect			Productivity effect		
	Total	own	imported	Total	own	imported
		USA				
Agriculture, forestry & fishing	-0.07	0.01	-0.09	0.31	0.28	0.02
Mining & quarrying	-0.04	-0.05	0.01	-0.15	-0.14	-0.00
Food, beverages & tobacco	-0.00	-0.02	0.01	0.20	0.15	0.05
Textiles, apparel & leather	-0.04	0.01	-0.06	0.57	0.49	0.08
Wood products & furniture	-0.00	-0.00	-0.00	0.32	0.23	0.09
Paper, paper products & printing	-0.00	-0.02	0.02	0.04	0.05	-0.00
Industrial chemicals	-0.09	0.01	-0.11	0.02	0.12	-0.10
Non-metallic mineral products	0.08	-0.00	0.09	0.04	0.09	-0.04
Basic metal Industries	0.06	-0.05	0.11	-0.10	-0.07	-0.03
Metal products machinery equipments	-0.02	0.04	-0.06	0.47	0.49	-0.02
Other manufacturing	-0.00	0.00	-0.01	0.19	0.17	0.02
Electricity, gas & water	-0.04	-0.07	0.03	-0.23	-0.19	-0.04
Construction	0.01	-0.01	0.03	-0.08	-0.13	0.05
Wholesale & retail trade	-0.02	0.00	-0.03	0.10	0.19	-0.08
Restaurants & hotels	0.00	-0.00	0.00	-0.09	-0.09	-0.00
Transport & storage	-0.04	0.02	-0.06	0.23	0.21	0.02
Communication	-0.04	0.00	-0.05	0.72	0.75	-0.03
Finance & insurance	-0.00	0.00	-0.00	0.05	0.11	-0.06
Real estate & business services	-0.01	-0.00	-0.00	-0.35	-0.36	0.00
Community, social & personal services	0.05	-0.01	0.06	-0.00	0.01	-0.02
Producers of government services	0	0	0	0.07	0.07	0
Other producers	0	0	0	-1.74	-1.74	0

			France			
Agriculture, forestry & fishing	-0.00	-0.01	0.00	0.70	0.69	0.00
Mining & quarrying	-0.09	-0.04	-0.05	1.49	1.50	-0.01
Food, beverages & tobacco	-0.12	-0.03	-0.09	0.22	0.14	0.08
Textiles, apparel & leather	-0.17	-0.01	-0.16	0.22	0.29	-0.06
Wood products & furniture	-0.11	-0.00	-0.11	0.45	0.39	0.06
Paper, paper products & printing	-0.13	-0.03	-0.09	0.21	0.26	-0.04
Industrial chemicals	-0.06	0.05	-0.11	0.68	0.43	0.25
Non-metallic mineral products	-0.08	-0.04	-0.03	-0.11	-0.17	0.05
Basic metal Industries	0.00	-0.02	0.03	0.99	0.75	0.24
Metal products machinery equipments	-0.22	-0.00	-0.21	0.24	0.32	-0.08
Other manufacturing	-0.21	-0.00	-0.21	0.18	0.20	-0.01
Electricity, gas & water	-0.06	0.06	-0.13	0.69	0.68	0.00
Construction	-0.33	-0.00	-0.33	-0.06	0.16	-0.23
Wholesale & retail trade	-0.15	-0.02	-0.13	0.01	0.18	-0.16
Restaurants & hotels	-0.07	-0.02	-0.04	-0.08	-0.01	-0.06
Transport & storage	-0.12	-0.00	-0.12	0.17	0.26	-0.08
Communication	-0.17	0.03	-0.20	1.22	1.41	-0.18
Finance & insurance	-0.06	-0.05	-0.00	-0.67	-0.68	0.00
Real estate & business services	0	0	0	0	0	0
Community, social & personal services	-0.05	-0.00	-0.05	0.06	0.15	-0.08
Producers of government services	0	0	0	0.14	0.14	0
Other producers	0	0	0	0	0	0

157

within industries. Technological progress seems to be the main source of productivity gains in the vertically integrated product sector.

Structural and productivity components can be further decomposed into an own and imported component (Table 8.5). The own structural component comprises the impact of changes in the employment share of a specific industry, whereas the imported component describes the changes of employment shares of other industries contributing to the final product sector. A similar distinction applies to the productivity component. Own productivity components tend to be larger both than imported productivity components and than structural effects (both own and imported components); on the other hand, imported structural components (although smaller than productivity effects) tend to be larger than own structural components.

The strength of own productivity components is evidence of the importance of the role of technological progress for productivity growth in vertically integrated product sectors.[8]

To summarize, outsourcing – although present – does not appear strong enough to cause the observed change in employment (decline in manufacturing, increase in services industry).[9] In our analysis outsourcing from manufacturing to services would account for a decline in manufacturing employment of –0.22 percentage points per year in France, –0.14 percentage points per year in Germany; –0.02 percentage points per year in the USA and +0.02 percentage points per year in Japan (insourcing). This clearly indicates that other structural economic dynamics must be at work.

5   ANALYSIS

To summarize the results of our analysis so far we concentrate on the aggregate manufacturing and service industry.

From the analysis in section 3 the following trends appear (see Table 8.2):

(i)   final demand shifted from manufacturing to services according to the final product approach, under the drive of private consumption;

(ii)   the employment share of manufacturing declines because of both the shift in final demand and unbalanced productivity growth;

(iii)   the manufacturing share in real output declines much less than in employment;

(iv)   purchased intermediate services are, against expectations, a lower share in manufacturing gross output in the USA than in Germany;

(v)   over almost two decades goods purchased form service industries in manufacturing gross output changed only marginally in the USA and Japan and somewhat more markedly in France and Germany.

Therefore, outsourcing alone cannot explain the structural changes in the industrialized economies.

The analysis of productivity effects showed that:

(vi)   the main source for productivity gains are productivity improvements within industries, that is technological progress is an important source for productivity gains.

A prime explanation for (vi) may be capital–labour substitution. Table 8.6 displays capital–labour ratios and their annual compound growth rates. The data reveals a striking difference between the USA and the other three countries. In general, capital–labour ratios grow much less in the USA. Leaving agriculture and mining aside, manufacturing experienced the highest growth rates. The capital–labour ratio grows especially slowly in the aggregate service industry.

Obviously:

(vii)   in manufacturing, capital has been substituted for labour (but levels are not high) and rationalization may be the main motivation for investments in this industry (see Malinvaud 1991).[10]

From Table 8.2 it is clear that a very likely candidate in driving sectoral employment growth is final demand. To gauge its importance on the employment growth of an industry we have performed a regression analysis using the compound growth rate employment as dependent variable, for each country separately. We have obtained the following results (standard errors in parentheses):

$$E\dot{M}P_i = 0.04\dot{K}P_i + 0.79\dot{F}D_i - 0.89F\dot{D}GO_i \quad R^2 = 0.64 \text{ USA} \qquad (8.9)$$
$$\phantom{E\dot{M}P_i = } (0.19) \quad\ \ (0.25) \quad\ \ (0.20) \qquad F = 10.04$$

$$E\dot{M}P_i = 0.28\dot{K}P_i + 0.58\dot{F}D_i - 0.64F\dot{D}GO_i \quad R^2 = 0.86 \text{ JAPAN} \quad (8.10)$$
$$\phantom{E\dot{M}P_i = } (0.09) \quad\ \ (0.09) \quad\ \ (0.28) \qquad F = 26.16$$

$$E\dot{M}P_i = 0.85\dot{K}P_i + 0.42\dot{F}D_i - 0.39F\dot{D}GO_i \quad R^2 = 0.69 \text{ FRANCE} \quad (8.11)$$
$$\phantom{E\dot{M}P_i = } (0.22) \quad\ \ (0.14) \quad\ \ (0.20) \qquad F = 11.25$$

$$E\dot{M}P_i = 0.50\dot{K}P_i + 0.08\dot{F}D_i - 0.45F\dot{D}GO_i \quad R^2 = 0.68 \text{ GERMANY} \quad (8.12)$$
$$\phantom{E\dot{M}P_i = } (0.18) \quad\ \ (0.24) \quad\ \ (0.26) \qquad F = 11.48$$

Where the '·' indicates annual compound growth rates, EMP = employment share of industry i, KP = capital stock share of industry i,[11] FD is industry

Table 8.6 The capital–labour ratio and its annual compound growth rate per aggregate industry

	USA			Japan			Germany			France		
	1972	1990	1972–90	1970	1990	1970–90	1978	1990	1978–90	1972	1990	1972–90
Agriculture, forestry & fishing	98.01	115.34	0.91	9.33	62.81	10.00	231.82	715.23	5.79	20.87	55.57	5.59
Mining & quarrying	498.77	678.76	1.73	24.79	103.36	7.39	4.10	17.23	7.44	11.13	29.60	5.58
Manufacturing	53.62	92.63	2.91	19.68	73.07	6.77	42.33	112.07	4.98	46.71	94.79	4.01
Electricity, gas & water	831.81	1063.97	1.38	231.82	715.23	5.79	81.24	122.82	3.50	571.96	776.88	1.71
Construction	19.73	14.63	–1.65	4.10	17.23	7.44	85.66	121.61	2.96	20.38	36.71	3.32
Services	162.24	168.27	0.20	42.33	112.07	4.98	47.68	56.66	1.44	143.70	187.67	1.49

Note: Capital stock is evaluated at constant prices in national currencies: USA: billions of 1982 $; Japan: trillions of 1985 Yen; Germany: billions of 1985 DM; France: billions of 1982 FF.

Table 8.7 Purchases of intermediate goods within the same aggregate industry and its annual compound growth rate

	USA			Japan			Germany			France		
	1972	1990	1972–90	1970	1990	1970–90	1978	1990	1978–90	1972	1990	1972–90
In levels												
Services	358313	860361	4.98	26369	80034	5.70	208437	402982	5.64	227118	706536	6.50
Manufacturing	671359	869365	1.44	68460	154046	4.14	596776	781614	2.27	562985	775168	1.79
Agriculture	57713	59342	0.15	2041	2186	0.34	9129	9558	0.38	38198	45707	1.00
Mining	9194	16461	3.28	9	6	2.01	10538	6458	-4.00	15384	27688	3.31
Construction	60455	20665	-5.78	133	403	5.7	10407	10436	0.02	4781	12317	5.39
Energy	112	811	11.62	55	316	9.14	3717	3661	-0.13	244	218	-0.62
% of gross output												
Services	16.98	21.67	1.37	19.31	22.83	0.84	17.53	22.20	1.99	14.73	23.02	2.51
Manufacturing	37.47	34.87	-0.40	43.80	43.54	-0.03	41.36	42.21	0.17	35.98	36.67	0.11
Agriculture	32.52	27.87	-0.85	12.64	12.98	0.13	13.11	11.59	-1.02	17.87	15.75	-0.70
Mining	4.43	7.04	2.61	0.42	0.50	0.87	22.97	19.12	-1.52	37.05	31.53	-0.89
Construction	14.48	3.94	-6.98	0.33	0.50	2.04	5.18	4.65	-0.89	1.27	2.62	4.13
Energy	0.05	0.37	11.76	0.60	1.42	4.43	3.86	3.03	-1.98	0.37	0.16	-4.52
Share of purchases of intermediate goods from services in total purchases of intermediate goods of the manufacturing sector												
Services/total	0.18	0.21	0.92	0.18	0.22	0.98	0.19	0.24	1.86	0.16	0.25	2.36

specific share in total final demand, and *FDGO* is the final demand to gross output ratio in industry *i*.

From the estimation results can be seen that the evolution of final demand appears to have a significant impact on sectoral employment growth. Furthermore, the share of final demand in gross output appears to have a negative impact on sectoral employment growth; this may signal the presence of outsourcing within industries as Table 8.7 makes clear.

6 CONCLUSIONS

Employment growth in the service industries has been caused by the following factors:

1. by a substantial increase in the final demand,
2. by a limited increase in the demand for services from the manufacturing industry,
3. by a limited increase in the demand of intermediate services in the production of services; that is services industries outsourcing activities to other service industries.

To investigate the importance of outsourcing activities out of manufacturing to the services industry as a source of change in the structure of employment, we use the concepts of final product productivity (FPP) and final product employment (FPE); productivity and employment within a vertically integrated product sector.

Our results show that while it is certainly present, the extent of outsourcing taking place does not warrant the shift in employment between manufacturing and the services industry. Moreover, there is little evidence that outsourcing became more important over the last two decades and, most important, the differences in the interindustry division of production do not support the often held view that there is a higher degree of specialization in the USA as compared to Europe. If anything, the reverse seems to be the case.

Furthermore, we find that structural dynamics in final demand do affect structural dynamics in employment. Changes in the structure of final demand and especially in consumption play an important role in determining the relative employment growth of industries.

To conclude, structural economic dynamics are not a myth; their working is the cause of the substantial change in the structure of employment observed in industrialized countries during the last two decades.

NOTES

1. The chapter has benefited from constructive comments by Andrew Glyn, Jan Reijnders, Tullio Gregori and participants at TSER workshops in Paris.
2. For a discussion of the underlying implicit assumption see Appelbaum and Schettkat (1997).
3. Of course, the first (no change in real shares) and the second (changes in shares explained by changes in the inter-industry division of labour) arguments are compatible only if the first argument is based on the final product demand concept.
4. Notice that, for individual firms, outsourcing may also take place within the same industry. Industry level data cannot reveal this phenomenon. However, if this process leads to productivity gains, the effect will be discovered in industry-specific productivity figures.
5. The aggregate service sector includes: wholesale retail and trade, restaurants and hotels, transport and storage, communication, finance and insurance, real estate and business services, community and social and personal services, producers of governmental services, other producers. The aggregate manufacturing sector includes: food, beverages and tobacco, wood products and furniture, paper products and printing, industrial chemical, non-metallic mineral products, basic metal industries, metal product machinery and equipment, other manufacturing.
6. Where ρ: correlation coefficient, *significant at 10 per cent confidence level. Moreover, we use the following abbreviations: Fr for France, Jpn for Japan, Ger for Germany, and USA for the United States.
7. A negative productivity effect may be caused by shorter average working hours.
8. ten Raa and Wolff (1996) investigate outsourcing in US manufacturing. To this end, the authors decompose total factor productivity growth in manufacturing into an industry-specific (manufacturing) component and a drag effect due to productivity stagnation in service industries. They find that outsourcing is present but industry-specific components mainly lead total factor productivity growth in US manufacturing.
9. Siegel and Griliches (1992) in their analysis of the productivity recovery in the US manufacturing sector for the period 1972–87, find that outsourcing (to services and abroad) does not seem to be correlated with productivity growth. Moreover, Morrison and Siegel (1997) find, in an analysis of employment composition in the US manufacturing industry in the period 1959–89, that outsourcing has a negative impact on labour demand across skill levels, but its impact is small when compared to the technological and trade impacts.
10. This may lead to a negative relationship between productivity growth and employment growth in manufacturing. However, capital stock and employment growth rates show a strong positive correlation ($\rho_{Ger} = 0.70^*$, $\rho_{US} = 0.47^*$, $\rho_{Jpn} = 0.54^*$, $\rho_{Fr} = 0.62^*$).
11. In the present analysis we have not distinguished between investment in machinery and investment in buildings.

REFERENCES

Appelbaum E. and R. Schettkat (1990), *Labor Market Adjustments to Structural Change and Technological Progress*, New York: Praeger.

Appelbaum E. and R. Schettkat (1994), 'The end of full employment? Economic developments in industrialized economies', *Intereconomics*, 29, 122–30.

Appelbaum E. and R. Schettkat (1995), 'Employment and productivity in industrialised economies', *International Labour Review*, 134, 605–23.

Appelbaum E. and R. Schettkat (1997), 'Are prices unimportant? The changing structure of the industrialised economies', AWSEB Discussion Paper, 97/10.

Baumol W.J., S.A.B. Blackman and E.N. Wolff (1989), *Productivity and American Leadership: The long view*, Cambridge: MIT Press.

DIW (1996), 'Deutsches Institut für Wirtschaftsforschung', report for Ministry Melkert.

Fuchs V.R. (1968), *The Services Economy*, New York: NBER, Distributed by Columbia University Press.

Leontief W. (1986), *Input–Output Economics*, New York: Oxford University Press.

Malinvaud, E. (1991), *Diagnosing Unemployment*, Cambridge: Cambridge University Press.

Momigliano F. and D. Siniscalco (1982), 'Note in Tema di Terziarizzazione e Deindustrializzazione' (Notes about terziarization and de-industrialisation), *Moneta e Credito*, pp. 143–81.

Morrison C.J. and D. Siegel (1997), 'The impact of technology, trade and outsourcing on employment and labor composition', University of California at Davis, Mimeo.

Pasinetti L. (1983), *Structural change and economic growth: an essay in the dynamics of wealth of nations*, Cambridge: Cambridge University Press.

Petit P., R. Schettkat and B. Verspagen (1997), 'Uneven growth, technology, and employment', Mimeo, CEPREMAP Paris.

Ramaswamy R. and R. Rowthorn (1997), 'Deindustrialization: causes and implications', IMF Working Paper, Washington DC (April).

Salter W.E.G. (1966), *Productivity and Technical Change*, Cambridge: Cambridge University Press.

Siegel D. and Z. Griliches (1992), 'Purchased services, outsourcing, computers, and productivity in manufacturing', in Z. Griliches (ed.), *Output Measurement in the Service Sectors*, Chicago: University of Chicago Press.

ten Raa T. and E.N. Wolff (1996), 'Outsourcing of services and the productivity recovery in US manufacturing in the 1980s', Tilburg University, CENTER Discussion Papers No. 9689.

APPENDIX: DATA DESCRIPTION

Input–output tables summarize the transaction between individual industries within a given economy (Leontief 1986). The input–output framework divides the economy into industries (or sectors) which at the same time buy products (inputs) from and deliver products (output) to the other industries and to final demand (households' consumption, investments, exports, imports, and government consumption). That is, Input–Output tables are double entry tables in which the cells show the transactions between industries. Read along the rows, figures show the output produced in a specific industry shipped to other industries (the output of one industry is thus the input for some other industries) and to final demand. Read along the columns, figures show the inputs received from other industries (input of production) and value-added. The structure of each industry's production process is represented by a vector of structural coefficients, which describe in quantitative terms the relationship between the inputs it absorbs and the output it produces. The interdependence among the sectors of a given economy is described by a set of linear equations expressing the balances between the total input and the aggregate output of each good and service produced and used. The technical structure of the economy is concisely summarized by the matrix of technical input–output coefficients.

The empirical analysis is based on two input–output tables for each country (USA, Germany, France and Japan). The tables refer to 1972 and 1990 for France and the USA, to 1970 and 1990 for Japan, and to 1978 and 1990 for Germany. The figures are given at constant prices (in millions of 1982 US dollars, billions of 1985 Yen for Japan, millions of 1985 DM for Germany, and 1982 FF for France). Each economy is divided into 22 industries (listed below) compatible with industry classification of the OECD's Industrial Structure DataBase (ISDB). Data on employment and gross fixed capital have been matched to the input–output data from the ISDB.

Notice that data on employment in the Financial and Business Service industry for Germany and in the Wholesale and Retail Trade industry for Japan were reported as missing values in the ISDB. Moreover, input–output tables decompose final demand into consumption, exports, investments, and government spending. Final demand plus (total) sales of intermediate goods (to the rest of the economy) minus imports gives industry's gross output. Gross output can also be obtained as value-added produced in a given industry plus the industry's purchases of intermediate goods (from the rest of the economy). The summation of gross output across industries produces national GDP.

Industries in the input–output database are classified as follows:

1. Agriculture forestry and fishing
2. Mining and quarrying
3. Food beverages and tobacco
4. Textile apparel and leather
5. Wood products and furniture
6. Paper paper products and printing
7. Industrial chemical
8. Non-metallic mineral products
9. Basic metal industries
10. Metal product machinery and equipment
11. Other manufacturing
12. Electricity gas and water
13. Construction
14. Wholesale and retail trade
15. Restaurants and hotels
16. Transport and storage
17. Communication
18. Finance and insurance
19. Real estate and business services
20. Community and social and personal services
21. Producers of government services
22. Other producers.

9. Income and price elasticities in different sectors of the economy: an analysis of structural change for Germany, the UK and the USA[1]

Joachim Möller

1 INTRODUCTION

The restructuring process in developing and advanced economies has been a major topic in economics in the last three or four decades. In the centre of the analysis stands the rise and fall of the manufacturing sector with respect to the employment share and the predominance of the service sector in the most advanced economies. The phenomenon of the secular decline in the share of manufacturing employment is also at the heart of the European unemployment debate. For many observers, Europe's persistent labour market problems are closely related to the inability to use the job potential of emerging markets for new services. Inflexibility, over-regulation and reluctance to accept more inequality are seen as major obstacles in this process.

Contrary to popular perceptions, it turns out that many facets of the restructuring process are not well understood. Even 30 years after the famous contributions of Kuznets (1966) and Baumol (1967), which pioneered the theoretical analysis on this topic, some of the basic facts are still open to debate. For example, there is a recent theoretical and empirical dispute whether the share of manufacturing in real value-added is declining, stagnating or rising with per capita income (see Gundlach 1994, 1996; Quibrai and Harrigan 1996). Although the hypothesis of a productivity bias in favour of manufacturing (Baumol's 'cost disease of stagnant services') is widely accepted, it is not evident whether this quasi-law will hold in the future, when new kinds of services being closely related to information technologies enter the scene.[2] It is also controversial whether productivity bias alone can explain the stylized facts or whether is has to be accompanied by an income or demand bias hypothesis (richer people spending more on services). Last but not least, an open question concerns the role of the price sensitivity of demand in the restructuring process (Appelbaum and Schettkat 1997). So it comes as no surprise that several recent papers indicate a renewed interest in the economics of structural change (see, among others, Falvey and Gemmell 1996; Ramaswamy and Rowthorn 1997; Saeger 1997).

. The aim of the present chapter is to contribute to the empirical analysis of price and income elasticities of various branches in the economy. Since a new theoretical approach for investigating the restructuring process centrally rests on the hypothesis of a long-run change in the price elasticity of product demand, special emphasis is laid on the time-varying structure of this important parameter. For this purpose a state-space model with maximum likelihood estimation of the variance components is used. The remainder of this chapter is organized as follows. The next section outlines a theoretical framework. In section 3 various concepts of demand analysis are discussed. Section 4 presents an empirical investigation using long-run industry-specific data for Germany, the UK and the USA. In section 5 these results are used for a deeper analysis of structural change. This analysis has to be confined to a comparison of Germany with the USA because of missing long-run data for the service sector in the UK. The chapter ends with some concluding remarks in section 6.

2   A THEORETICAL FRAMEWORK

In a series of papers Appelbaum and Schettkat[3] argue that, in recent years, productivity gains in the manufacturing sector have led to a reduction in employment while in the fifties or sixties gains in output per worker translated into more employment. According to this approach, the basic reason for this phenomenon stems from changes in product markets' behaviour, caused by a shift in the price elasticity of demand. Assuming that productivity gains exert a dampening effect on prices, a highly price-elastic product demand gives rise to an increase in output strong enough to over-compensate the labour-saving effect of productivity progress. By contrast, in the event of a price-inelastic demand, employment losses dominate.

The basic relationships can be clarified with a simplified version of the Appelbaum and Schettkat (1997) approach. This consists basically of three elements: the definition of labour productivity, a Blanchard–Kiyotaki function of product demand,[4] and a price-setting (mark-up) equation widely used in macroeconomic modelling.[5] Let Q, P, Π, W, L, Y stand for output (demand), prices, productivity, employment, wages and national income. Using small letters for logs, a hat for first differences and denoting the industry by subscript i, one gets the following equations

$$\hat{q}_i = \hat{\ell}_i + \hat{\pi}_i \tag{9.1}$$

$$\hat{q}_i = -\varepsilon_i(\hat{p}_i - \hat{p}) + \eta_i \hat{y} \tag{9.2}$$

$$\hat{p}_i = \hat{w}_i - \hat{\pi}_i \tag{9.3}$$

The parameters of the model are the price elasticity ε_i and the income elasticity η_i. With labour mobility between industries and competitive labour markets, industry-specific and aggregate wages will follow the same growth path as income and output:

$$\hat{w}_i = \hat{w} = \hat{y} = \hat{q} \tag{9.4}$$

Some algebraic manipulation of (9.2) and (9.3) then leads to

$$\hat{q}_i - \hat{q} = \varepsilon_i(\hat{\pi}_i - \hat{\pi}) + (\eta_i - 1)\hat{y} \tag{9.5}$$

and together with (9.1) one obtains

$$\hat{\ell}_i - \hat{\ell} = (\varepsilon_i - 1)(\hat{\pi}_i - \hat{\pi}) + (\eta_i - 1)\hat{y} \tag{9.6}$$

Hence the employment performance of an industry relative to the aggregate is determined by three factors:

- productivity bias: $\hat{\pi}_i \neq \hat{\pi}$,
- income-elasticity-of-demand bias: $\eta_i \neq 1$,
- price-elasticity-of-demand bias: $\varepsilon_i \neq 1$.

As can be verified easily, (9.6) captures the basic argument from above. Other things being equal, the employment share of industry i increases (shrinks) with relative productivity gains if the demand reaction is price-elastic (inelastic). To put it differently: In the event of a positive productivity bias, the employment performance of a given industry increases with the price elasticity of demand and *vice versa*. A price-elasticity of unity implies that productivity bias exerts a proportional effect on relative output growth, but no effect on employment shares. In the absence of productivity bias, changes in the price elasticity have no relevance for relative output and employment growth.

The second term in (9.5) and (9.6) relates to the Engel-curve effect. Other things being equal, the real output and employment share in a given industry increases if the Engel curve is convex ($\eta_i > 1$) and *vice versa*.

The simple framework presented here encompasses the different views of the main determinants underlying the process of structural change. It remains an empirical matter to evaluate the explanatory power of each of these approaches with respect to the secular decline in the employment share of manufacturing industries – the so-called de-industrialization process. In what follows, we concentrate on the estimation of productivity bias, income, and price effects to assess their quantitative importance. Since these calculations require the knowledge of price and income elasticities, concepts of demand analysis are discussed in the next section.

3   CONCEPTS OF DEMAND ANALYSIS

3.1   Marshallian Demand Functions

Standard microeconomics (utility maximization under budget constraint) lead to the Marshallian demand functions, where quantities demanded are functions of (nominal) income X and a vector of *all* prices relevant for a specific household. Let $\mathbf{q}$ and $\mathbf{p}$ be n-dimensional vectors of quantities and prices with typical element Q_i and P_i. The system of Marshallian demand function can be written as

$$Q_i = Q_i(\mathbf{p}, X), \quad i = (1,\ldots,n) \qquad (9.7)$$

with the budget constraint

$$\mathbf{p}'\mathbf{q} = X \qquad (9.8)$$

Equation (9.7) forms a demand system. In empirical demand analysis income and the price vector are taken as exogenous. Econometric techniques are applied to obtain estimates of income as well as own and cross price elasticities. Knowledge of these parameters can be used to characterize the behaviour of consumers and to classify goods.

The approach outlined so far can be criticized for a number of theoretical reasons. The most important aspects are the following:

- dynamic aspects are neglected; no adjustment processes are modelled although it seems plausible that expectation errors and the like can draw individuals away from optimal behaviour;
- income might be endogenous via the labour supply decision;
- prices can be considered endogenous if product markets are not perfectly competitive, because then the behaviour of consumers feeds back to the pricing behaviour of firms;
- applications of the approach neglect the aggregation problem.

Moreover, several complications arise from a more practical point of view. For example, the number of relevant prices, in general, is much too high for all to be included in econometric estimates. Since the movement of prices is highly correlated in many cases, empirical estimates have to deal with multicollinearity. Methodological problems also arise in connection with the restrictions imposed by the theory of demand. These restrictions involve

- homogeneity: since demand functions are homogeneous of order zero in prices and income, the sum of uncompensated price elasticities and the income elasticity should be equal to zero; let ε_{ij} be the elasticity of good i with respect to the price of good j, and ε_i the income elasticity of good j; homogeneity requires $\Sigma_j \varepsilon_{ij} + \eta_i = 0$;
- adding up: $\Sigma_i S_i \eta_i = 1$, where S_i is the expenditure share of good i;
- symmetry: the compensated price effects (as elements of the Slutsky matrix) should be symmetrical;
- negativity: the compensated own-price elasticities should be negative.

Applied demand analysis typically reveals that one or more of these conditions are violated.

3.2   Almost Ideal Demand Systems

An attractive approach for the estimation of demand systems is given by the Almost Ideal Demand System (AIDS) developed by Deaton and Muellbauer (1980).

This approach starts from a logarithmic cost function

$$c(u,\mathbf{p}) = \varphi_1(\mathbf{p}) + \varphi_2(\mathbf{p})u \tag{9.9}$$

where u stands for utility and φ_1 and φ_2 are two functions. The budget share of this good is given by

$$S_i := \frac{Q_i P_i}{X} = \frac{\partial c(u,\mathbf{p})}{\partial p_i} \tag{9.10}$$

This relation is derived by using Shephard's lemma and noting that total costs are equal to nominal income:

$$\frac{\partial C(u,\mathbf{p})}{\partial p_i} = \frac{\partial c(u,\mathbf{p})}{\partial P_i} \frac{P_i}{C(u,\mathbf{p})} = \frac{Q_i P_i}{X}$$

Since total expenditures are equal to total costs it follows from (9.9) that

$$u(x,\mathbf{p}) = \frac{x - \varphi_1(\mathbf{p})}{\varphi_2(\mathbf{p})} \tag{9.11}$$

For a constant price vector one obtains

$$S_i = \alpha + \beta_i x \tag{9.12}$$

which can be interpreted as logarithmic Engel curves. The coefficient β_i can be taken as a characteristic of good i. Luxury goods have $\beta_i > 0$, whereas necessities or inferior goods are characterized by $\beta_i < 0$.

As a special choice for the general functions φ_1 and φ_2, Deaton and Muellbauer suggest a translog formulation:

$$\varphi_1(\mathbf{p}) = \alpha_0 + \sum_k \alpha_k p_k + 0.5 \sum_k \sum_\ell \gamma^*_{k\ell} p_k p_\ell \tag{9.13}$$

and

$$\varphi_2(\mathbf{p}) = \beta_0 \prod_k P_k^{\beta_k} \tag{9.14}$$

Substituting these functions into equation (9.9), taking derivatives with respect to p_i to calculate the budget shares and replacement of u yields

$$S_i = \alpha_i + \sum_j \gamma_{ij} p_j + \beta_i y \tag{9.15}$$

where $y := \ln(X/P)$ stands for the log of real income and $\gamma_{ij} = 0.5(\gamma^*_{ij} + \gamma^*_{ji})$. Note that the general price index is defined here as

$$P = \alpha_0 + \sum_k \alpha_k p_k + 0.5 \sum_k \sum_\ell \gamma^*_{k\ell} p_k p_\ell \tag{9.16}$$

Adding a disturbance term to equation (9.15) leads to an equation suitable for estimation.

3.3 Demand Analysis for Industry Data in an Open Economy

The demand analysis framework aims at analysing private household expenditures. Although this could give some important insights with respect to economic behaviour, the more relevant analysis in our context concerns price and income elasticities at the industry or sector level.

In principle, one can think of a combination of household demand framework with input–output (I–O) analysis to see how demand behaviour spills over to the production sector. Unfortunately, several problems arise with such an approach. The first is that standard I–O analysis neglects substitution processes within the production sector. The effects of changes in relative prices are relevant, however, if the focus is on the structure of production. Moreover, it seems to be a formidable task to carry over the sophisticated analysis of demand systems (think of the cross equation restrictions imposed by theory) to such an extended approach. And finally, problems posed by the openness of the economy come into play. For example, if an industry domestically exhibits a strong decline because of low international competitiveness of this industry, it may well be that this decline is more than compensated by imports. For an open economy, the fact that a class of production is *inferior in production* does not imply that it is *inferior in consumption* as well. It is also the case that imported and exported goods of the same industry typically are not homogenous (for example, with respect to technological standards, quality, capital intensity of production and so on).[6] To put it differently: most industries are producing for a world market and production shares do not necessarily reflect expenditure shares of domestic consumers. In principle, expenditure patterns for consumers all over the world have to be taken into account in an open economy. Therefore, a combination of genuine demand system analysis with an investigation at the industry level appears to be hardly feasible. In my view, an analysis of income and price elasticities at the industry or sector level being rigorously founded in microeconomic analysis of consumer behaviour is not realistic at the present stage, especially if further complications are involved, for example because of a time-varying structure of demand.

One possibility of overcoming the dilemma is to use demand theory as an 'as-if' approach. Assume that a typical firm or industry reacts to changes in behaviour of a representative 'consumer'. The latter must be thought of as composed of foreign or domestic firms demanding intermediate or investment goods, as well as foreign or domestic households demanding final goods. The rationale behind this heuristic approach is simply to have a guideline for the investigation of income and price elasticities. Of course, some of the restrictions stemming from classical utility-based demand analysis are no longer directly applicable in this setting.

As pointed out above, a complete modelling of substitution processes would require to include *n* price variables in each estimation equation, where *n* is the number of industries. With a limited number of observations available, this strategy is not feasible. As has been proposed in the literature, one way to save degrees of freedom would be to constrain the model to substitution possibilities between similar groups of products. Since the focus here is on branches of the economy, however, this seems unreasonable. Assume instead that products of each industry are substituted against a composite good (that is, a product mixture of all other industries).[7] If furthermore a specific industry can be taken as small against the aggregate, then a suitable estimation approach based on a Marshallian type of approach is as follows:[8]

$$y_{it} = \alpha_{0i} + \alpha_{1i}(p_{it} - p_t) + \alpha_{2i}y_t + \varepsilon_{it} \tag{9.17}$$

where y and y_i are aggregate and industry real output, p and p_i the aggregate and industry price level (all variables in logs) and ε_i is a disturbance term with the usual assumptions.[9] Note that equation (9.17) is rather similar to a specification based on the AIDS approach. To see this, take the log of the expenditure share $S_i = P_i Y_i/(PY)$ and subtract $p_i - p - y$ on both sides of equation (9.15). A re-parameterization yields a specification comparable to equation (9.17).

The coefficient α_{1i} gives the price elasticity and α_{2i} the elasticity with respect to aggregate value-added. Neglecting the difference between gross domestic product and national income, the latter can also be taken approximately as an income elasticity. Two caveats are in order here. Firstly, since product demand is partly from abroad, one has also to assume that national and world market consumers are identical. Secondly, industrial output is only partly in the form of final products. Hence the income elasticity concept is applied here also to intermediate goods.

One would expect the price elasticity α_{1i} to be typically negative. The parameter α_{2i} is equal to unity if the output of the respective industry keeps pace with the aggregate, and is smaller (greater) than unity for (relatively) shrinking (expanding) industries.

Although the outlined heuristic approach is not completely satisfactory from a rigorous theoretical standpoint, it has the advantage of leading to a feasible estimation approach, the outcome of which can be interpreted in analogy to demand analysis.

3.4   Estimation of Time-varying Elasticities

As described in the introduction, there is special interest in the question of whether price (and perhaps also income) elasticities change over time. In the literature of applied demand system analysis only few attempts to estimate time-varying elasticities are found. Despite a vast econometric literature in that field and a variety of methods to test for the stability of a regression model over time, most of these estimates use a rather simplistic econometric methodology, for example split-sample or moving-windows estimates.

The most common econometric tests for parameter instability are (i) Chow-F-tests (structural-break test); (ii) analysis of recursively estimated regression coefficients (Recursive Ordinary Least Squares, ROLS) and (iii) analysis of one-step-ahead forecast errors (CUSUM tests and different variants).[10]

The application of stability tests to estimates of special price and income elasticities indicates that these parameters did change over time. For example, Hackl and Westlund (1996) in their study on international telecommunication demand, conclude that '... the assumption of a unique, constant value of the regression coefficient and particularly of the price elasticity is not realistic' (p. 249).

Also in this context, one could suggest that price elasticities for two subsequent sample periods could be estimated, and then these estimates compared with each other. Chow-F-tests (structural-break test) could be performed to calculate whether these changes are significant or not. Such an approach would be easy to implement since standard regression software could be used. But there are severe shortcomings. The problem is not where to split the sample (the most likely breakpoint could be calculated in a slightly extended approach). The more critical problem appears to be the presumption that the change has occurred abruptly instead of gradually (*natura non facit salta*). A severe objection is that more complicated patterns of change (such as U- or hump-shaped developments) cannot be detected. Perhaps the most important argument in this respect is that the split-sample approach does not use the available information efficiently. This is especially critical because consistent time series for the estimation of elasticities are typically short. It seems barely reasonable to compare estimates that are extremely imprecise because of a short sample size. This argument also applies to moving-windows (or local) regression techniques.[11]

In my view, a clearly preferable econometric approach in this respect would be to use a state-space model with the estimation based on the Kalman filter and smoothing algorithm. The state-space model consists of two parts, the *measurement equation* and the *state equation*. The former is similar to a familiar multivariate regression equation in econometrics

$$\mathbf{y}_t = \mathbf{X}_t \boldsymbol{\beta}_t + \boldsymbol{\varepsilon}_t \qquad (9.18)$$

with **y** as a vector of dependent variables, **X** as a corresponding matrix of explanatory variables and ε as a vector of stochastic disturbances. In contrast to the standard approach, however, the coefficient vector $\boldsymbol{\beta}$ is supposed to be time-varying. The state equation specifies the stochastic variation of the coefficient vector. Here it is assumed that the coefficient vector follows a stochastic trend.[12]

$$\boldsymbol{\beta}_t = \boldsymbol{\beta}_{t-1} + \mathbf{v}_t \qquad\qquad (9.19)$$

The disturbances in equation (9.18) and equation (9.19) ε_t and $\mathbf{v}_t$ should be independent identical distributed with covariance matrices $\mathbf{R}$ and $\mathbf{Q}$, respectively. To keep the number of parameters small, a diagonal form for both covariance matrices is assumed. Note that the corresponding parameter β_i is invariant over time if the element Q_{ii} is equal to zero. Once the *hyperparameters*, that is the matrices $\mathbf{R}$ and $\mathbf{Q}$, are specified and the initial values $\boldsymbol{\beta}_0$ as well as the corresponding covariance matrix $\mathbf{P}_0$ are given, the Kalman filter and smoothing algorithm provides consistent and efficient estimates for $\boldsymbol{\beta}_t$ and $\mathbf{P}_t$ ($t = 1,...,T$). As discussed, for example, by Harvey (1989), several methods are available to estimate the hyperparameters of the model. In what follows, a maximum likelihood approach based on the scoring method is used.[13]

Note that the measurement equation of the model (9.18) is also suitable for a panel data structure. By allowing the diagonal elements of $\mathbf{R}$ to differ, heteroscedasticity between industries can explicitly be taken into account.

4   ESTIMATION OF PRICE AND INCOME ELASTICITIES

4.1   Data and Methodology

The following investigation uses long-run data from the OECD industrial structural database for employment, real and nominal value-added on two-digit industry level for three countries (Germany, United Kingdom (UK) and the United States (USA)). From the real and nominal value-added, the implicit value-added deflator was calculated. The data set comprises 23 industries from the primary and secondary sector as well as from services. The time period is from 1960 to the early 1990s, except for data on UK service industries that only start in 1973. Estimates of the Marshallian type approach outlined above suffer from an endogeneity problem. If the industry is small compared to the aggregate this does not apply to the aggregate price and output variable in the estimated equation but to the sector price variable p_{it}. Therefore, the estimates were based on 2SLS with one-period lagged output, aggregate and industry prices, a linear and a quadratic time trend as instruments. The approach was applied to each industry separately before the panel structure of the data was explicitly taken into account.

4.2   Results of Industry-specific Estimates

For the industry-specific approach, we estimated the state-space model with the measurement equation

$$y_{it} = \alpha_{0i} + \alpha_{1i,t}(p_{it} - p_t) + \alpha_{2i}y_t + \varepsilon_{it} \qquad (9.20)$$

where sector-specific prices were instrumented as described above. Note that the price elasticity parameter is allowed to vary over time while the income elasticity parameter is restricted to be constant.[14] Conventional 2SLS estimates were calculated as a reference.

Table 9.1 shows the log likelihood for the state-space model λ and a Likelihood Ratio (LR) test statistic

$$LR = -2(\lambda - \lambda_c) \qquad (9.21)$$

where λ_c denotes the log likelihood of the constant coefficient 2SLS model. The test statistic follows a χ^2 distribution with one degree of freedom. According to this test statistic, a constant price elasticity can be rejected at a high level of significance in most of the estimates. Only for one industry (Agriculture, Forestry & Fishing) does the evidence support the hypothesis of constant parameters in all three countries. For not more than three industries (Metal Products, Other Manufacturing and Construction) the state-space model with time-varying parameters gives no significant improvement in two of the three countries. A closer analysis for the manufacturing sector reveals that for Germany and the UK the hypothesis of a constant price elasticity is rejected at least at the 10 per cent level in ten out of 13 industries, while for the USA this is the case in six out of 13.

The results for the income elasticity for the two variants of the estimated model are presented in Table 9.2. In what follows, we refer to the constant-coefficient estimates only if the state-space model gives no superior results according to the LR test. The estimated income elasticity is typically positive, but there are some exceptions. To obtain an overview, all estimates together with a 95 per cent confidence interval are plotted in Figure 9.1. It turns out that only in the case of Mining & Quarrying in Germany, Basic Metal Industries in the USA and Metal Products in the UK, is the elasticity significantly negative. These industries are known for their marked decline during the last two or three decades.

On the other side of the spectrum, the estimated income elasticity significantly exceeds unity in only a few industries of the Primary and Secondary Sector. According to Figure 9.1 this is the case for Mining & Quarrying, Industrial Chemical and Data Processing/Precision & Optical Instruments in the UK, for Electrical Goods in Germany and the USA as well as for Transport Equipment in Germany. Typically the estimates for the income elasticity in the primary and secondary sector are found in the range between zero and one in all three countries, indicating that these industries are growing less than proportionally with national income.

Table 9.1 Log likelihood and Likelihood-Ratio statistic by industry (state-space model vs. 2SLS)

Industry	Germany		UK		USA	
	ln Lik.	LR-test	ln Lik.	LR-test	ln Lik.	LR-test
Primary Sector						
Agricult., Forestry, Fishing	50.630	–[a]	49.559	–[a]	41.760	–[a]
Mining, Quarrying	41.246	–[a]	30.393	7.179**	57.734	26.338**
Manufacturing						
Food, Beverages, Tobacco	62.876	6.606**	82.453	13.741**	75.026	–[a]
Textile, Apparel, Leather	65.053	48.026**	40.079	22.780**	62.032	10.360**
Wood Products, Furniture	39.306	2.847(*)	24.458	3.122(*)	38.783	6.766**
Paper, Printing	59.012	18.228**	53.594	20.780**	73.786	–[a]
Industrial Chemical	56.498	10.766**	63.461	21.467**	58.172	–[a]
Non-Metallic Mineral Prod.	47.744	21.366**	43.528	9.459**	34.865	1.607
Basic Metal Industries	54.584	7.677**	31.172	14.044**	11.460	–[a]
Metal Products	41.870	–[a]	25.296	2.176	52.618	4.147*
Machinery	48.952	12.199**	26.487	–[a]	36.351	4.567*
Data Proc., Prec. & Opt. Instr.	46.891	20.968**	38.828	23.875**	48.610	1.171
Electrical Goods	56.794	–[a]	58.091	16.852**	52.421	7.906**
Transport Equipment	50.811	20.264**	36.261	–[a]	31.574	3.094(*)
Other Manufacturing	40.168	–[a]	38.296	23.999**	45.610	–[a]

Energy and Construction

Electricity, Gas, Water	52.249	14.608**	40.159	7.273**	73.883	28.628**
Construction	43.365	1.732	45.722	12.220**	48.308	2.106
Services						
Wholesale and Retail Trade	75.189	5.292*	$-^b$		77.394	$-^a$
Restaurant and Hotels	66.027	18.033**	$-^b$		63.501	$-^a$
Transp., Storage, Communic.	81.431	15.040**	$-^b$		86.454	$-^a$
Financial Inst., Insurance	67.306	10.425**	$-^b$		70.792	14.683**
Real Estate, Business Serv.	51.716	$-^a$	$-^b$		74.723	21.460**
Community, Social & Pers. Serv.	57.216	34.473**	$-^b$		84.459	16.178**

Notes:
Sample period: 1961–1991 (Germany), 1961–1992 (UK, Manufacturing), 1973–1992 (UK, Services), 1961–1993 (USA);
ln Lik.: log Likelihood of the state space model;
LR-test: Likelihood Ratio test of state space model versus constant coefficient model; estimation method: Two Stage Least Squares; instruments used: lagged aggregate and sector prices and output, linear and quadratic trend;
a: State space model yields no improvement in likelihood;
b: State space model not calculated because of shorter sample size; **, *, (*) significant at 1%, 5% and 10% level.

Table 9.2   Estimated price elasticities by industry

Industry	Germany		UK		USA	
	2SLS	Kalman	2SLS	Kalman	2SLS	Kalman
Primary Sector						
Agricult., Forestry, Fishing	0.384*	–[a]	0.389**	–[a]	0.432**	–[a]
Mining, Quarrying	–0.909**	–[a]	1.647**	1.633**	0.292**	0.381**
Manufacturing						
Food, Beverages, Tobacco	0.279**	0.256**	0.516**	0.404**	0.472**	–[a]
Textile, Apparel, Leather	0.210	–0.057	–0.036	–0.146	1.029***	0.833**
Wood Products, Furniture	0.594***	0.508***	–0.222	–0.278	0.927**	0.843**
Paper, Printing	0.680***	0.502***	0.647***	0.908***	0.837***	–[a]
Industrial Chemical	0.719***	0.700***	1.118***	1.177***	1.158***	–[a]
Non-Metallic Mineral Prod.	0.504***	0.247*	0.268***	0.265***	0.378***	0.246*
Basic Metal Industries	0.883***	0.836***	–0.120	0.681***	–0.516***	–[a]
Metal Products	0.480**	–[a]	–0.493**	–0.557***	1.066**	0.964**
Machinery	0.928**	0.597**	0.021	–[a]	0.941**	0.536**
Data Proc., Prec. & Opt. Instr.	1.559***	1.354***	1.068***	2.186***	1.162**	1.138***
Electrical Goods	1.767**	–[a]	0.930***	0.884***	1.788**	1.627**
Transport Equipment	1.715***	1.779***	–0.159*	–[a]	0.884**	0.910**
Other Manufacturing	0.438**	–[a]	0.174(*)	0.494**	0.635**	–[a]

Energy and Construction

Electricity, Gas, Water	1.505**	1.749**	0.877**	0.929**	1.202**	1.132**
Construction	0.264**	0.272**	1.000**	1.163**	0.458**	0.380**
Services						
Wholesale and Retail Trade	0.958**	1.022**	1.204**	$-^b$	1.124**	$-^a$
Restaurant and Hotels	0.393**	0.629**	0.983**	$-^b$	1.202**	1.205**
Transp., Storage, Communic.	0.988**	1.139**	1.293**	$-^b$	1.133**	$-^a$
Financial Inst., Insurance	1.846**	1.465**	2.451**	$-^b$	1.360**	1.313**
Real Estate, Business Serv.	1.535**	$-^a$	1.884**	$-^b$	1.467**	1.600**
Community, Social & Pers. Serv.	2.554**	1.841**	2.584**	$-^b$	1.243**	1.064**

Notes:
2SLS: Two Stage Least Squares estimates;
Kalman: State space model estimates assuming time-varying price elasticities;
a: State space model yields no improvement in likelihood;
b: State space model not calculated because of shorter sample size; **, *, (*) significant at 1%, 5% and 10% level.; for further notes see Table 9.1.

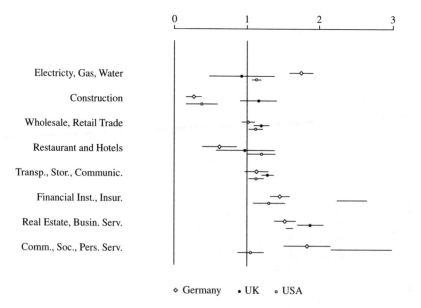

*Figure 9.1   Income elasticities by industry and 95 per cent confidence
              bounds*

Comparing the results for Germany, the UK and the USA, one finds strong similarities between the estimated income elasticities only for Agriculture/Forestry & Fishing, Food/Beverages & Tobacco, Non-Metallic Mineral Products and Other Manufacturing. Striking differences in the results can be detected for Mining & Quarrying (sharp decline of this industry in Germany, strong increase in the UK) and for Transport Equipment (just the reverse pattern). For Textile/Apparel & Leather the income elasticities for Germany and the UK are rather similar (both seem to be stagnating or decreasing with aggregate output), whereas the coefficient is not significantly different from unity in the USA. Output for the Electricity/Gas & Water industry is income-elastic in Germany and the USA, while for Construction it is inelastic. For the UK both estimates are not significantly different from unity. In general, the results indicate that country-specific influences are important, for example the exploitation of North-Sea oil in the UK or the high competitiveness of German car industries (in contrast to the long-run decline of this industry in the UK).

For the service industries the estimates typically exceed unity. If changes in relative prices are controlled for, the only service industry that definitely grows less than proportionally with respect to aggregate output is the Restaurant & Hotels sector in Germany. In three cases (Wholesale & Retail Trade and Transport/Storage & Communication in Germany, Restaurant & Hotels in the UK and Community/Social & Personal Services in the USA) the estimates are not significantly different from unity. For the majority of service industries, however, the estimates clearly indicate that output is income-elastic.

Table 9.3 shows the estimates for the price-elasticity coefficient. While for Germany and the UK the evidence mostly favours the hypothesis of a time-varying price elasticity (16 out of 23 cases and 13 out of 17 cases, respectively), the state-space model yields superior results in only 11 out of 23 cases for the USA. We first concentrate on the industries with a constant price elasticity. As mentioned above, Agriculture/Forestry & Fishing is the only industry where the time-varying-elasticity hypothesis is rejected in all three countries. The estimates corroborate the view that demand in this industry is price-inelastic (with the lowest value found for Germany).

For manufacturing industries with constant price elasticities, the estimates are typically between zero and minus unity. The price elasticity coefficient for Metal Products is negative, but not significantly different from zero in Germany and the UK. The same is true for Electrical Goods in Germany and for Basic Metal Industries and Non-Metallic Mineral Products in the USA. The price elasticity of Other Manufacturing in Germany and the USA, as well as Machinery and Transport Equipment in the UK is relatively high and not significantly different from unity. In the USA we find a significant con-

Table 9.3   Estimated income elasticity coefficients by industry (2SLS)

Industry	Germany		UK		USA	
	coeff.	t-stat.	coeff.	t-stat.	coeff.	t-stat.
Primary Sector						
Agricult., Forestry, Fishing	-0.231	1.689	-0.534	4.917	-0.514	6.874
Mining, Quarrying	-0.383	3.994	0.555^{vv}	8.576	-0.094^{vv}	2.646
Manufacturing						
Food, Beverages, Tobacco	-0.516^{vv}	2.996	-0.199^{vv}	2.462	-0.486	8.604
Textile, Apparel, Leather	1.143^{vv}	2.913	0.138^{vv}	0.623	0.175^{vv}	1.378
Wood Products, Furniture	-1.996^{v}	7.006	-0.553^{v}	1.525	-0.135^{vv}	0.354
Paper, Printing	-0.253^{vv}	0.844	-0.635^{vv}	2.626	-0.392	4.841
Industrial Chemical	-1.602^{vv}	11.835	-0.573^{vv}	4.136	-0.402	2.350
Non-Metallic Mineral Prod.	-0.244^{vv}	0.783	-0.739^{vv}	6.281	0.156	0.423
Basic Metal Industries	0.887^{vv}	2.180	0.282^{vv}	1.548	-0.400	1.063
Metal Products	-0.081	0.199	-0.393	1.109	1.113^{v}	4.503
Machinery	-0.921^{vv}	3.140	-1.090	3.092	-0.212^{v}	1.353
Data Proc., Prec. & Opt. Instr.	-0.105^{vv}	0.933	-0.969^{vv}	6.058	-0.699	3.642
Electrical Goods	0.036	0.180	-0.324^{vv}	2.144	-0.152^{vv}	0.688
Transport Equipment	-0.894^{vv}	2.375	-0.836	2.555	0.212^{v}	0.793
Other Manufacturing	-0.858	4.470	-0.322^{vv}	3.031	-0.946	3.722

Energy and Construction

Electricity, Gas, Water	-0.573^{vv}	2.845	-0.842^{vv}	11.034	-0.537^{vv}	9.747
Construction	0.126	0.377	-1.151^{vv}	5.582	-0.566	4.789

Services

Wholesale and Retail Trade	0.018^{v}	0.137	$-0.044^{\#}$	0.226	-0.628	5.501
Restaurant and Hotels	-0.211^{vv}	0.823	$-0.060^{\#}$	0.557	-0.238	2.250
Transp., Storage, Communic.	-0.845^{vv}	9.786	$-0.303^{\#}$	2.770	-0.568	5.869
Financial Inst., Insurance	0.156^{vv}	1.370	$0.223^{\#}$	1.135	-0.300^{vv}	3.623
Real Estate, Business Serv.	-0.586	4.011	$-0.661^{\#}$	6.707	-0.258^{vv}	2.388
Community, Social & Pers. Serv.	-1.548^{vv}	3.662	$-0.214^{\#}$	1.771	-0.306^{vv}	3.702

Notes:

coeff.: Two-Stage-Least-Squares estimates of price elasticity (constant parameter case);

t-stat.: t-statistic in absolute value;

vv, v, (v): corresponding coefficient is time-varying according to a Likelihood Ratio test at least at the 1%, 5 % and 10% level;

#: state space model not calculated because of shorter sample size; for further notes see Tables 9.1 and 9.2.

stant price elasticity also for Food/Beverages & Tobacco (estimated coefficient about –0.5), Paper & Printing and Industrial Chemical (estimated
coefficient in both cases about –0.4) and Data Processing/Precision & Optical
Instruments (estimated coefficient about –0.7) .

A price sensitivity of output in the Construction sector cannot be detected
in Germany. By contrast, the estimated effect for the USA is –0.57 and highly
significant. For service industries we find constant and highly significant
price elasticities which are comparable to this value for Real Estate & Business Services in Germany, and for Wholesale & Retail Trade as well as for
Transportation, Storage & Communication in the USA. A lower, but also
significant elasticity is estimated for Restaurant & Hotels in the USA (–0.24).
Hence the results are roughly similar to what is found for Manufacturing. The
estimates typically indicate an inelastic reaction of output to price changes.

4.3   Changes in Price Elasticities over Time

In this subsection, we include the results for the time-varying price elasticities
as estimated from the state-space model. Since this model was not calculated for service industries in the UK, a total of 63 industries can be
considered.

To give an overview, the estimates were classified into five categories:

i.   the coefficient is significantly negative throughout the observation
       period;
ii.   the coefficient is negative when significantly different from zero;
iii.   the evidence is inconclusive, either because the estimated coefficient is
       not significantly different from zero throughout the observation period,
       or it is partly negative, partly positive when significantly different from
       zero;
iv.   the coefficient is positive when significantly different from zero;
v.   the coefficient is significantly positive throughout the observation
       period.

Table 9.4 indicates that in none of the estimates is an atypical positive sign
found throughout the observation period. Episodes of a positive relationship
between output and relative prices occur in some of the industries. These
deviations from the typical results are concentrated in the following three
industries:

1.   Textile/ Apparel & Leather,
2.   Basic Metal Industries,
3.   Metal Products.

In all three countries the estimates in these cases are either positive when significant or not significantly different from zero throughout the observation period. For Textile/Apparel & Leather in Germany and the UK, Basic Metal Industries in the USA and Metal Products in the UK, this is accompanied by a negative income elasticity. Such a result indicates that these industries are shrinking over time. In the terminology of demand analysis these industries produce inferior, or Veblen goods, respectively.

Table 9.4 shows that in 39 out of 63 cases the results fall into categories (i) or (ii) which are in line with the theoretical requirement of a negative own price elasticity. Typically the estimated coefficients are between zero and minus unity. But there are also several industries with at least some episodes of a price-elastic output. These include Wood Products & Furniture in Germany, Paper & Printing in Germany and the UK, Industrial Chemical in Germany, Machinery in all three countries, Non-Metallic Mineral Products in the UK and Transport Equipment in Germany, Construction in the UK and Real Estate & Business Services in the USA.

From a theoretical point of view there is special interest in the question of whether a trend in the estimated price elasticities can be detected or not. To assess the empirical evidence, we consider only estimates where the state-space model gives superior results. We also exclude categories (iv) and (v) and those of the estimates in category (iii) that are not significantly different from zero throughout the sample. Confining the analysis to the 19 remaining industries in the manufacturing sector, one finds the highest price elasticities in the early or mid-sixties in 14 cases. Hence the empirical evidence supports the view that output (demand) has become less price elastic in several industries of the manufacturing sector since the beginning of our sample period.

A more or less monotonous trend is apparent in the following industries in Germany

- Wood Products & Furniture,
- Paper & Printing,
- Industrial Chemical,
- Non-Metallic Mineral Products.

For the UK, a similar trend pattern is visible in

- Food, Beverages, Tobacco,
- Wood Products & Furniture,
- Paper & Printing,
- Non-Metallic Mineral Products,
- Electrical Goods.

Table 9.4 *Classification of estimated price elasticities by industry*

Industry	Estimated price elasticity				
	signif. neg. throughout	negative if signif.	inconclusive	positive if signif.	signif. pos. throughout
Primary sector					
Agricult., Forestry, Fishing	UKᶜ, USAᶜ		Gᶜ		
Mining, Quarrying	Gᶜ	USA		UK	
Manufacturing					
Food, Beverages, Tobacco	USAᶜ	G, UK		G, UK, USA	
Textile, Apparel, Leather			USA		
Wood Products, Furniture	G	UK	$G^{+/-}$		
Paper, Printing	USAᶜ	UK	$UK^{+/-}$		
Industrial Chemical	G, USAᶜ	G, UK, USA			
Non-Metallic Mineral Prod.		G, UK, USA			
Basic Metal Industries			USAᶜ	G, UK	
Metal Products			Gᶜ, UKᶜ	USA	
Machinery	UKᶜ	G, USA		G	
Data Proc., Prec. & Opt. Instr.	UK, USAᶜ		Gᶜ		
Electrical Goods		UK, USA			
Transport Equipment	UKᶜ		USA, $G^{+/-}$		
Other Manufacturing	Gᶜ, USAᶜ	UK			

Energy and construction					
Electricity, Gas, Water	USA^c	UK, USA	$G^{+/-}$		
Construction		UK	G^c		
Services					
Wholesale and Retail Trade	USA^c			G	
Restaurant and Hotels	USA^c	G			
Transp., Storage, Communic.	USA^c	G			
Financial Inst., Insurance		USA	$G^{+/-}$ $USA^{+/-}$		
Real Estate, Business Serv.	G^c		$G^{+/-}$		
Community, Social & Pers. Serv.		USA			
Total	19	20	15	9	0

Notes:
+/-: Estimates partly significantly positive, partly negative;
G: Germany; UK: United Kingdom; USA: United States;
c: constant coefficient estimates;
sample period: 1961–91 (Germany); 1961–92 (UK, Manufacturing);
UK: Services excluded because of the shorter time period.

and for the USA in

- Non-Metallic Mineral Products,
- Machinery,
- Data Processing/Precision & Optical Instruments.

Although the manufacturing sector as a whole seems to be characterized by declining price elasticities, there are some exceptions to the rule. For example, the important machinery industry in Germany was price-elastic during most of the 1970s, but not at the beginning and the end of the observation period. Such a U-shaped development is also found for Electrical Goods in the USA and – less pronounced – for Data Processing/ Precision and Optical Instruments in the UK. Although there are further cases where the price elasticity follows no simple trend (for example Industrial Chemical in Britain shows a hump-shaped pattern), the only industry where output changes clearly turn from price-inelastic to price-elastic is Transport Equipment in Germany.

For the service industries the evidence is not clear-cut. For Germany we find a positive trend for Restaurants & Hotels and Community/Social & Private Services, a negative one for Financial Institutions & Insurance and a U-shaped development for Transport/Storage & Communication. For US data a clear trend towards price-elastic output is apparent in Real Estate & Business Services, while the estimates for Community/Social & Private Services and Financial Institutions & Insurance are not significantly different from zero for most of the observation period. In these cases the highest elasticities are found for the early 1980s.

4.4   A Panel Data Approach with Time-varying Coefficients

It can be argued that estimating the price elasticity of industrial output is difficult because of the small variance in the time series prices and the corresponding problem of identification. An alternative to industry-specific estimates is to use a panel data approach with the price elasticity coefficient restricted to be equal across industries. This should yield a reliable average estimate of this important structural coefficient for the industries contained in the sample. On the other hand, it would be less reasonable to restrict the income elasticities to be equal across industries (because this parameter is well identified and varies widely). Again the possibility for the income elasticity to vary over time is excluded. Hence the a priori restrictions of the empirical model are as shown in Table 9.5.

As a compromise to preserve the information content of the cross sectional dimension on the one hand and the need to constrain the estimated coeffi-

Table 9.5   Assumptions for the estimated model

	Variation across industries	Time-varying estimates
Income elasticities	yes	no
Price elasticities	no	yes

cients to a reasonable number on the other hand, we disregard information for the Food/Beverages & Tobacco industry as well as for the three industries that tended to give atypical results in all countries (Textile/Apparel & Leather, Basic Metal Industries and Metal Products). Moreover, Data Processing/ Precision & Optical Instruments was merged in Electrical Goods. We also neglect Transport Equipment, since this industry showed a reverse trend in the estimates at least for Germany. Hence the estimates with pooled data in a multivariate approach rest on the following industries in the manufacturing sector:

- Wood Products & Furniture,
- Paper & Printing,
- Industrial Chemical,
- Non-Metallic Mineral Products,
- Machinery,
- Data Processing /Precision & Optical Instruments and Electrical Goods,
- Other Manufacturing.

Basic results of the estimates are presented in Table 9.6. According to the ML estimation of the hyperparameters of the model, the variance of the price-elasticity coefficient in the state equation is positive in all three countries. Hence the findings, in general, give rise to the assumption that the price elasticities are changing over time. According to the LR test, however, the hypothesis of constant coefficients can only be rejected for Germany and the UK, while the superiority of the time-varying model is not evident for the USA. Furthermore, the variances in the measurement equation are quite different between industries. This is especially true for the USA where variances differ by a factor of about 15, and in Germany they differ by a factor of about 6.

The results for the GDP-elasticities are plausible. For Germany and the USA, we find positive values that are significantly different from zero (the only exception being Non-Metallic Mineral Products in Germany). For the UK, the income elasticity is negative for Wood Products & Furniture and Machinery, but not significantly different from zero in both cases. The in-

Table 9.6 Value-added of industries included in the estimates and results of the state-space model for pooled data

Industry	Value-added in 1991		Variance meas. eq. ×100	Constant term		Income elasticity	
	nominal[a]	real[b]		coef.	t-stat.	coef.	t-stat.
			Germany				
Wood Products/Furniture	25.990	180.4	0.860	0.172	3.095	0.515	5.609
Paper/Printing	37.110	223.4	0.209	0.180	6.084	0.546	11.570
Industrial Chemical	138.100	376.9	0.147	0.661	13.749	0.808	11.704
Non-Metallic Mineral Products	30.100	194.7	0.369	0.581	9.925	0.031	0.374
Machinery	89.772	180.2	0.728	-0.219	3.689	1.045	11.188
Data Proc. & Electr. Goods	125.384	502.8	0.216	0.440	8.431	1.204	17.144
Other Manufacturing	5.220	141.5	0.465	-0.245	4.122	0.609	7.248

variance price elasticity coefficient (state equation, × 100): 0.863
Log Likelih.: var. coeff.: 296.96, const. coeff.: 283.56
Likelihood Ratio-test [$\chi^2(1)$]: 26.80**

Industry	Value-added in 1992		Variance meas. eq. ×100	Constant term		Income elasticity	
	nominal	real		coef.	t-stat.	coef.	t-stat.
			UK				
Wood Products/Furniture	3.16	117.3	1.276	0.372	5.642	-0.222	-1.540
Paper/Printing	13.12	154.2	0.350	-0.111	-3.043	0.663	8.694
Industrial Chemical	20.49	314.2	0.148	0.304	7.862	1.134	14.977
Non-Metallic Mineral Products	4.26	131.3	0.586	0.203	4.765	0.275	2.909

		Variance	Constant term		Income elasticity	
Machinery	12.52	109.9	1.230	0.236	3.840	-0.006	-0.043
Data Proc. & Electr. Goods	14.07	318.8	0.193	0.383	6.689	0.983	8.975
Other Manufacturing	1.41	118.9	0.928	0.016	0.265	0.279	2.271

variance price elasticity coefficient (state equation, × 100): 0.106
Log Likelih.: var. coeff.: 268.67, const. coeff.: 265.06
Likelihood Ratio-test [$\chi^2(1)$]: 7.22**

USA

Industry	Value-added in 1993		Variance meas. eq. × 100	Constant term		Income elasticitiy	
	nominal	real		coef.	t-stat.	coef.	t-stat.
Wood Products/Furniture	53.00	236.8	0.679	0.266	5.090	0.796	9.811
Paper/Printing	128.20	225.8	0.056	0.101	6.844	0.825	34.563
Industrial Chemical	207.80	367.8	0.153	0.273	6.451	1.121	19.866
Non-Metallic Mineral Products	26.10	151.8	0.813	0.209	4.205	0.216	2.573
Machinery	108.40	346.9	0.750	0.245	4.704	0.822	9.345
Data Proc. & Electr. Goods	154.40	563.4	0.201	0.341	5.503	1.389	15.777
Other Manufacturing	22.40	262.3	0.338	0.116	3.135	0.799	13.595

variance price elasticity coefficient (state equation, × 100): 0.035
Log Likelih.: var. coeff.: 341.28, const. coeff.: 340.62
Likelihood Ratio-test [$\chi^2(1)$]: 1.32

Notes:
a: Nominal value added in billions of home countries currency;
b: index of real value added (1960 = 100); meas. eq.: measurement equation.
For further notes see Tables 9.1 and 9.2.

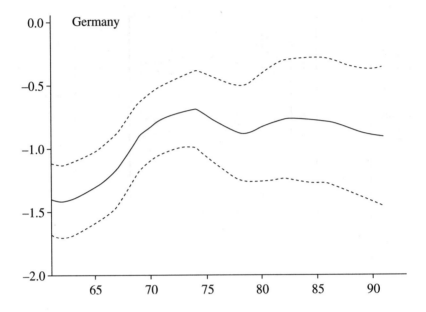

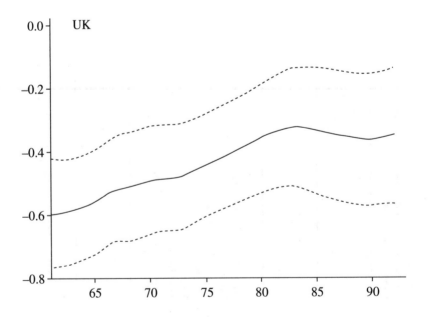

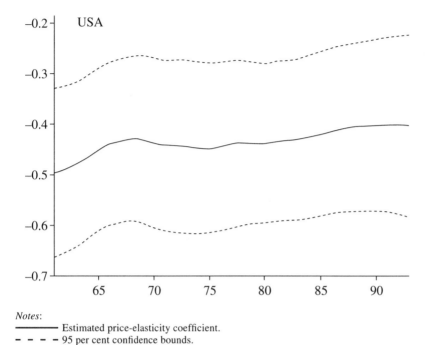

Notes:
——————— Estimated price-elasticity coefficient.
− − − − − 95 per cent confidence bounds.

Figure 9.2   Time-path of estimated price-elasticity coefficient and 95 per cent confidence bounds for Germany, UK and USA

come elasticity is very close to and not significantly different from unity for Machinery in Germany, as well as for Data Processing & Electric Goods and Industrial Chemical in the UK. In three cases (Data Processing & Electric Goods in Germany and the USA, and Industrial Chemical in the USA) output appears to be income-elastic.

Of special interest are the results for the time-varying coefficients related to the price elasticities. The time path of these coefficients is shown in Figure 9.2 together with a 95 per cent confidence interval. According to the Kalman-smoother estimates, the coefficients are significantly negative throughout the sample and exhibit a trend pattern in all countries. At the beginning of the sample, the elasticity is highest in all cases (0.5 in the USA, 0.6 in the UK and 1.4 in Germany). By the early 1990s the price elasticity of manufacturing output has only slightly fallen to 0.4 in the USA, but markedly in the UK (to about 0.3) and even more sharply in Germany (to 0.8).

While in the UK and the USA the erosion of the price elasticity was a rather smooth process, this is not the case for Germany, where a profound change took place from the mid-1960s to the mid-1970s. Since the mid-1970s the development appears to be rather flat in this country.

5   AN ANALYSIS OF STRUCTURAL CHANGE FOR GERMANY AND THE USA

Given the knowledge of price and income elasticities of the various branches of the economy, it is possible to decompose the change in the structure of employment. Since data on the service sector for the 1960s are not available for the UK, the following analysis has to be confined to Germany and the USA. An investigation of aggregate sector data reveals some striking similarities and differences between these two countries. The upper part of Figure 9.3 shows the development of employment in total manufacturing and in those manufacturing industries that were selected in the previous section. Note that these indices are calculated *relative to the development of employment in the aggregate economy*. Until the early 1980s, the time-path of the indicators for Germany and the USA is roughly comparable. Employment in German manufacturing has kept pace with the aggregate until the mid-1970s and then declined in relative terms. In the USA the falling trend in the employment share of manufacturing set in about five years earlier. As the decline for Germany was somewhat steeper, the deterioration in the relative employment position of manufacturing was more or less the same in both economies by the early or mid-1980s. Compared to the beginning of the sample period, this decline amounts to about 15 percentage points in 1985 for total manufacturing and was even more pronounced in the selected manufacturing industries.

Since the mid-1980s, however, the development in Germany and the USA diverges. While the erosion of the relative employment position of the manufacturing sector in the USA continued at almost the same rate, the structural change evidently decelerated in Germany.

In the lower part of Figure 9.3 the development of relative productivity growth in total manufacturing and selected manufacturing industries is depicted. Although the productivity bias phenomenon is clearly apparent in both countries, the phenomenon is more significant in the USA. While there are only minor differences in the 1960s and 1970s, the discrepancy is quite substantial in the last decade. Since the beginning of the 1980s the productivity bias for German manufacturing industries was small or even slightly negative. By contrast, the productivity advantage of manufacturing kept on rising in the USA during the 1980s and early 1990s.

Figure 9.4 shows a productivity index for manufacturing and non-manufacturing industries in both countries and the manufacturing/non-manufacturing productivity ratio. It turns out that productivity in manufacturing grew faster in Germany than in the USA, with the gap between the two series widening in the 1970s and somewhat closing again in the 1980s and early 1990s. Figure 9.4 also reveals, however, that the main difference between Germany and the USA is not in the productivity development in manufacturing but in non-manufacturing industries. While productivity in German non-manufacturing industries almost doubled from the early 1960s to the early 1990s, the corresponding index for the USA shows an only modest increase (less than 20 per cent). As a consequence, the manufacturing/non-manufacturing productivity ratio grew steadily in the USA throughout the sample period. Although the development of this ratio for Germany was very similar until the late 1970s, it then ceased to rise and even fell back. Average manufacturing productivity in Germany reached 90 per cent of the non-manufacturing sector in the mid-1980s but never exceeded this benchmark. By contrast, this indicator exceeds unity since the mid-1980s in the USA.

It seems worthwhile to analyse the process of structural change by means of a decomposition. As outlined in section 2, an important determinant of changes in relative employment growth is the productivity bias which is closely related to the price-elasticity-of-demand effect. Figure 9.5 shows the smoothed productivity growth relative to the aggregate economy, the estimated price elasticity and the combined effect for the selection of manufacturing industries described above. As measured by the corresponding index, the productivity bias in Germany was nearly constant at a high level during the 1960s and then strongly declined. In combination with price-elastic demand, the result was a positive effect on the employment share of manufacturing industries.

As a mirror of this, the fall-back of relative productivity growth in manufacturing in the second half of the 1980s in combination with a price elasticity below unity, also led to a (slightly) positive effect on the relative employment performance of manufacturing industries. From the late 1960s to the early 1980s, however, the combination of productivity bias and price-inelastic demand typically resulted in a negative effect on the employment share of manufacturing industries.

The situation for the USA appears to be quite different. Price-inelastic demand and significant productivity bias led to a negative effect on relative employment growth of manufacturing industries throughout the sample period. The only exception to this can be found around the year 1980, where relative productivity growth of manufacturing industries temporarily declined markedly. It should be stressed that the depressing effects on the employment share of manufacturing industries was especially strong since the mid-1980s (although the price elasticity somewhat declined).

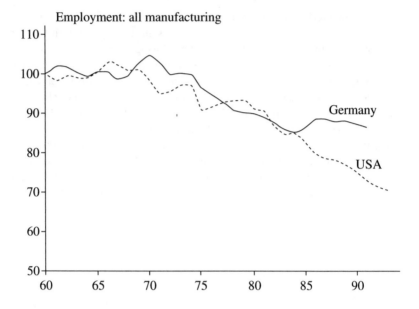

Employment: all manufacturing

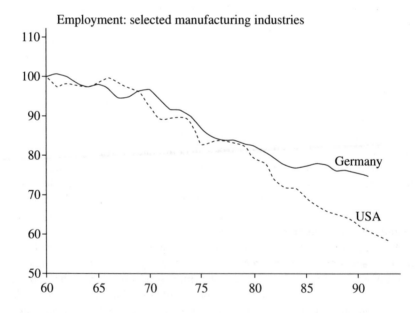

Employment: selected manufacturing industries

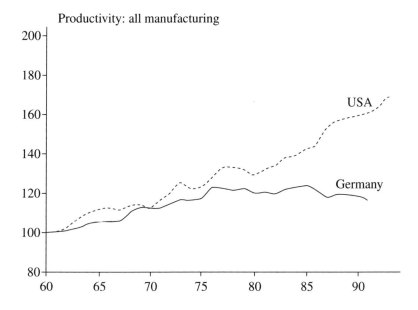

Productivity: all manufacturing

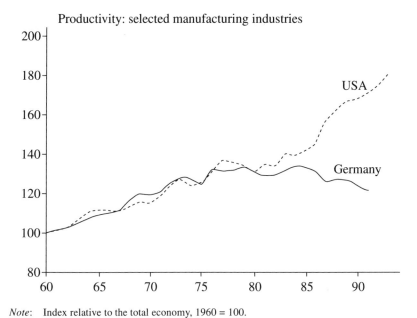

Productivity: selected manufacturing industries

Note: Index relative to the total economy, 1960 = 100.

*Figure 9.3   Employment and productivity development in Germany and
USA: all manufacturing and selected manufacturing industries*

Productivity index: manufacturing

Productivity index: non-manufacturing

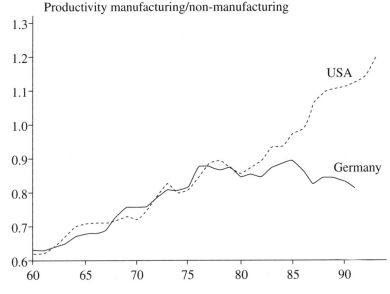

Productivity manufacturing/non-manufacturing

Notes: Index 1960 = 100

Figure 9.4   *Productivity of manufacturing and non-manufacturing*
industries and manufacturing/non-manufacturing productivity
ratio for Germany and USA

Figure 9.6 shows the effect on employment stemming from the income effect together with the combined price elasticity and productivity bias effect. It is evident that the income effect is clearly negative in both countries. This means that in the absence of productivity bias, the employment share of manufacturing industries declines. In Germany the price elasticity and productivity bias effect counteracts this negative tendency for employment in the manufacturing sector during the 1960s and (to a much smaller extent) at the end of the observation period. This is in contrast to the USA, where – with the exception of the year 1980 – both effects always worked in the same direction.

Some further insights are given in Figure 9.7. It shows the development of the actual relative employment index together with the *cumulative* income and price elasticity/productivity bias effect. It can be seen that for Germany the latter was a strong counter-force against relative employment losses of manufacturing in the 1960s, but was not able to prevent the manufacturing employment share from falling since the mid-1970s. In combination, both effects lead to a satisfactory description of changes in the structure of

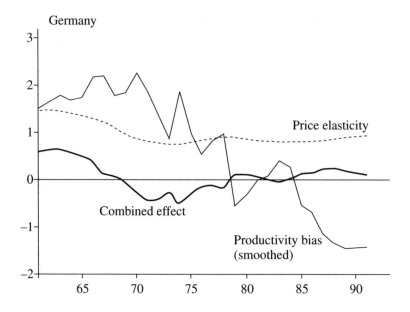

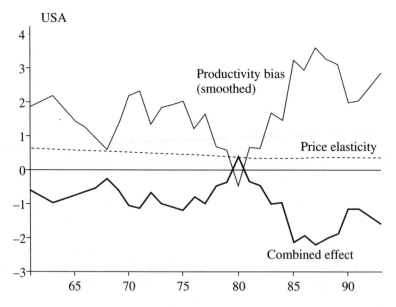

*Figure 9.5 Productivity bias, price elasticity and the combined effect on
         relative employment growth for selected manufacturing
         industries, Germany and USA*

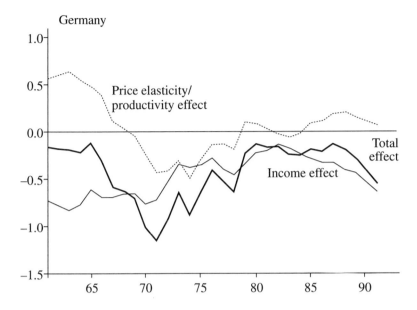

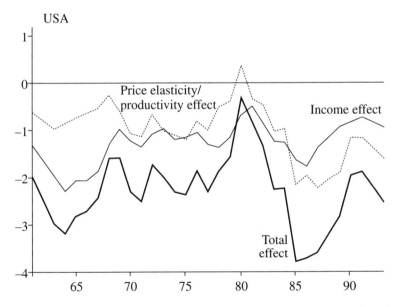

Figure 9.6   *Income effect, price elasticity/productivity bias effect and total*
               effect on relative employment growth for selected
               manufacturing industries, Germany and USA

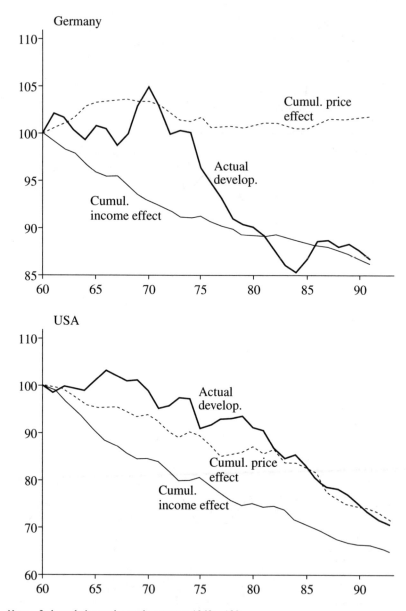

Note: Index relative to the total economy, 1960 = 100.

*Figure 9.7   Actual development, cumulative price elasticity/productivity
             bias and income effect on employment for selected
             manufacturing industries, Germany and USA*

German employment. For the USA, however, the approach seems to over-state the process of structural change: Taken together, the cumulative income and price elasticity/productivity bias effect tend to predict a relative employment decline that markedly exceeds the decrease that is actually observed.

6   SUMMARY AND CONCLUSIONS

Our investigation is based on a simple theoretical framework for analysing structural change. According to the approach, the (real) output and labour share of a sector or an industry can be decomposed into three components: productivity bias and two effects related to the price and income elasticity of product demand. For a deeper understanding of structural change it is necessary to determine these components quantitatively. As a pre-requirement of such a decomposition, one has to estimate the price- and income elasticities for specific industries. Using long-run industry data for Germany, the USA and the UK, the present chapter contributes to this empirical analysis.

Since an important hypothesis in the debate on structural change postulates a decline in the price-elasticity parameter for manufacturing industries, the focus here is on the time-varying estimates using a Kalman filter approach. The findings support the view that output in the manufacturing sector has become less price-elastic from the 1960s to the 1990s. Disregarding a small group of strongly declining industries that tend to show an atypical positive price coefficient (Textile/Apparel & Leather and Metal Industries), the estimates for the price elasticity of output in most manufacturing industries are highest in the 1960s. Estimates with pooled data for major manufacturing industries corroborate these results.

The evidence in favour of a declining trend in the price elasticity of output is especially strong for Germany and the UK, whereas the corresponding elasticity parameter has only slightly changed for the USA. The results for Germany indicate that the price elasticity of industrial output exceeded unity in the 1960s. This helps us to understand why in this country the share of labour employed in manufacturing stayed at comparatively high levels until the early 1970s.

The second piece of evidence presented here concerns the income elasticity of output. Although there are some industries that resist the overall trend, the income effect is clearly unfavourable for the employment share of total manufacturing in all countries under investigation. Since there is no effective counter-balance for a price-stimulated demand increase, the income bias effect dominates since the early 1970s in all countries. As a consequence, the employment share of manufacturing industries shrinks.

A closer comparison between Germany and the USA reveals a major difference concerning the productivity bias effect. For both countries the development in this respect is rather similar in the 1960s and 1970s. Since the late 1970s, however, the productivity bias effect in favour of manufacturing is weak or even reversed in Germany. By contrast, productivity in US manufacturing industries kept on growing relative to the service sector. The analysis shows that the basic reason for the different evolution of the two economies can be found not in manufacturing, but in the service sector. During the 1980s and early 1990s average productivity growth in the US service sector was quite low, while output per worker in German service industries kept pace with manufacturing. To put it differently: the German society was not willing or not able to create a large number of low-productivity jobs in service industries.

NOTES

1. An earlier version of this contribution was presented at the workshop Structural Change and Employment in Felix Meritis, Amsterdam, October 30–31, 1998. I would like to thank all participants of the workshop for valuable comments and suggestions. Special thanks to Eileen Appelbaum, William Baumol, Thijs ten Raa, Giovanni Russo, and Ronald Schettkat. The usual disclaimer applies.
2. See Mattey (1998).
3. See Appelbaum and Schettkat (1994), (1995), (1997).
4. See Blanchard and Kiyotaki (1987). Note that the Blanchard–Kiyotaki demand function is here applied to a sector or an industry, not to a specific firm. For the optimization problem to be solvable, the price elasticity of demand *for the individual firm* has to exceed unity. This requirement is not necessary if the concept is applied to the aggregate.
5. See Layard, Nickell and Jackman (1991) or Beißinger and Möller (2000), for instance. It can be shown that the price-setting equation corresponds to mark-up on marginal costs for a CES production function with Hicks-neutral technical progress.
6. This line of argument is developed, among others, by Wood (1994).
7. Note that this assumption requires separability of the utility function.
8. The approach here is similar to that used in other recent studies. Falvey and Gemmell (1996) present an overview of different specifications used in cross-country studies.
9. Equation (9.17) fulfils the homogeneity restriction by construction. Deaton and Muellbauer (1980) have shown, however, that a log-linear approach violates the adding-up condition. Hence, the approach suggested here has to be considered as an approximation to a rigorously founded demand equation.
10. For an overview of the various test strategies in the regression model see Krämer and Sonnberger (1986).
11. Beside this, a window width has to be chosen a priori in such an approach. For an application and discussion of this method see Hackl and Westlund (1996). These authors also present a state-space estimator as an alternative.
12. This expresses the plausible assumption that stochastic shocks have permanent effects on the parameter vector.
13. Note that the score can be calculated by extending the filter algorithm. The computer programs are written by the author using GAUSS.
14. At least to some extent this can be justified on empirical grounds. An analysis not to be documented here shows that the correlation between split sample estimates is relatively

high for the income-elasticity estimates, but is not significantly different from zero for the estimated price elasticities.

REFERENCES

Acemoglu, D. (1998), 'Why do new technologies complement skills? Directed technical change and wage inequality', *Quarterly Journal of Economics*, **113**, 1055–89.

Appelbaum, E. and R. Schettkat (1994), 'The end of full employment? Economic developments in industrialized economies', *Intereconomics*, **29**, 122–30.

Appelbaum, E. and R. Schettkat (1995), 'Employment and productivity in industrialised countries', *International Labour Review*, **134**, 605–23.

Appelbaum, E. and R. Schettkat (1997), 'Are prices unimportant? The changing structure of industrialised countries', AWSEB Discussion Paper 97/10, Utrecht.

Baumol, W.J. (1967), 'Macroeconomics of unbalanced growth: the anatomy of urban crisis', *American Economic Review*, June, **57**, 415–26.

Baumol, W.J., S.A.B. Blackman and E.N. Wolff (1989), *Productivity and the American Leadership: The Long View*, Cambridge, MA: MIT Press.

Beißinger, T. and J. Möller (2000), 'Unemployment – theoretical explanations', in H. Wagner (ed.), *Globalization and Unemployment*, Berlin, Heidelberg, New York: Springer, pp. 89–133.

Blanchard, O. and N. Kiyotaki (1987), 'Monopolistic competition and the effects of aggregate demand', *American Economic Review*, **77** (4), 647–66.

Deaton, A. and J. Muellbauer (1980), *Economics and Consumer Behavior*, Cambridge: Cambridge University Press.

Falvey, R.E. and N. Gemmell (1996), 'Are services income-elastic? Some new evidence', *Review of Income And Wealth*, **42** (3), Sept., 257–69.

Gundlach, E. (1994), 'Demand bias as an explanation for structural change', *Kyklos*, **47**, 249–67.

Gundlach, E. (1996), 'Demand bias as an explanation for structural change – reply', *Kyklos*, **49**, 249–67.

Hackl, P. and A.H. Westlund (1996), 'The demand for international telecommunication time-varying price elasticity', *Journal of Econometrics*, **70**, 243–60.

Harvey, 1989, *Forecasting, Structural Time Series Models and the Kalman Filter*, Cambridge: Cambridge University Press.

Krämer, W. and H. Sonnberger (1986), *The Linear Regression Model Under Test*, Heidelberg, Wien: Physica.

Kuznets, S. (1966), *Modern Economic Growth*, New Haven: Yale University Press.

Layard, R., S. Nickell and R. Jackman (1991), *Unemployment*, Oxford: Oxford University Press.

Mattey, J.P. (1998), 'Will the new information economy cure the cost disease in the US?', Paper presented at the Workshop on Structural Change and Employment, October 30–31, Amsterdam: Felix Meritis.

Quibrai, M.G. and F. Harrigan (1996), 'Demand bias and structural change, comment', *Kyklos*, **49**, 205–13.

Ramaswamy, R. and R. Rowthorn (1997), 'Deindustrialisation: causes and implications', *IMF Working Paper*, WP/ 97/42, Washington, DC.

Saeger, S.S. (1997), 'Globalization and deindustrialization: myth and reality in the OECD', *Weltwirtschaftliches Archiv*, **133**, 579–608.

Wood, A. (1994), *North-South Trade, Employment and Inequality: Changing Fortunes in a Skill Driven World*, Oxford: Clarendon.

PART V

Conclusions

10. Light on the mystery of service sector growth: some stylized facts

Thijs ten Raa and Ronald Schettkat

The work in this volume illuminates the mystery of the service sector, which attracts a rising share of nominal output even though relative prices of services are rising. This is a fundamental puzzle for economics, which pays so much attention to the impact of relative prices. Even more surprising – although a less well-established fact – is the rising service share in real output over recent decades. Why doesn't demand shift away from products that continually rise in price? The development process of industrial economies has been described in classic contributions such as Salter (1960) as following the law of negative correlation between price and quantity demanded. Industries with a higher rate of productivity growth and thus declining relative prices (technologically progressive industries) will attract demand and should therefore also expand in employment terms. Yet, we observe that the contrary occurs in the industrialized world. High productivity growth manufacturing industries decline everywhere in employment while service industries suffering from 'Baumol's cost disease' expand. This is a mystery, which is clearly present in contradictory 'facts' and rival explanations in the literature. One of the most fundamental contradictory 'facts' is whether the share of service industries in real output actually expands, remains constant, or shrinks.

The works presented in this volume investigate the various hypotheses and mysteries ranked around the development of the service sector. Complex theoretical issues and measurement problems are involved in evaluations of the development of the service sector and, not surprisingly, the views on these fundamental questions are extremely heterogeneous in the literature. It is all the more surprising, therefore, that a clear picture emerges from the collected contributions in this volume, despite the fact that they use different methodology, different data sets and include various countries. All the chapters point to a product market explanation: income effects have diminished the demand for manufactures, which broadly speaking became a satiated market whereas the expansion, especially of personal services, suffers from rising relative prices.

In the following we summarize the main stylized facts, which can be derived from the work collected in this volume. A substantial number of stylized facts can be grouped under the heading 'conceptual frame and measurement error', which affects both the input and output side of service production. A second group of stylized facts may be classified as 'final demand shifts' with a domestic and an international demand component.

Our interpretation of the data, which leads to widely believed 'facts', is affected by a multitude of conceptual and measurement issues: output measurement (real output of service industries, quality measurement), input measurement (labour versus total production factors), the appropriate definition of the production unit, theoretical concepts about the relative importance of price and income effects; all these issues may affect our perception of the 'facts'. Mismeasurement of both the output and the input of service industries may affect the perceived productivity trends and may lead to a downward bias in service sector productivity and an upward bias in manufacturing productivity. Measurement bias can be caused by difficulties in determining the real output of service industries, but it can also be related to conceptual problems concerning productivity measures and the definition of industries.

Measurement of real service output has been one of the most important issues in the debate on inflation-bias in the US consumer price index (CPI). If real output of services is systematically underestimated, productivity and price increases will be overestimated as a result. If such mismeasurement occurs on a grand scale, service sector expansion may not be a mystery at all. While it is true that quality improvements are extremely difficult to estimate, for example in the medical industry, it is also true that these problems are less severe in other services. Moreover, they are not unique to the service sector but occur with manufactures as well. Joe Mattey points out clearly that even if real output growth of service industries is underestimated, the puzzle remains as to why the nominal share of services increases with price.

Stylized fact 1:

The possible underestimation of real output of service industries leaves us with the puzzle that nominal demand for services rises with price.

Another reason why productivity differentials between manufacturing and service industries are overestimated is the common use of labour productivity instead of total factor productivity measures. It is the classical Baumol argument that some services suffer from the absence of technological progress – which in turn seems substantially related to capital–labour substitution. If capital–labour substitution occurs, labour productivity will overestimate efficiency gains in the production of manufacturing goods where capital–labour substitution is more important than in most service industries. An important cause of the cost disease of services is the limited possibility of mechanization in several, although not all, services. In other words, production functions of service industries may not allow for the same degree of capital–labour substitution as in manufacturing industries, which seems to be apparent in the long-run data (Erdem and Glyn). In this case labour productivity overestimates actual productivity gains in manufacturing and thus overestimates the productivity differential between manufacturing and service industries. Although studies in this volume (ten Raa and Mohnen, Russo and Schettkat) find evidence that productivity differentials between manufacturing and service industries, measured by total factor input (total factor productivity, TFP) are lower than differentials measured by labour productivity, the differential nevertheless remains.

Stylized fact 2:

The productivity differential between manufacturing and service industries estimated by labour productivity seems to overestimate the true differential. It is smaller when measured by total factor inputs but it does not disappear.

Service industries are heterogeneous with respect to capital–labour substitution. Some service industries experience high substitution (like data processing, banking) while others, especially personal services, are lacking this opportunity to increase productivity.

Stylized fact 3:

The service sector is heterogeneous with respect to productivity growth and capital–labour substitution. Some service industries seem to be similar to manufacturing with respect to capital–labour substitution whereas others are clearly distinct from manufacturing in this respect.

Another source for industry-specific productivity growth may be outsourcing of less productive activities. If manufacturing industries outsource low productive activities to service industries this alone would lead to a rising productivity differential between manufacturing and services. Thus data based on National Income and Product Accounts statistics measure productivity as value-added in an industry over inputs in that industry, and this may be a misleading measure if outsourcing of low productivity activities from manufacturing to services occurs. When integrating over the production chain (so-called vertically integrated sectors) productivity (final product productivity) would be unchanged in this case. On the other hand, outsourcing may very well lead to actual efficiency gains (that is, a rise in final product productivity) because of specialization, economies of scale and so on. At the same time, outsourcing will affect the size of the industries and outsourcing may explain shrinking manufacturing employment and simultaneously rising service employment. Part of the changing industrial structure may thus be related to a reorganization of production between industries rather than to shifts in final demand. The contributions by ten Raa and Mohnen as well as Russo and Schettkat found that while outsourcing occurs in the described direction, it is not substantial and fails as a major explanation for productivity growth as well as for the changing weights in industry structure. Productivity growth occurs mainly within industries.

Stylized fact 4:

The changing division of labour between industries (outsourcing) is apparent but not strong enough to explain the differential in productivity growth. Only a small share of productivity growth in a final product productivity measure (integrating all stages of production) can be attributed to outsourcing.

Stylized fact 5:

Productivity growth takes place within each industry and thus seems to be mainly related to technological progress. High growth in manufacturing productivity is no artifact, but real.

R&D stock is a more direct measure of technological progress than TFP or labour productivity. Using this measure Mohnen and ten Raa find that R&D stock is developing favourably in services but declines sharply in manufacturing. This indicates that the cost disease of services may in part be overcome by innovative production techniques.

Stylized fact 6:

The share of R&D stocks in manufacturing dropped sharply but rose in services indicating that innovative activity shifted in favour of the service industries.

Machin finds that industry-specific R&D expenditures are highly correlated between countries and that these seem to increase the share of non-production workers in the industry wage bill. This finding is interpreted as skill-biased technological change that upgrades the skill requirements of the workforce. This is another piece of evidence in favour of the argument that it is mainly technological progress rather than international trade, which reshapes skill requirements. In their long-run, multi-country analysis, Erdem and Glyn find that service employment expansion seem to be bigger in countries in which the labour reserves in agriculture or in non-participation are higher. Services may serve as a sponge for an excess supply of labour. The changing industry structure affects male employment negatively, which tends to be concentrated in manufacturing, but it favours the employment of women. However, not only is tertiarization taking place through inter-industry employment shifts, but also the non-production workforce is expanding within each industry (Machin).

Stylized fact 7:

Employment expansion in service industries favours the employment of women, whereas the decline in manufacturing affects male employment negatively. The shift to non-production jobs is apparent in each industry. It is more likely that skill-biased technological change rather than trade restructures the skill requirements of the workforce. The impact that skill restructuring has on inequality seems to depend substantially on the institutional frameworks of countries.

The shift in economic structure to services is less dramatic when measured in real output shares rather than in nominal output shares or in employment shares. Consequently the decline in the real output share of manufacturing is less severe than the drop in employment share or nominal output share. Also, the shift to services is weaker when measured by the final product concept as compared to shifts measured by the industry concept (value added) in National Income and Product Account statistics, which confirms the fact that some outsourcing of productive activities from manufacturing to services takes place. However, there seems to be a clear shift in private consumption towards services.

Stylized fact 8:

The slight expansion of services is not a statistical artifact inherent in the industry concept of the National Income and Products Accounts, but it can also be found in final demand. It is due mainly to private consumption, which shifts to services.

There is also a slight trend to services in the exports of the highly industrialized countries, but Mohnen and ten Raa as well as Russo and Schettkat find that this is not substantial at all. Trade is still dominated by 'tradables', that is, manufactures. The expansion of services and/or decline in manufacturing is a phenomenon related to domestic demand rather than international trade.

Stylized fact 9:

International trade shifted only marginally to services. It is still the 'tradables' (manufactures), which dominate trade.

Why, then, is demand for manufactures lagging behind its potential growth as determined by the rise in productivity? Demand for manufacturing gets satiated as demand for agricultural products did many decades ago (Baumol). Satiated demand together with ongoing productivity growth leads to the fall in manufacturing employment, which has been experienced in all industrialized economies. Demand for services seems far from being satiated, but rising relative prices slow the expansion of service demand. Appelbaum and Schettkat show that the demand trends in services are the net effect of a positive income effect partly compensated by a negative price trend. In the case of services, the positive income effect seemed to have balanced the negative price effect during the long periods when the income effect was strong due to high rates of income growth as in the 1960s and early 1970s. The puzzle is, however, why services continued to expand while the rate of income growth slowed down from the mid-1970s onwards. Since productivity growth is still concentrated in manufacturing, the price effect of services should have come to dominate the income effect, which does not seem to be the case. It is therefore very likely that demand conditions changed.

Stylized fact 10:

Income and price effects work in opposite directions for services. Since service demand tended to remain stable or even grew while the rate of income growth slowed down, it is very likely that demand condition changed.

Indeed the econometric work by Joachim Möller shows that price elasticity of demand for manufactures has declined over time, thus explaining employment stability in manufacturing until the 1970s or so as well as the subsequent decline in manufacturing employment. The falling relative price for manufactures lost its role in stimulating product demand and thus the labour-saving effect of productivity growth in manufacturing could no longer fully be compensated by the demand-stimulating effect. The consequence is falling manufacturing employment (Appelbaum and Schettkat).

Stylized fact 11:

Price elasticity of demand for manufactures seem to have fallen over time, that is, the positive price effect in the demand for manufactures shrunk over time and thus may explain the decline in manufacturing employment.

Although the chapters in this volume use different methodological approaches and data sets for different industrialized countries, all results point in the same direction: the growth of the service sector is real, although much overstated in nominal terms and employment shares. As long as some activities show productivity growth, the production frontier of the economy expands allowing also for consumption of luxury products, such as high-priced services. But demand for services is not automatically activated, and consequently we see a huge inter-country variation in the expansion of service industries.

REFERENCE

Salter, W.E.G. (1960), *Productivity and Technical Change*, Cambridge: Cambridge University Press.

Index